THE STRANGE CASES OF DR. STANCHON

BY

JOSEPHINE DASKAM BACON

JOSEPHINE DASKAM BACON

THE KEY

The young doctor stamped vehemently up the marble steps, to warm his feet, and once in the warm, flower-scented halls, let a little shiver escape him. The butler was new—he was always new, the doctor thought—and actually didn't know him.

"Mrs. Allen is at bridge, sir, with a party: she asks to be excused," he began mechanically.

(*"That's good!" Stanchon felt tempted to say, "and I hope the girls are out, too!"*) As if in answer to this indiscretion, the new butler droned on:

"Miss Alida is at her riding-lesson and Miss Suzanne is—is engaged——"

(*"Now, what particular infernal idiocy is Suzanne at, I wonder?" Stanchon pondered, still smiling lightly at the butler and warming himself at every breath.*)

"Mr. Edmund is—I think he could be found, sir," the voice went on.

(*"I don't doubt it," Stanchon agreed mentally, "at the side board, no doubt; a nice time of day for a lad of twenty to be hanging about the house!"*)

But all he said was:

"I am the doctor. I called to see Miss Mary."

"Oh!" Even this new butler assumed a look of burdened intelligence; he leaned toward the visitor, "Oh, yes, sir—Miss Mary. I understood that it wouldn't be possible for Miss Mary to see anybody, sir, but I suppose, the doctor——"

"Certainly," said Stanchon curtly. "Please send word to her nurse that I am here."

"Yes, sir," but the man hesitated, even as he took the hat held out to him, "yes, sir, but—but ... it isn't Dr. Jarvyse, is it, sir?"

A slow, dark red spread over Stanchon's forehead.

(*"So they've sent for Jarvyse—well, I might have known. Nice, tactful crowd, aren't they!"*)

He scowled slightly and set his jaw.

"No, I'm Dr. Stanchon," he said. "Dr. Jarvyse is coming later, I suppose. Kindly let Miss Jessop know that I am here, will you? I haven't much time."

The man sped swiftly down the hall, after depositing his hatless charge in a blue satin reception-room, and Stanchon stared, unseeing, at the old Chinese panels and ivory figures that dotted its walls and tables. The strong odour of freesias and paper-narcissus hung heavy in the room; the roar of the great, dirty, cold city was utterly shut away and a scented silence, costly and blue and drowsy, held everything.

Presently the nurse stood before him, smiling, and he saw that her usual modish house dress was changed for the regulation white duck and peaked cap of her profession.

"What's all this?" he asked, and she shrugged her broad shoulders.

"She told me to put it on to-day. 'You're really a nurse, you know, Miss Jessop,' she said, 'and if I require one, it might as well be known.' Of course, I had it here, so I got it right out. Poor Miss Mary!"

"I see they've sent for Jarvyse?"

She nodded uncomfortably.

"Then it's all over but the shouting, I suppose?" Again she shrugged. The fatalism of her training spoke in that shrug, and the necessity for taking everything as it comes—since everything is bound to come!

"H'm..." he meditated deeply, and all the youth went out of his face, suddenly: he might have been forty-five or fifty. At such times the nurses and the other doctors always watched him eagerly; it was supposed that it was then that those uncanny intuitions came to him, that almost clairvoyant penetration of the diseased minds that were his chosen study.

"How is she?" he asked abruptly.

"Oh, very much the same, doctor. I can't see much difference."

"But you see a little?"

She moved uncomfortably.

"I don't say that ... it's nothing she says or does—but—sometimes I think she's a little more—a little less..."

"A little less normal?"

She rested, relieved.

"Yes, just that."

Across the broad halls came a wave of sudden sound: movement of drapery, faint clashes of metallic substances and glass, broken feminine cries and light, breathy laughter. A difference in the air became noticeable, new perfumes floated in to the little blue room, perfumes and the odour of expensive, warm fur.

—"You don't mean to say that you discard from a strong suit—always?"

"My dear, I had nothing but that queen—nothing!"

—"And that's why, as Elwell says...."

—"And so he absolutely refuses to play with women!"

Evidently a door had been opened, somewhere. The next moment brought a new whiff of cold, fresh air and the sound of a motor, then silence again, sudden and profound, from the street-side. A deep, almost dramatic voice silenced the confused babble.

"My dear, I'm frightfully sorry, but I simply could *not* manage to get here before! Why weren't any of you at the lecture? *Moyen Age* house-furniture and decoration—terribly interesting. It's a shame to miss a thing like that. Is my table all made up? Never mind, I can cut in any time. Yes, Mrs. Allen, I know, but really, you ought not to neglect the intellectual side, entirely, you know!"

The door closed instantly, and again they stood alone in the heavy silence. It was as if a curtain had been lifted swiftly on some bustling, high-lighted scene and dropped as swiftly. Only a strong, heady scent floated in on them, troubling, suggestive, complicated.

"What is that?" Stanchon asked, sniffing.

"Oh, one of those new Russian perfumes," the nurse said. "I hate them."

"Russian?" he looked puzzled.

"Don't you know it's a Russian season?" she instructed him. "Dancers and music and hats—those high fur ones—and perfumes? And all that Byzantine embroidery? You must have noticed!"

"Oh!" He considered thoughtfully. "I *had* noticed the perfumes. But I didn't know why it was.... Well, am I to see Miss Mary?"

"I don't know why not, doctor," she said. "She always likes to see you. And I suppose you'll consult with Dr. Jarvyse, won't you?"

"I suppose so," he agreed, "though, of course, nobody's asked me. Is she going out, this weather?"

"No: I wish she would. She says it tires her too much. It's a pity she hates the South so."

They walked to the tiny tapestried lift, beyond the curve of the great stairs, and she pressed the ivory button that sent them up. At the fourth floor the car settled lightly and they stepped out.

"She's not speaking much," the nurse warned him, "but of course she may, for you. Very gloomy, for two days, she's been."

She knocked lightly at a door and entered without waiting. The room was very light, with bowls of cut flowers everywhere and a pair of green love-birds billing eternally on a brass standard: they chirped softly now and then. A miniature grand piano filled one corner, and the light fell richly on the tooled leather of low book-cases, and slipped into reflected pools of violet, green and blood-red on the polished floor. A great tiger skin stretched in front of a massive, claw-legged davenport, and in the corner of it, away from the cheerful, crackling fire, a black-haired woman sat, tense and silent, her eyes fixed in a brooding stare. She was all in delicate, cunningly mingled tints of mauve, violet and lavender; near her neck tiny diamond points winked; magnificent emeralds edged with diamonds lay like green stains on her long white hands. In her dark immobility, among the rich, clear objects scattered so artfully about the sun-lighted chamber, she had a marvellous effect of being the chief figure in some modern French artist's impressionistic "interior." She gave a distinct sense of having been bathed and dried, scented and curled, dressed—and abandoned there, between the love-birds and the polished piano: a large gold frame about the room would have supplied the one note lacking.

"Well, Miss Mary, and how goes it?" Dr. Stanchon said, sitting beside her and taking her hand easily, since she failed to notice his own outstretched.

She lifted her eyes slightly to his, moved her lips, then sighed a little and dropped her lids. She might have been a young-looking woman of forty, or a girl of twenty-five who had been long ill or distressed.

"Come, now, Miss Mary, I hear you've given me up—wasn't I high priced enough for you? Because I can always accommodate, you know, in that direction," Stanchon went on persuasively.

Again she raised her eyes, swallowed, appeared to overcome an almost unconquerable lethargy of spirit, and spoke.

"It's no use, doctor, all that. I've given up. It's all one to me, now. Don't bother about me."

Stanchon looked genuinely concerned. He had worked hard over this case, and it cut his pride to have the great specialist, with his monotonous inflexible system, summoned against his express wish. That meant they were all tired, disgusted, sick of the whole business. They were determined to be rid of her.

"I wish you wouldn't look at it that way, Miss Mary," he said gently. "I don't believe you need give up—if you'll only make an effort. But it's fatal to give 'way: I've always told you that."

"Yes. You always told me that. You were always open and fair," she said wearily, "but now you see it is fatal, for I *have* given 'way. Please go," she added nervously. "I feel more like crying. Ask him to go, Miss Jessop..."

Her voice grew peevish and uncontrolled, and he bowed slightly and left her. It was too bad, but there was nothing to do. Once or twice in his brilliant career he had felt that same heavy hopelessness, realized, to his disgust, that the patient's dull misery was creeping over him, too, and that he had no power to help.

"Oh, well, you can't win out all the time," he said to himself philosophically, "and it isn't as if she wouldn't have every comfort. Old Jarvyse looks after them well: I'll say that for him."

The new butler met him as the lift reached the drawing-room floor.

"Mr. Edmund would like to see you a moment, sir," he murmured. "He's—he's in the dining-room, doctor."

Stanchon turned abruptly and plunged into the great, dim leather-hung apartment. He always felt as if he were entering into some vast cave under the sea, when he crossed the threshold of this room, and the peculiar odour of the leather always caught at his breath and choked him for a moment. Edmund looked sulkier and more futile than usual, even, and the cigarette that dropped from his trimmed and polished hand had a positively insolent angle.

"Oh! How do!" he said discontentedly. "Been upstairs, I hear?"

"Yes," Stanchon answered briefly.

"Well, ... how about it?"

"I'm sorry to say your aunt is a little worse to-day; it may be, probably is, nothing but a passing phase——"

"Ah, go on!" Edmund burst out. "Phase, nothing! She's as dippy as they make 'em, Stanchon, and I'm through with it!"

The older man looked his disgust, but Edmund scowled and went on.

"After day before yesterday afternoon, I told Suzanne I'd come to the end of my rope, and I meant it. I suppose you heard about it?"

"No."

"Oh, Miss Jessop knows. Upsetting a whole luncheon, and one the girls had worked over, too, I can tell you! Why, they had three reporters on their knees to hear about that luncheon!"

"Really?" Stanchon inquired politely.

"Yes. But Alida wouldn't let mother say a word. And that was all right, too. And then what does Aunt Mary do but say she's coming? And mother weakened and said we'd have to let her, because either she is all right or she isn't, and according to you, we're not to admit she isn't—yet. So she comes, and what does she do but insult two of the biggest swells there, right to their face! And when Suzanne tried to carry it off, she just turns stubborn and never opens her mouth again. Queered the whole thing. Broke the women all up. Suzanne says, never again! And I'm with her.

I had Jarvyse called in and he's going to make his final decision today. Of course, if he wants to consult, we'll be glad——"

"Dr. Jarvyse and I will settle all that, thanks," Stanchon interrupted coldly. "I regret that your sisters should have been annoyed, but as I explained to your mother, inconveniences of this sort would be bound to occur, and the only question was——"

"The only question is," Edmund blustered, "are we to be queered in New York for good by a woman who ought to have been shut up long ago! It's up to me, now, as the man of the house, and I say, no."

He dabbed his cigarette viciously into a wet ring on the silver tray beside him and filled a tiny glass from a decanter; his hand shook.

Stanchon's mounting wrath subsided. The boy became pathetic to him; behind his dapper morning clothes, his intricate studs and fobs and rings, his reedy self-confidence, the physician saw the faint, grisly shadow of a sickly middle-age, a warped and wasted maturity.

"I'm sorry for you all," he said kindly. "Don't think I don't appreciate the strain ... your mother has tried her best, I'm sure. And—and go slow on those cigarettes, Allen, why don't you? They won't help that cough, you know. And you told me you'd cut out the Scotch."

"Oh, that's all right," Edmund assured him. "I was seasoned in the cradle, doc! Remember the old man's cigars?"

Stanchon put on his gloves.

"Your father was a very strong man," he said quietly, "and a hard worker. And I've already reminded you that he didn't inhale. And for more years than you've lived, Allen, he worked out of doors. I don't want to nag at you, but just give it a thought now and then. And let me know if I can do anything for you, ever. My regards to your sisters."

As he paused at the curb, a short man in heavy motoring furs stumbled out of a luxurious landaulet and would have gone down on the treacherous pavement without Stanchon's quick arm.

"All right, doctor, all right," he smiled, as he braced himself for the little man's weight. "Glad I was here. I've just left Mary—she's getting a little unmanageable, I hear."

"Yes, yes," the little man panted, "she'll do better out of the family. Yes, yes. They often do, you know. Position's perfectly anomalous here, you know—constant friction."

"I see," said Stanchon. "Let me walk up to the door with you—I've practiced on the steps, once today. You make it ..."

"Oh, clear paranoia," Jarvyse finished the sentence promptly. "They go right along, you know. Perfectly typical. Good days—yes. Of course. Everybody encouraged. Come to a ladies' luncheon—fat in the fire directly. No keeping servants, you know. All that sort of thing. Ever show you my card-catalogue of women between thirty-eight and thirty-nine? No? Ask me some day."

The younger man pressed the electric button and turned the bronze knob of the outer door, wrought and decorated like some great public tomb.

"Thanks, I'd be interested," he said.

"You knew the brother, didn't you?" Jarvyse went on, breathing easier in the warmth of the vestibule. "Nothing out of the way there?"

"Absolutely not. He had the constitution of a bull. But I fear he's not handed it on to his son."

"Ugh, no! Nasty little cub. Those families don't last. Daughters always stronger. I give him fifteen ... eighteen years," the alienist said placidly.

The inner door opened and Stanchon turned to go.

"Come up and see the patient," Jarvyse suggested, over his shoulder, one glove already off. "Pleased to have you, and so would she, of course. You'll find her much happier."

But Miss Mary was not happier. Freed of the contemptuous *brusquerie* of Edmund, the thinly-veiled dislike of the girls, the conscience-stricken attempts of her sister-in-law, she had felt for a time the relief of a strain abandoned, the comfort of a definite position. They had come to see her, too, and their timid overtures of interest, their obvious surprise at the ease with which this great change had been effected, their frank amazement at the luxury and silken routine in which they found her, had almost established relations long since fallen out of use. But the novelty had faded, the visits grew fewer and shorter, the very telephone messages languished; and as she sat brooding alone, in the few unoccupied half-hours that the omniscient System left her, a slow, sure conviction dropped like an acid on the clouded surface of her mind: she was alone. She was no longer a part of life as it was ordinarily lived. She and the others who shared that rich, tended seclusion were apart from the usages and responsibilities of the World that was counterfeited there. They were unreal. Through all the exercise and repose, the baths and manipulations, the music and the silences, the courtesies and the deprecations, the flowers and the birds that brought an artificial summer within the thick walls, one idea clanged like a bell through her weary mind: *This is not real.*

To Dr. Stanchon, who came in the intervals allowed by his work, she seemed sadly changed. It was not that her face looked heavier and more fretfully lined; not that her voice grew more monotonous; not that she seemed sunk in the selfish stupor that her type of suffering invariably produces. He had seen all this in others and seen it change for a better state. No; in Miss Mary the settled pessimism of a deep conviction had an almost uncanny power of communicating itself to those about her.

"She's in bad, that one," one of the gardeners said to him, on a windy March day when he had hunted for her over half-a-dozen guarded acres, and found her sitting in one of her heavy silences under a sunny ledge of rock.

"She's quiet and easy, but she's one of the worst of 'em, in my opinion."

And when she turned to him a moment later and said quietly: "Tell me, once for all, Dr. Stanchon, do you consider me insane?" his voice expressed all the simple sincerity of his eyes.

"Miss Mary, I tell you the truth—I don't know."

"But you know they'll never let me out?"

He braced himself. "How can they, Miss Mary, when you won't promise——"

"Why should I promise anything, if I'm not insane? Would you promise never to state your opinion in your own house?"

He shrugged his shoulders helplessly.

"You see!" he said gently.

Beyond them the gardener struggled with a refractory horse that refused to draw his load of brush and dead leaves. She stared at the group dully: six months ago she would have flinched at the great clambering hoofs and the man's danger.

"And even if I did give up and promise everything, do you believe I'd get out, doctor?"

"I see no reason——"

"You don't need to lie to me," she interrupted. "When I signed that paper, they fooled me: it was for good. It said six months—but it was for good."

He felt a great sympathy for her. It was hard, very hard. And yet, what they had been through with her!

"If only you hadn't refused to travel," he began.

"But I agreed to—I agreed to, last month," she cried, "even though I'm never well travelling, I agreed to—and what happened? Dr. Jarvyse said it wouldn't be best for me! And you did nothing..."

"How could I, Miss Mary?" he urged. "You know the only reason I see you so often is that I acquiesce and don't interfere. The moment I thought it would do any good——"

"You mean you're not sure, yourself!" she said keenly.

He sighed.

"You know I'm your friend," he said simply.

Her whole face changed. An almost disconcerting brightness flashed over it. Through all the heaviness and fatigue and despair that had yellowed her skin, dulled her eyes, and taken, it seemed, the very sheen from her black hair, her lost girlhood flared a moment. With the inconstant emotion of a child she smiled at him.

"I know you are," she murmured confidingly, "and I'll tell you something, because you are."

"What is it, Miss Mary?" he said, but he sighed as he said it.

"Do you see how I'm dressed?" she half whispered. He looked, uncomprehending, at the long light ulster she wore.

"Underneath, I'm in black," she said softly, "a whole suit. I have a little bag packed right under this rock, and I have ninety dollars in my bag, here." She tapped her waist, where a small shopping bag dangled. "And I have an umbrella. I always sit near this gate."

"Why do you do such things, dear Miss Mary?" he said sadly. "It does you no good—please try to believe me!"

"I never did, until I had the dream," she answered calmly. "This is the third night I've had it. I dreamed I was near some gate, and I looked down, and right before me on the path I saw a key—a great, brown key! So I started to pick it up, and then I realised that I wasn't prepared, that I had no money, and that I'd just be caught and brought back. Then I woke. But I dreamed it over again the next night, so I packed the bag and got it out here under this steamer-rug, and asked for some money to buy presents when that embroidery woman came from Lakewood. And I got it, of course, and bought some. She said she was coming again. So I got more. Last night I dreamed it again, and it looked like this gate, in the dream. That's three times. Suzanne has those dreams, you know—she's like me, Suzanne—and they always happen. So perhaps mine will. I tell you, because you're my friend. And you would never have put me here."

Stanchon bit his lip. A sudden disgust of everything seized him.

"No, I wouldn't have put you here—once," he said slowly, then rose abruptly.

"Hi, there, hold him! hold him, you fool!" he shouted. "Sit on his head!"

The gardener's horse, beyond all control, now, was rolling furiously, neighing and snapping. The man clung to the reins, keeping his distance, but as the animal gained his feet with a lurch, his finger slipped and he, too, rolled over and over down the little slope to the gravelled path. Stanchon was after the horse before the attendant had picked himself up and was calling him angrily.

"Don't be alarmed, miss," the man panted. "The doctor and I can settle him!" and staggering to his feet made off to the rescue. As he ran, something clinked and rattled about his boots, and a bunch of keys lay quiet on the gravel.

Miss Mary rose instantly, walked to them and put her foot over them, but the man was several yards away and Stanchon and the horse were struggling towards the wagon. Miss Mary stooped down and lifted the keys; all had metal tags and the one in her hand read, *East Gate, by shrubbery*. She stepped to the ledge, drew out a fair sized black hand-bag, tucked her umbrella under her arm and looked about her. The nearest gate, set in dense shrubbery, lay in a direct line with the ledge, and as she slipped behind it the two men and the horse were wiped out of her vision. With her usual quiet, long step she reached the gate, fitted the key, turned it and opened the gate. She closed it behind her, considered a moment, then tossed the keys back among the thick, glossy rhododendrons.

"Just as I dreamed," she muttered, "but where is the carriage?"

She stood on the edge of a road she had never seen, a quarter of a mile from the great wrought-iron entrance that had closed behind her half a year ago, and looked vaguely about her, at the mercy of Fate. And Fate, that quaint old lady who holds you and me and Miss Mary in the hollow of her hand, smiled and gave a tiny pat and a push to the shiny little electric run-about of Miss Winifred Jarvyse, a handsome young Diana, who had never seen the inside of the great walled estate next her father's private grounds, so that she waved her hand cordially, stopped out of pure good feeling for the absent-minded stranger in the beautiful coat, and asked if she could drop her at the station!

"Why, yes, thank you," said Miss Mary, still vaguely.

"It's going to rain and I've no cover on," said Winifred. "It's a pity about your coat."

"I can turn it," said Miss Mary, and standing up for a moment she slipped the sleeves of the ulster, shook herself slightly and sat down a totally different woman. So that when (such was the perfection of the System) a quick call to the ticket office set the agent searching twenty minutes later for a tall woman in a light tan coat, alone, without luggage, he replied very truly that no such person had entered his station. Only a friend of Miss Jarvyse had come to the 2:15, a lady in a dark plaid ulster with bag and umbrella, in Miss Jarvyse's car.

"I hope you found your friends—er—doing well?" said Miss Jarvyse delicately.

"Thank you, they were very well," said Miss Mary gravely. And she took the 2:15 for New York.

Nothing further than the immediate moment was in her mind. To her thought, long confused and fleeting, the dreamlike character of this sudden change seemed natural and simple. She had no plan of campaign, no route of escape, no future. Her mind, relaxed from the quick decision that had cleared its mists in the moment of action, began to dull and settle and fall into its old rut of mechanical despair, when suddenly the voices of two women in the seat behind her grew louder and rose above the jar of the train.

"And so she decided to get it over while he was in the hospital. She thought the dye would have to wear off gradually, but there's a place on West Twenty-eighth Street—near Sixth Avenue, I think—where a French woman guarantees to remove any dye, perfectly harmlessly, in two hours. So she had it done, and he was delighted. My dear, she was fifty, and the grey hair really was more becoming to her. Everybody thinks so. But nobody knew her—I never saw such a change, at first. If you know anybody who wants it done, just send them there. Some French name."

And just as Miss Mary was drifting off to that dull world of grievances in which she dwelt habitually, a new idea, as strong and definite as that which took her through the gate caught and held her, and she wrote in a little leather book in her bag, "28th St. west, near Sixth." Some primitive instinct of caution directed her to a street car in preference to a hansom or taxi-cab, and she found the French woman's small, musty establishment with an ease that surprised her. Her coat, obviously "imported," the elegance of her bag and umbrella, the air of custom with which she submitted to others' ministrations, brought her quick service, and in less than the guaranteed two hours she left Madame, whose very considerable fee she paid with gloved hands, thus, through sheer inadvertence, concealing the one trace of her identity—her massive and beautiful rings. For no one of Dr. Jarvyse's detectives could be expected to look at an iron-grey woman in black, when searching for a black-haired woman in blue plaid. And none of them, not the great Jarvyse, nor her maid even, knew that Miss Mary had dyed her hair for ten years!

As she stood by a little optician's, on one of the great avenues, later, gazing fascinated at her strange reflection in a large glass there, terrified at her daring, doubtful if her freedom could endure, two errand-girls, peering in with her in the imitative New York fashion, held her with an idle sentence.

"Did you know Miss Mahoney with those glasses? I nearly fell over when I seen her, honest! She was awful cross—the boss himself cut her dead!"

"Say, what do you think of that now?"

"An' they're only window-glass, too! She told one o' the fitters. She can stare at the ladies better she says, when they try to beat her down."

They moved on, but Miss Mary entered the shop.

"Can I get a pair of eye-glasses made of window-glass?" she asked him simply.

"Certainly, madam," and one would have supposed that leaders of fashion generally were wearing these articles, so swiftly and unsmilingly did he produce them and adjust them to her strong, dark eyes.

"Wonderful how they change a person, though," he admitted. "You wouldn't believe it."

The price seemed very small to Miss Mary, whose last purchase in that line had been a tortoise-shell lorgnette for her sister-in-law.

She had eaten very lightly at luncheon, for food was tasteless to her, of late, and she had been so followed, tended and directed in all the operations of life that she actually failed to recognise her sensations as those of hunger. But her unwonted exertions, the strain on her flagging brain, the stimulus of this unprecedented day, all combined to flush her cheek feverishly and she felt strangely weak. For the first time it flashed over her cleared faculties that she must go somewhere and at once. New York was too dangerous for her; she must leave it.

A very panic of terror seized her and she half expected to hear Dr. Jarvyse's soft voice at her shoulder. She started from the shop like one pursued, and hurried foolishly on and on in an ecstasy of flight. The streets were now dark, and Miss Mary, who had begun life in New York with her own private hansom, felt singularly out of place in the jostling crowd.

She stopped at the foot of an elevated railway station, and more because she was pushed up the steps by the hurrying mass of humanity that scurried like ants up and down, than for any other reason, climbed wearily up. As she sat pressed against a dirty man with a bundle, a sudden inconsequent thought struck her, and she removed her gloves in a leisurely way, took off her rings, dropped them into a roll of chamois-skin in the large bag, added to them a diamond cross and pendant from the lace at her neck and put on her gloves again. The dirty man stared at her.

Then she lifted her eyes to a large sign above the car-windows and the sign read:

Avoid the biting March winds. You will find quiet, an even temperature and perfect seclusion among the pines at restful Lakewood. Take the ferry at 23d St.

So that when the guard announced Twenty-third Street, Miss Mary got up, went down the stairs, tumbled with surprising facility upon a cross-town car and made for the ferry. And the dirty man went down the stairs with her.

Fate put Miss Mary on just the right boat for a Lakewood Special, and hunger cleared her mind to the extent of throwing her card-case over the rail on the way across. Her umbrella and ulster she had left behind on the elevated train, not being accustomed to carry such things, and they were found by a thrifty old lady in the second-hand-clothing line, who annexed them silently and forever. So that when she arrived at the Lakewood Station and fell among the cabbies and hotel touts she was the perfect type of the no-longer-young spinster, unaccompanied, awkward and light of luggage, presumably light of purse. The cabbies left her therefore, unchallenged, to a lad as shy and awkward as herself, who mumbled something about quiet, reasonable rooms, and received her yielded bag with a surprise as great as her own.

Miss Mary was by now almost light-headed from hunger and excitement. At the slightest pressure she would have told her story to the first interested stranger, and thus ended her adventure, most surely. But Fate led her to the door of one too full of trouble to heed Miss Mary's. To Mrs. Meeker she was a lodger certainly, a boarder possibly—in any event, a source of income. So long had she been waiting for Miss Mary that she fairly snatched her bag from her and pushed her up the faded, decent stairs into the faded, decent bedroom with the cracked china toilet-set. Any one, *any one* would have been welcome to Mrs. Meeker, and Miss Mary's quiet elegance and handsome travelling-bag were far beyond her hopes.

"A real lady," she whispered to her nephew. "Ask if she'd like a little something on a tray, Georgie. I could poach that egg, and there's tea. I won't say anything about a week in advance. She looks tired to death."

Miss Mary's famishing senses cried out loudly at sight of the meagre tray, and as the egg and tea passed her lips a strange, eager sensation was hers, a delicious, gratified climax of emotion: Miss Mary was glad she was alive! She savoured each morsel of the pitiful meal; she could have wished it doubled; the cheap tea filled her nostrils with a balmy odour; she was hungry.

And hardly had the food satisfied her when her eyelids fell, her head dropped forward. Approaching oblivion drugged her ere it reached her and she dozed in her chair. But some instinct forced her to her feet as the landlady appeared, and fumbling in her bag for her card-case and pocketbook, she held herself awake.

"I'd like to pay," she murmured, "and then I'll—I'll go to bed. Will you send some one, please?"

She meant some one to undress her, but Mrs. Meeker did not know this.

"It's—it's twelve a week, with board," she said, her eyes lighting at the yellow bills in her lodger's hand, "and—oh, dear, yes, two weeks is ample, Miss—Miss——"

"My cards are lost," said Miss Mary fretfully. "I can't think where I left them. The man or somebody will know. Ask——"

She started to say, "Ask the doctor," for her memory was swallowed, nearly, by sleepiness, and a curious woman would have had her secret in a twinkle. But Mrs. Meeker was too thankful to be curious.

"Certainly, Miss—Miss——"

"Miss Mary," said the other, yawning, and the landlady repeated, "Yes, Miss Merry. Can't I help you, you being so tired and all?"

"And she stuck out her feet for her shoes, just like a baby," she confided to Georgie, later. "She went off before I got her undressed, really; her folks ought to 've sent some one with her, worn out as she was! You go 'round the first thing in the morning and tell the agent I've got a fine boarder, and more expected. I feel real encouraged."

And all that night and all the next day Miss Mary slept dreamlessly, for the first time in years without a drug to help her.

It did not seem unusual that Mrs. Meeker should have unpacked her few things and laid them in the drawer of the battered bureau: some one always unpacked her things. And when, strangely weak and relaxed, she lay for three days more and ate dutifully from the tray, dozing between whiles, nobody questioned her.

On the fourth day she woke into a grey, despondent world again. The old angry, purposeless tears beset her and she felt that terrible dumbness settling over her. She had long ceased to fight it, now; she only wondered what Mrs. Meeker would do with her. But she never knew what Mrs. Meeker would have done, for when the tired, drudging little woman brought her breakfast tray she held it in dingily gloved hands; she was dressed for a journey.

"My brother's down with a stroke," she said abruptly, "Georgie's father, and wants to see me. I'll have to nurse him, prob'ly, and I s'pose his sending means he's friendly again. It may just be I won't need to come back, and I'm glad, of course, for I'm worth my keep to him any day, and he'd ought to have took Georgie long ago. I'll soon know, and I'll write you, and what I wanted to ask was, would you be willin' to wait till I find out? It might be only temp'ry, and then I'd be sorry to lose a boarder. Will you stay till you hear, anyway?"

Miss Mary nodded dumbly. She could not speak and she was ashamed that she could not; *she had never been ashamed before.*

"That's good," said Mrs. Meeker quickly, "and the lady next door'll give you meals. I'll settle with her—Mrs. Palmer. Her board's good, and I'll only charge you five for the room. That makes a month you've paid for. D'you see?"

Again, Miss Mary nodded.

"Then I'll get right off. It's Philadelphia I'm going to, and I'll write you as soon's I know. But I count on you to stay."

"Yes, I'll stay."

Miss Mary forced the words harshly and it seemed that they would tear her lips, so hard they came. But they came, and they sufficed for Mrs. Meeker, who went out of her solitary lodger's life as quickly as she had come into it, for Miss Mary never saw her again.

On that day she dressed herself slowly, and with a certain clumsiness, took her little shopping bag and bought, with economy and taste, a very fair outfit of simple clothing for the seventy dollars she had gained on the strength of the peddler of embroideries; she passed the peddler's very shop on her way. Underwear, a black dress, rubber overshoes and a plain umbrella—nothing was forgotten.

"When my money is all gone, I will begin to sell the jewelry," she thought, for she knew that she could live comfortably for the rest of her life on less than the value of the emeralds and diamonds. She did her shopping in a public victoria and brought the parcels home in it: it was her only extravagance that day.

As she got out at the door of the little faded house and paid the driver, it occurred to her that she had left it unlocked during her absence, and in her remorse over this and the bustle of going to the strange dining-room for luncheon, whither she was summoned by a slatternly waitress, she forgot completely that on this day she had sworn to stay alone in her room, to conceal from strangers her malady of melancholy dumbness.

"But I'm *not* that way—I'm *not*!" she whispered to herself in amazement, "why, I talked to the clerks all the morning!" And so she had, and none of the dozen at Mrs. Palmer's table that noon remarked anything further than that Miss Merry seemed a quiet, shy sort of person with a tendency to vagueness and little idea of passing the butter dish.

She sorted and arranged her purchases all the afternoon; the little roll of chamois-skin she kept carefully in the wrist-bag which never left her arm.

At dinner Mrs. Palmer took her aside and with the touch on her arm Miss Mary's blood turned to water. "She knows about me!" she thought and nearly fell to the ground from weakness.

"I'm sorry I startled you," said Mrs. Palmer, "Mrs. Meeker said you weren't any too strong, I remember. I only wanted to say that I've sent three more roomers over to your house—she'll be only too glad, I know. You don't mind, Miss Merry?"

"No. I don't mind," she answered, and her heart gave a great pump of relief.

"It'll be more comfortable at night, too," said Mrs. Palmer. "That makes the four rooms full, now, and I'll see that your room gets done up every day with the others. I presume we'll hear from her soon."

The next day she approached Miss Mary with an open letter in her hand.

"Mrs. Meeker's to live with her brother, now, he's paralysed," she announced. "She's sent me a check for the rent and you've paid twenty-four dollars, I see. I'm going over to pack up her stuff and she'll sell me the rest reasonable enough. I'm going to take her house, too. There's a new roomer comes to-day—I think I'll put him in her old room. Or if you," with a shrewd glance at Miss Mary, "wanted to economise at all. I'd rent you hers for four dollars and give this gentleman yours. And I'm usually paid in advance, so if you could make it convenient——"

"I'll attend to it," said Miss Mary, "but I'll keep the room, I think. I don't like change."

She went up to her room, and Dr. Jarvyse would have been amazed at the easy quickness of her gait. She had it all planned, now—the diamonds should go first, and then she would buy some fruit and a plant for her room. She liked her room very much; she did as she pleased in it and no one spied on her or suggested ways of passing the time. Was it some faint memory of her room as a girl, before her brother made his great fortune, that found this dull, half-worn chamber so home-like and soothing? Every afternoon she dusted it, as the chambermaid suggested most ladies expected to, and once she had turned the mattress and made the bed, when the girl felt ill. It gave her a sense of competence and executive ability.

Now she went to the little chamois skin roll, unpicked the tight knots carefully, opened it—and dropped on her knees. The roll was empty. On the compartment where the diamond cross had fitted, stretched a soiled, streaked thumb mark; mechanically she sniffed it—it smelled of tar. The dirty fellow with the bundle who had followed her down the elevated steps had smelled of tar, too, had Miss Mary remembered it.

Well, it was over. She never had a moment's doubt. She had no means, she could not starve, nobody would keep her, and she must go back to Dr. Jarvyse. She groaned in anguish as she looked about her dear, safe room and thought of the horrible luxury of that guarded prison, the birds and the flowers and cruel kindness of those strangers who knew every corner of her bureau, every word of her letters. Still, it must be. The Allens would never take her back, and after this, she would be watched as never before. It must be.

She met Mrs. Palmer on the threshold of what she had begun to call her home. Mrs. Palmer looked worried and spoke sharply to the untidy cleaning-woman behind her.

"Now, I do hope I can trust you," she said, "for I can't stay here to watch. Three new gentlemen for meals, and I have no table for them! And this whole house to be cleaned! And not a girl to be hired in the town! I wish I had another room—I could rent it this afternoon."

"You can have mine," said Miss Mary quietly. "I have no money and I must go."

Mrs. Palmer looked shrewdly at her.

"What made you think you had, before?" she said.

"I had some valuable jewelry—I expected to sell it. It must have been stolen before I got here. I have nothing here to pay with, but I can send it back to you from New York."

"Folks rich?" asked Mrs. Palmer.

Miss Mary nodded carelessly. That people should be rich was nothing to her, and the practiced landlady saw this in a twinkling: no protestations could have proved so much.

"But you don't get on well, I s'pose," she suggested.

"No. We don't get on well," Miss Mary repeated dully.

"I guess it's often so," said the other. Her placid acceptance of these facts was very comforting to Miss Mary. She did not realise how different she herself was from the vague, scared woman of a week ago; nor how her quiet, well-dressed taciturnity impressed Mrs. Palmer.

"You find this agrees with you here, don't you?" the landlady asked, tapping her teeth with a key, thoughtfully.

"Oh, yes, I like it here. I would have liked to stay."

"Well, Miss Merry, how'd you like to stay and help me?" said the landlady. "To tell the truth, I've bit off more than I can chew, as they say. I never had such a run of boarders, and it's all the girl can do to look after the other house. What keeps my people is the cooking, you see, and that I do mostly myself. I'm not fit to talk to the ladies and gentlemen, with my hair all stringy, and smelling of cooking. I know it well enough. I had some thought of asking Mrs. Meeker to go in with me and look after this house and take the head of the table, and keep the books. But you could do it, if you wanted, and you'd look more—more—not that Mrs. Meeker wasn't a lady, of course, but—well, some people look the part better than others."

Miss Mary's brain whirled. The head of the table! The books! It was impossible. Why, the woman didn't realise that she was talking to a—a—Patient, then! (They were never called anything but Patients at Dr. Jarvyse's.)

"I—I'm afraid I haven't the experience," she began tremulously. "I—sometimes my head—I can't always talk to people——"

"Oh, you talk enough," Mrs. Palmer interrupted, kindly. "That's just what it is: some talk too much. Mr. Swartout (that's the literary gentleman in brown—the one with the grey moustache) said you were so quiet and dignified. You know you sat at the end, today, for breakfast, and he said to me it would be pleasant if you kept that place. That's what put it into my head, really. And I guess you've had experience enough. Miss Jenny, that went with you through the store when you bought those clothes (I know her, you see) said she'd never seen seventy dollars used with more judgment nor made to go further. I noticed what she said." She nodded shrewdly, as one who knew the world.

"Well, I don't want to urge, but will you or won't you? I'd give board and lodging and, say, twenty-five a month, till I could do better. The Palmer House has just got to the point where there'll have to be a change, or it'll get second-class."

"Very well, I will try," said Miss Mary huskily, and in a moment she was alone, for Mrs. Palmer was half across the side-yard.

"Just boss that woman, then, and see if she can get the house clean by evening," she called over her shoulder. "I leave her to you, Miss Merry, and it's a weight off me, I can tell you!"

If Miss Mary had paused to think, she would have collapsed into tears and sent for the doctor, but she could not stop, for the cleaning-woman addressed her briskly.

"I suppose everything better come right out and get a good beating?" she said, shouldering her mop; and Miss Mary controlled her quivering lips, pressed her hands to her head, which must not, *could not* fail her now, and agreed.

Late in the afternoon Mrs. Palmer dashed over, her hair flying, her dress untidy.

"Well, how'd you get along?" she began, but paused in the doorway of the fresh, aired house, taking in, at one eagle glance, the white curtains behind shining panes, the polished woodwork, the re-arranged furniture.

"I guess that cleaning-woman met her match," she announced dryly. "You must be nearly dead, Miss Merry! And all ready for dinner, too! I've had a clean table cloth put on, and what do you think that Delia said? 'I'll just rub out me apron an' press it off,' she said, 'for if *she's* to head the table, I can see she'll be particular!'"

Nothing could have kept Miss Mary up but the fact that her own room was yet uncleaned. The lust of soap and water had entered into her, and she ate and answered and passed the butter dish like one in a dream, looking forward with the last of her strength to sleeping in an immaculate chamber. And at half-past one in the morning, she did so. The warm bath in the painted tin tub was a luxury she had never imagined; as the sheets received her tired body, aching in every joint, she tasted for the one moment before sleep blotted out consciousness the ecstasy of earned rest after steady, worried toil, and it was very sweet. Privilege of the clumsiest hod-carrier, it was utterly new to Miss Mary, and she in her innocence, thought it due to delight at the prospect of board and lodging and, say, twenty-five dollars a month!

She did not know that she had hummed, unconsciously, during the afternoon, a song of her early girlhood; nor that the blood, long stagnant, that had raced through every vein as she stooped and beat and lifted and cleansed, was driving the crawling vapours from that mysterious grey tissue in her skull that had so long plagued and confused her.

Nor did she know that the flowers on the table, the fresh chintz covers for the worn lodging-house furniture, so recklessly provided by her, the quick neatness of an apotheosised Delia and the gentle, reserved welcome of the new housekeeper herself, were lifting the commonplace boarding-house to a higher and still higher level. She only knew that she worked harder and harder and never wept nor shuddered nor looked out of black apathy into a cruel tantalizing world, whose inhabitants had evil thoughts of her and wished and worked her ill.

"It's just as I always say," Mrs. Palmer observed, one afternoon in May, as, resting in frank gingham and enveloping apron, she permitted herself the luxury of a cup of tea in Miss Mary's own room. "What's bred in the bones comes out in the blood. I had a gift for cooking since I was ten, and there's little I'll thank a French chef to tell me, Miss Merry. But I can't impress the boarders. I never could. And I can't get the work out of servant-girls without screaming at 'em—never could. And look at you! Every man of 'em—that we wanted—coming up two dollars a week, like gentlemen. And all for the privilege of having this house bachelor. I thought they would. And every man Jack of 'em booked for November first again. I tell you what, Miss Merry, we'll paint both houses this fall, and I wouldn't wonder, what with this spring being so backward and the season so long, if we could paint and paper inside, right through, would you?"

"No," said the housekeeper, rocking gently, luxuriating in the half-hour rest after a hard day on her feet with one servant gone. "No, I wouldn't. That would be nice. I have something saved. You can take that."

"Look at you!" cried Mrs. Palmer. "Saving on thirty a month! We'll pretty near go halves, Miss Merry, from next November. What's bred in the bone, as I said—you were born for the business!"

And the sister of Hiram Z. Allen, late Captain of Finance, blushed with pleasure.

It was in March of the next year, as she sat at her neat desk in the little room they had made into an office when they created a sun parlour out of the side verandah, that Delia, responsible head of three maids now, ushered a gentleman in to her.

"The doctor, Miss Merry, that came yesterday about the rooms for his patient in the cottage," said Delia softly. "I can't seem to get the name, ma'am."

"Very well," said Miss Mary and rose, plumper by eight or ten pounds than she had been, dignified in black broadcloth, only enough of reserve and weighing of her words about her to mark her off slightly from the most of her sex and business.

"Miss Merry? I am Dr. Stanchon, I have been recommended most strongly——"

She swayed before him, then sank into her chair, grasping the arms. He looked courteously alarmed, stared, stared again, then snatched her hand.

"It's not—it can't be—why, Miss Mary!" She gasped and trembled. The year dropped off from her like a loosened cloak.

"Oh, Dr. Stanchon, don't, *don't* tell him!" she moaned.

"Him? him?" he repeated. "Why, Miss Mary, were you here all the time? And your hair—you were ill?"

"It used to be coloured—you never knew," she murmured. "I mean Dr.—Dr. Jarvyse."

"But you are the one Swartout described to me—the one he's in love with? Miss Mary, it was wrong of you—I looked for months. It was cruel. And when they found the emeralds and the cross——"

"Did they find them?"

"Why, certainly—the stones were all listed, you know. Didn't you read it in the papers?"

"I never see them," she said quietly. She had gathered herself together for what must be the struggle of her life.

"Will you tell him? I can't go back. I'd die first!" she cried.

"But why should you go back?" he asked in amazement. "Surely you'll let them know? They gave up hope long ago. You needn't go back to them, if you're happy here, of course, and indeed, I wouldn't, Miss Mary——"

"I don't mean go back *there*," she interrupted gently, "I mean to the—to—Dr.——"

He stared.

"You know, of course, what's the matter," she said quietly, "but nobody here does. They think I'm—I'm like anybody else. I don't mind any more, since I've been so busy. I haven't had time to worry over it. But still, I know it.—And so I told Mr. Swartout it would be impossible. It wouldn't be right."

Stanchon seized both of her hands.

"For heaven's sake, Miss Mary, what do you think's the matter with you?" he cried, his voice breaking in spite of himself.

"Isn't it so?" she queried wistfully. "Do you really mean it?—But who cured me, then?"

"If you are the wonderful person I've been hearing about all this time from Swartout," Stanchon said, trying to speak lightly, his grey eyes firm on her anxious brown ones, "I should say that working for your living did it, Miss Mary!"

And it may be he was right: as a diagnostician he has been widely commended.

THE CHILDREN

It all came over me, as you might say, when I began to tell the new housemaid about the work. Not that I hadn't known before, of course, what a queer sort of life was led in that house; it was hard enough the first months, goodness knows. But then, a body can get used to anything. And there was no harm in it—I'll swear that to my dying day! Although a lie's a lie, any way you put it, and if all I've told—but I'll let you judge for yourself.

As I say, it was when I began to break Margaret in, that it all came over me, and I looked about me, in a way of speaking, for how I should put it to her. She'd been house-parlor-maid in a big establishment in the country and knew what was expected of her well enough, and I saw from the first she'd fit in nicely with us; a steady, quiet girl, like the best of the Scotch, looking to save her wages, and get to be housekeeper herself, some day, perhaps.

But when Hodges brought the tray with the porringers on it and the silver mug, for me to see, and said, "I suppose this young lady'll take these up, Miss Umbleby?" and when Margaret looked surprised and said, "I didn't know there were children in the family—am I supposed to wait on them, too?"—then, as I say, it all came over me, and for the first time in five years I really saw where I stood, like.

I stared at Hodges and then at the girl, and the tray nearly went down amongst us.

"Do you mean to say you haven't told her, Sarah?" says Hodges (and that was the first time that ever he called me by my given name).

"She's told me nothing," Margaret answers rather short, "and if it's invalid children or feeble-minded, I take it most unkind, Miss Umbleby, for I've never cared for that sort of thing, and could have had my twenty-five dollars a month this long time, if I'd wanted to go out as nurse."

"Take the tray up this time, yourself, Mr. Hodges, please," I said, "and I'll have a little talk with Margaret," and I sat down and smoothed my black silk skirt (I always wore black silk of an afternoon) nervously enough, I'll be bound.

The five years rolled away like yesterday—as they do now—as they do now——

I saw myself, in my mind's eye, new to the place, and inclined to feel strange, as I always did when I made a change, though I was twenty-five and no chicken, but rather more settled than most, having had my troubles early and got over them. I'd just left my place—chambermaid and seamstress—in a big city house, and though it was September, I was looking out for the country, for I was mortal tired of the noise and late hours and excitement that I saw ahead of me. It was parties and balls every night and me sitting up to undress the young ladies, for they kept no maid, like so many rich Americans, and yet some one must do for them. There was no housekeeper either, and the mistress was not very strong and we had to use our own responsibility more than I liked—for I wasn't paid for that, do you see, and that's what they forget in this country.

"I think I've got you suited at last, Sarah," the head of the office had said to me, "a nice, quiet place in the country, good pay and light work, but everything as it should be, you understand. Four in help besides the housekeeper and only one in family. Church within a mile and every other Sunday for yourself."

That was just what I wanted, and I packed my box thankfully and left New York for good, I hoped, and I got my wish, for I've never seen the inside of it since.

A middle-aged coachman in good, quiet country livery, met me at the little station, and though he was a still-mouthed fellow and rather reserved, I made out quite a little idea of the place on the way. The mistress, Mrs. Childress, was a young widow, deep in her mourning, so there was no company. The housekeeper was her old nurse, who had brought her up. John, who drove me, was coachman-gardener, and the cook was his wife—both Catholics. Everything went on very quiet and regular and it was hoped that the new upstairs maid wouldn't be one for excitement and gaiety. The inside man had been valet to Mr. Childress and was much trusted and liked by the family. I could see that old John was a bit jealous in that direction.

We drove in through a black iron gate with cut stone posts and old black iron lanterns on top, and the moment we were inside the gates I began to take a fancy to the place. It wasn't kept up like the places at home, but it was neat enough to show that things were taken thought for, and the beds of asters and dahlias and marigolds as we got near the house seemed so home-like and bright to me, I could have cried for comfort. Childerstone was the name of the place; it was carved on a big boulder by the side of the entrance, and just as we drove up to the door John stopped to pick some dahlias for the house (being only me in the wagon) and I took my first good look at my home for twenty years afterward.

There was something about it that went to my heart. It was built of grey cut stone in good-sized blocks, square, with two windows each side the hall door. To some it might have seemed cold-looking, but not to me, for one side was all over ivy, and the thickness of the walls and the deep sills looked solid and comfortable after those nasty brown-stone things all glued to each other in the city. It looked old and respectable and settled, like, and the sun, just at going down, struck the windows like fire and the clean panes shone. There was that yellow light over everything and that stillness, with now and then a leaf or so dropping quietly down, that makes the fall of the year so pleasant, to my mind.

The house stood in beeches and the trunks of them were grey like the house and the leaves all light lemon-coloured, like the sky, and that's the way I always think of Childerstone—grey and yellow and clean and still. Just a few rooks (you call them crows here), went over the house, and except for their cry as they flew, there wasn't a sound about the place. I can see how others might have found it sad, but it never seemed so to me.

John set me down at the servants' entrance and there, before ever I'd got properly into the hall, the strangeness began. The cook in her check apron was kneeling on the floor in front of the big French range with the tears streaming down her face, working over her rosary beads and gabbling to drive you crazy. Over her stood a youngish but severe-appearing man in a white linen coat like a ship's steward, trying to get her up.

"Come, Katey," he was saying, "come, woman, up with you and help—she'll do no harm, the poor soul! Look after her, now, and I'll send for the doctor and see to madam—it's only a fit, most like!"

Then he saw me and ran forward to give a hand to my box.

"You're the chambermaid, Miss, I'm sure," he said. "I'm sorry to say you'll find us a bit upset. The housekeeper's down with a stroke of some sort and the madam's none too strong herself. Are you much of a hand to look after the sick?"

"I'm not so clumsy as some," I said. "Let me see her," and so we left the cook to her prayers and he carried my box to my room.

I got into a print dress and apron and went to the housekeeper's room. She was an elderly person and it looked to me as if she was in her last sickness. She didn't know any one and so I was as good as another, and I had her tidy and comfortable in bed by the time the doctor came. He said she would need watching through the night and left some medicine, but I could see he had little hope for her. I made up a bed in the room and all that night she chattered and muttered and took me for different ones, according as her fever went and came. Towards morning she got quiet, and as I thought, sensible again.

"Are you a nurse?" she says to me.

"Yes, Mrs. Shipman, be still and rest," I told her, to soothe her.

"I'm glad the children are sent away," she went on, after a bit. "'Twould break their mother's heart if they got the fever. Are the toys packed?"

"Yes, yes," I answered, "all packed and sent."

"Be sure there's enough frocks for Master Robertson," she begged me. "He's so hard on them and his aunties are so particular. And my baby must have her woolly rabbit at night or her darling heart will be just broken!"

"The rabbit is packed," I said, "and I saw to the frocks myself."

There's but one way with the sick when they're like that, and that's to humour them, you see. So she slept and I got a little nap for myself. I was glad the children were away by next morning, for she was worse, the cook lost her head, and managed to break the range so that the water-back leaked and John and Hodges were mopping and mending all day. The madam herself had a bad turn and the doctor (a New York doctor for madam, you may be sure!) brought out a handsome, dark woman, the trained hospital nurse, with him. Madam wasn't allowed to know how bad her old nurse was.

So it turned out that I'd been a week in the house without ever seeing my mistress. The nurse and I would meet on the stairs and chat a little, evenings, and once I took a turn in the grounds with her. She was a sensible sort of girl, not a bit above herself, as our English nursing-sisters are, sometimes, but very businesslike, as they say, and a good, brisk way with her. She saw a lot more than she spoke of, Miss Jessop did, I'll warrant!

"It's a good thing the children are sent away," I said. "They always add to the bother when there's sickness."

"Why, are there children?" says she. "Oh, yes, a boy and a girl," I answered, "poor old Mrs. Shipman is forever talking about them. She thinks she's their nurse, it seems, as she was their mother's."

"I wish they were here, then," says she, "for I don't like the looks of my patient at all. She doesn't speak seven words a day, and there's really little or nothing the matter with her, that I can see. She's nervous and she's low and she wants cheering, that's all. I wonder the doctor doesn't see it."

That night, after both patients were settled, she came up to my room and took a glance at the old lady, who was going fast.

"Mrs. Childress will soon have to know about this," she said and then, suddenly, "Are you sure about the children, Sarah?"

"Sure about them?" I repeated after her. "In what way, Miss Jessop?"

"That there are any," says she.

"Why, of course," I answered, "Mrs. Shipman talks of nothing else. They're with their aunty, in New Jersey, somewhere. It's a good thing there are some, for from what she says when she's rambling, the house and all the property would go out of the family otherwise. It's been five generations in the Childress family, but the nearest now is a cousin who married a Jew, and the family hate her for it. But Master Robertson makes it all safe, Mrs. Shipman says."

"That's a queer thing," said she. "I took in a dear little picture of the boy and girl this afternoon, to cheer her up a bit, and told her to try to think they were the real ones, who'd soon be with her, for that matter, and so happy to see their dear mamma, and she went white as a sheet and fainted in my arms. Of course, I didn't refer to it again. She's quiet now, holding the picture, but I feared they were dead and you hadn't known."

"Oh, no," said I. "I'm sure not," and then I remembered that I'd been told there was but one in family. However, that's often said when there's a nurse to take care of small children (though it's not quite fair, perhaps), and I was certain of the children, anyway, for there were toys all about Mrs. Shipman's room and some seed-cookies and "animal-crackers," as they call those odd little biscuits, in a tin on her mantel.

However, we were soon to learn something that made me, at least, all the more curious. The doctor came that morning and told Miss Jessop that her services would be no longer required, after he had seen her patient.

"Mrs. Childress is perfectly recovered," he said, "and she has unfortunately conceived a grudge against you, my dear girl. I need you, anyway, in town. Poor old Shipman can't last the night now, and I want all that business disposed of very quietly. I have decided not to tell Mrs. Childress until it is all over and the funeral done with. She is in a very morbid state, and as I knew her husband well I have taken this step on my own responsibility. Hodges seems perfectly able to run things, and to tell the truth, it would do your mistress far more good to attend to that herself," he said, turning to me.

"It would be a good thing for the poor woman to have some one about her, Dr. Stanchon," the nurse put in quietly. "If there were children in the house, now——"

"Children!" he cried, pulling himself up and staring at her. "Did you speak to her about them? Then that accounts for it! I should have warned you."

"Then they did die?" she asked him. "That's what I thought."

"I'm afraid not," he said, shaking his head with a queer sort of sad little smile. "I forgot you were strange here. Why, Miss Jessop, didn't you know that——"

"Excuse me, sir, but there's no sign of your mare about—did you tie her?" says Hodges, coming in in a great hurry, and the doctor swore and ran off and I never heard the end of the sentence.

Well, I'm running on too long with these little odds and ends, as I'm sure Margaret felt when I started telling her all about it. The truth is I dreaded then, just as I dread now, to get at the real story and look our conduct straight in the face. But I'll get on more quickly now.

Old Mrs. Shipman died very quiet in her sleep and madam wasn't told, which I didn't half like. The doctor was called out of those parts to attend on his father, very suddenly, and Hodges managed the funeral and all. It was plain to see he was a very trusty, silent fellow, devoted to the family. I took as much off him as I could, and I was dusting the drawing-room the day of the funeral, when I happened to pick up a photograph in a silver frame of the same little fellow in the picture the nurse had shown me—a dear little boy in short kilts.

"That's Master Robertson, isn't it?" I said, very carelessly, not looking at him—I will own I was curious. He gave a start.

"Yes—yes, certainly, that's Master Robertson—if you choose to put it that way," he said, and I saw him put his hand up to his eyes and his mouth twitched and he left the room.

I didn't question him again, naturally; he was a hard man to cross and very haughty, was William Hodges, and no one in the house but respected him.

That day I saw Mrs. Childress for the first time. She was a sweet, pretty thing, about my own age, but younger looking, fair, with grey eyes. She was in heavy crêpe and her face all fallen and saddened like, with grief and hopelessness—I felt for her from the moment I saw her. And all the more that I'd made up my mind what her trouble was: I thought that the children were idiots, maybe, or feeble-minded, anyhow, and so the property would go to the Jew in the end and that his family were hating her for it! Folly, of course, but women will have fancies, and that seemed to fit in with all I'd heard.

She'd been told that Shipman was away with some light, infectious fever, and she took it very mildly, and said there was no need to get any one in her place, at present.

"Hodges will attend to everything," she said, in her pretty, tired way; "not that there's much to do —for one poor woman."

"Things may mend, ma'am, and you'll feel more like having some friends about you, most likely, later on," I said, to cheer her a bit.

She shook her head sadly.

"No, no, Sarah—if I can't have my own about me, I'll have no others," she said, and I thought I saw what she meant and said no more.

That night the doctor and the legal gentleman that looked after the family affairs were with us and my mistress kept them for dinner. I helped Hodges with the serving and was in the butler's pantry after Mrs. Childress had left them with their coffee and cigars, and as Hodges had left the door ajar I couldn't help catching a bit of the talk now and then.

"The worst of it is this trouble about the children," said the doctor. "She will grieve herself into a decline, I'm afraid."

"I suppose there's no hope?" said the other gentleman.

"No hope?" the doctor burst out. "Why, man, Robertson's been dead six months!"

"To be sure—I'd forgotten it was so long. Well, well, it's too bad, too bad," and Hodges came back and closed the door.

I must say I was thoroughly put out with the doctor. Why should he have told me a lie? And it was mostly from that that I deliberately disobeyed him that night, for I knew from the way he had spoken to the nurse that he didn't wish the children mentioned. But I couldn't help it, for when I came to her room to see if I could help her, she was sitting in her black bedroom gown with her long hair in two braids, crying over the children's picture. "Hush, hush, ma'am," I said, kneeling by her and soothing her head, "if they were here, you may be sure they wouldn't wish it."

"Who? Who?" she answers me, quite wild, but not angry at all. I saw this and spoke it out boldly, for it was plain that she liked me.

"Your children, ma'am," I said, softly but very firm, "and you should control yourself and be cheerful and act as if they *were* here—as if it had pleased God to let you have them and not *Himself*!"

Such a look as she gave me! But soon she seemed to melt, like, and put out her arm over my shoulders.

"What a beautiful way to put it, Sarah!" says she, in a dreamy kind of way. "Do you really think God has them—somewhere?"

"Why, of course, ma'am," said I, shocked in good earnest. "Who else?"

"Then you think I might love them, just as if—just as if——" here she began to sob.

"Why, Mrs. Childress," I said, "where is your belief? That's all that's left to mothers. I know, for I've lost two, and their father to blame for it, which you need never say," I told her.

She patted my shoulder very kindly. "But oh, Sarah, if only they*were* here!" she cried, "really, really here!"

"I know, I know," I said, "it's very hard. But try to think it, ma'am—it helped me for weeks. Think they're in the room next you, here, and you'll sleep better for it."

"Shall I?" she whispered, gripping my hand hard. "I believe I would—how well you understand me, Sarah! And will you help me to believe it?"

I saw she was feverish and I knew what it means to get one good refreshing night without crying, and so I said, "Of course I will, ma'am; see, I'll open the door into the next room and you can fancy them in their cribs, and I'll sleep in there as if it was to look after them, like."

Well, she was naught but a child herself, the poor dear, and she let me get her into bed like a lamb and put her cheek into her hand and went off like a baby. It almost scared me, to see how easy she was to manage, if one did but get hold of the right way. She looked brighter in the morning and as Hodges had told me that Shipman used to do for her, I went in and dressed her— not that I was ever a lady's maid, mind you, but I've always been one to turn my hand easily to anything I had a mind to, and I was growing very fond of my poor lady—and then, I was a little proud, I'll own, of being able to do more for her than her own medical man, who couldn't trust a sensible woman with the truth!

She clung to me all the morning, and after my work was done, I persuaded her to come out for the air. The doctor had ordered it long ago, but she was obstinate, and would scarcely go at all. That day, however, she took a good stroll with me and it brought a bit of colour into her cheeks. Just as we turned toward the house she sat down on a big rock to rest herself, and I saw her lip quiver and her eyes begin to fill. I followed her look and there was a child's swing, hung from two ropes to a low bough. It must have been rotted with the rains, for it looked very old and the board seat was cracked and worn. All around—it hung in a sort of little glade—were small piles of stones and bits of oddments that only children get together, like the little magpies they are.

There's no use to expect any one but a mother or one who's had the constant care of little ones to understand the tears that come to your eyes at a sight like that. What they leave behind is worse than what they take with them; their curls and their fat legs and the kisses they gave you are all shut into the grave, but what they used to play with stays there and mourns them with you.

I saw a wild look come into her eyes, and I determined to quiet her at any cost.

"There, there, ma'am," I said quickly, "'tis only their playthings. Supposing they were there, now, and enjoying them! You go in and take your nap, as the doctor ordered, and leave me behind..."

She saw what I meant in a twinkling and the colour jumped into her face again. She turned and hurried in and just as she went out of sight she looked over her shoulder, timid like, and waved her hand—only a bit of a wave, but I saw it.

Under a big stone in front of me, for that part of the grounds was left wild, like a little grove, I saw a rusty tin biscuit box, and as I opened it, curiously, to pass the time, I found it full of little tin platters and cups. Hardly thinking what I did, I arranged them as if laid out for tea, on a flat stone, and left them there. When I went to awaken her for lunch, I started, for some more of those platters were on the table by her bed and a white woolly rabbit and a picture book! She blushed, but I took no notice, and after her luncheon I spied her going quickly back to the little grove.

"Madam's taking a turn for the better, surely," Hodges said to me that afternoon. "She's eating like a Christian now. What have you done to her, Miss Umbleby?" (I went as "Miss" for it's much easier to get a place so.)

"Mr. Hodges," I said, facing him squarely, "the doctors don't know everything. You know as well as I that it's out of nature not to mention children, where they're missed every hour of the day and every day of the month. It's easing the heart that's wanted—not smothering it."

"What d'you mean?" he says, staring at me.

"I mean toys and such like," I answered him, very firm, "and talk of them that's not here to use them, and even pretending that they are, if that will bring peace of mind, Mr. Hodges."

He rubbed his clean shaven chin with his hand.

"Well, well!" he said at last. "Well, well, well! You're a good girl, Miss Umbleby, and a kind one, that's certain. I never thought o' such a thing. Maybe it's all right, though. But who could understand a woman, anyway?"

"That's not much to understand," said I, shortly, and left him staring at me.

She came in late in the afternoon with the rabbit under her arm and there was Mr. Hodges in the drawing-room laying out the tea—we always had everything done as if the master was there, and guests, for the matter of that; she insisted on it. He knew his place as well as any man, but his eye fell on the rabbit and he looked very queer and nearly dropped a cup. She saw it and began to tremble and go white, and it came over me then that now or never was the time to clinch matters or she'd nearly die from shame and I couldn't soothe her any more.

"Perhaps Hodges had better go out and bring in the rest of the toys, ma'am," I says, very careless, not looking at her. "It's coming on for rain. And he can take an umbrella ... shall he?"

She stiffened up and gave a sort of nod to him.

"Yes, Hodges, go," she said, half in a whisper, and he bit his lip, and swallowed hard and said, "Very good, madam," and went.

Well, after that, you can see how it would be, can't you? One thing led to another, and one time when she was not well for a few days and rather low, I actually got the two little cribs down from the garret and ran up some white draperies for them. She'd hardly let me leave her, and indeed there was not so much work that I couldn't manage very well. She gave all her orders through me and I was well pleased to do for her and let Mr. Hodges manage things, which he did better than poor old Shipman, I'll be bound. By the time we told her about Shipman's death, she took it very easy—indeed, I think, she'd have minded nothing by that time, she had grown so calm and almost healthy.

Mr. Hodges would never catch my eye and I never talked private any more with him, but that was the only sign he didn't approve, and he never spoke for about a month, but joined in with me by little and little and never said a word but to shrug his shoulders when I ordered up a tray with porringers on it for the nursery (she had a bad cold and got restless and grieving). I left her in the nursery with the tray and went out to him, for I saw he wished to speak to me at last.

"Dr. Stanchon would think well of this, if he was here. Is that your idea, Miss Umbleby?" he said to me, very dry. (The doctor had never come back, but gone to be head of a big asylum out in the west.)

"I'm sure I don't know, Mr. Hodges," I answered. "I think any doctor couldn't but be glad to see her gaining every day, and when she feels up to it and guests begin to come again, she'll get willing to see them and forget the loss of the poor little things."

"The loss of *what*?" says he, frowning at me.

"Why, the children," I answered.

"What children?"

"Master Robertson, of course, and Miss Winifred," I said, quite vexed with his obstinacy. (I had asked her once if the baby was named after her and she nodded and went away quickly.)

"See here, my girl," says he, "there's no good keeping this up for my benefit. *I'm* not going into a decline, you know. I know as well as you do that she couldn't lose what she never had!"

"Never had!" I gasped. "She never had any children?"

"Of course not," he said, steadying me, for my knees got weak all of a sudden. "That's what's made all the trouble—that's what's so unfortunate! D'you mean to say you didn't know?"

I sank right down on the stairs. "But the pictures!" I burst out.

"If you mean that picture of Mr. Robertson Childress when he was a little lad and the other one of him and his sister that died when a baby, and chose to fancy they was *hers*," says he, pointing upstairs, "it's no fault of mine, Miss Umbleby."

And no more it was. What with poor old Shipman's ramblings and the doctor's words that I had twisted into what they never meant, I had got myself into a fine pickle.

"But what shall I do, Mr. Hodges?" I said, stupid-like, with the surprise and the shock of it. "It'd kill her, if I stopped now."

"That's for you to decide," said he, in his reserved, cold way, "I have my silver to do."

Well, I did decide. I lay awake all night at it, and maybe I did wrong, but I hadn't the heart to see the red go out of her cheek and the little shy smile off her pretty mouth. It hurt no one, and the mischief was done, anyway—there'd be no heir to Childerstone, now. For five generations it had been the same—a son and a daughter to every pair, and the old place about as dear to each son, as I made out, as ever his wife or child could be. General Washington had stopped the night there, and some great French general that helped the Americans had come there for making plans to attack the British, and Colonel Robertson Childress that then was had helped him. They had plenty of English kin and some in the Southern States, but no friends near them, on account of my mistress's husband having to live in Switzerland for his health and his father dying young (as he did) so that his mother couldn't bear the old place. But as soon as Mr. Robertson was told he was cured and could live where he liked, he made for Childerstone and brought his bride there— a stranger from an American family in Switzerland—and lived but three months. If anybody was ever alone, it was that poor lady, I'm sure. There was no big house like theirs anywhere about— no county families, as you might say—and those that had called from the village she wouldn't see, in her mourning. And yet out of that house she would not go, because he had loved it so; it was pitiful.

There's no good argle-bargling over it, as my mother used to say, I'd do the same again! For I began it with the best of motives, and as innocent as a babe, myself, of the real truth, you see.

I can shut my eyes, now, and it all comes back to me as it was in the old garden, of autumn afternoons—I always think of Childerstone in the autumn, somehow. There was an old box hedge there, trimmed into balls and squares, and beds laid out in patterns, with asters and marigolds and those little rusty chrysanthemums that stand the early frosts so well. A wind-break of great evergreens all along two sides kept it warm and close, and from the south and west the sun streamed in onto the stone dial that the Childress of General Washington's time had had brought over from home. It was set for Surrey, Hodges told me once, and no manner of use, consequently, but very settled and home-like to see, if you understand me. In the middle was an old stone basin, all mottled and chipped, and the water ran out from a lion's mouth in some kind of brown metal, and trickled down its mane and jaws and splashed away. We cleaned it out, she and I, one day, *pretending we had help*, and Hodges went to town and got us some gold fish for it. They looked very handsome there. Old John kept the turf clipped and clean and routed out some rustic seats for us—all grey they were and tottery, but he strengthened them, and I smartened them up with yellow chintz cushions I found in the garret—and I myself brought out two tiny arm-chairs, painted wood, from the loft in the coach house. We'd sit there all the afternoon in September, talking a little, me mending and my mistress embroidering on some little frocks I cut out for her. We talked about the children, of course. They got to be as real to me as to her, almost. Of course at first it was all what they *would* have been (for she was no fool, Mrs. Childress, though you may be thinking so) but by little and little it got to be what they *were*. It couldn't be helped.

Hodges would bring her tea out there and she'd eat heartily, for she never was much of a one for a late dinner, me sewing all the time, for I always knew my place, though I believe in her kind heart she'd have been willing for me to eat with her, bless her! Then she'd look at me so wistful-like, and say, "I'll leave you now, Sarah—eat your tea and don't keep out too late. Good-bye— good-bye..." Ah, dear me!

I'd sit and think, with the leaves dropping quiet and yellow around me and the water dripping from the lion's mouth and sometimes I'd close my eyes and—I'll swear I could hear them playing quietly beyond me! They were never noisy children. I'll say now something I never mentioned, even to her, and I'd say it if my life hung by it. More than once I've left the metal tea-set shut in the biscuit box and found it spread out of mornings. My mistress slept in the room next me with the door open, and am I to think that William Hodges, or Katey, crippled with rheumatism, or that lazy old John came down and set them out? I've taken a hasty run down to that garden (we called it the children's garden, after a while) because she took an idea, and seen the swing just dying down, and not a breath stirring. That's the plain gospel of it. And I've lain in my bed, just off the two cribs, and held my breath at what I felt and heard. She knew it, too. But never heard so much as I, and often cried for it. I never knew why that should be, nor Hodges, either.

There was one rainy day I went up in the garret and pulled the old rocking-horse out and dusted it and put it out in the middle and set the doors open and went away. It was directly over our heads as we sat sewing, and—ah, well, it's many years ago now, a many and a many, and it's no good raking over too much what's past and gone, I know. And as Hodges said, afterward, the rain on the roof was loud and steady....

I don't know why I should have thought of the rocking-horse, and she not that was always thinking and planning for them. Hodges said it was because I had had children. But I could never have afforded them any such toy as that. Still, perhaps he was right. It was odd his saying that (he knew the facts about me, of course, by that time) being such a dry man, with no fancy about him, you might say, and disliking the whole subject, as he always did, but so it was. Men will often come out with something like that, and quite astonish one.

He never made a hint of objection when I was made housekeeper, and that was like him, too, though I was, to say so, put over him. But he knew my respect for him, black silk afternoons or no black silk, and how we all leaned on him, really.

And then Margaret came, as I said, and it was all to tell, and a fine mess I made of it and William Hodges that settled it, after all.

For Margaret wanted to pack her box directly and get off, and said she'd never heard of such doings and had no liking for people that weren't right.

"Not right?" says Hodges, "not right? Don't you make any such mistake, my girl. Madam attends to all her law business and is at church regularly, and if she's not for much company—why, all the easier for us. Her cheques are as sensible as any one's, I don't care who the man is, and a lady has a right to her fancies. I've lived with very high families at home, and if I'm suited, you may depend upon it the place is a good one. Go or stop, as you like, but don't set up above your elders, young woman."

So she thought it over and the end of it all was that she was with us till the last. And gave me many a black hour, too, poor child, meaning no harm, but she admired Hodges, it was plain, and being younger than I and far handsomer in a dark, Scotch way, it went hard with me, for he made no sign, and I was proud and wouldn't have showed my feelings for my life twice over.

Well, it went on three years more. I made my little frocks longer and the gold fish grew bigger and we set out new marigolds every year, that was all. It was like some quiet dream, when I've gone back and seemed a girl again in the green lanes at home, with mother clear-starching and the rector's daughter hearing my catechism and Master Lawrence sent off to school for bringing me his first partridge. Those dreams seem long and short at one and the same time, and I wake years older, and yet it has not been years that passed but only minutes. So it was at Childerstone. The years went by like the hours went in the children's garden, all hedged in, like, and quiet and leaving no mark. We all seemed the same to each other and one day was like another, full, somehow, and busy and happy, too, in a quiet, gentle way.

When old Katey lay dying she spoke of these days for the first time to me. She'd sent up the porringers and set out glasses of milk and made cookies in heart shapes with her mouth tight shut for all that time, and we never knowing if she sensed it rightly or not. But on her deathbed she told me that she felt the Blessed Mary (as she called her) had given those days to my poor mistress to make up to her for all she'd lost and all she'd never had, and that she'd confessed her part in it and been cleared, long ago. I never loved any time better, looking back, nor Hodges either. One season the Christmas greens would be up, and then before we knew it the ice would be out of the brooks and there would be crocuses and daffodils for Mr. Childress's grave.

She and I took all the care of it and the key to the iron gate of it lay out on her low work table, and one or other of us always passing through, but one afternoon in summer when I went with a basket of June roses, she being not quite up to it that day, there on the flat stone I saw with my own eyes a little crumpled bunch of daisies—all nipped off short, such as children pick, and crushed and wilted in their hot little hands! And on no other tomb but his. But I was used to such as that, by then....

Margaret was handy with her needle, and I remember well the day she made the linen garden hat with a knot of rose-colour under the brim.

"You don't think this will be too old, do you, ma'am?" she said when she showed it to my mistress, and the dear lady was that pleased!

"Not a bit, Margaret," she said and I carried it off to Miss Winifred's closet. Many's the time I missed it after that, and knew too much to hunt. It was hunting that spoiled all, for we tried it....

And yet we didn't half believe. Heaven help us, we knew, but we didn't believe: St. Thomas was nothing to us!

Margaret was with us three years when the new family came. Hodges told us that Hudson River property was looking up and land was worth more every year. Anyway, in one year two families built big houses within a mile of us and we went to call, of course, as in duty bound. John grumbled at getting out the good harness and having the carriage re-lined, but my mistress knew what was right, and he had no choice. I dressed her very carefully, and we watched her off from the door, a thought too pale in her black, but sweet as a flower, and every inch full of breeding, as Hodges said.

I never knew what took place at that visit, but she came back with a bright red circle in each cheek and her head very high, and spent all the evening in the nursery. Alone, of course, for I heard little quick sounds on the piano in the drawing-room, and the fairy books were gone from the children's book-shelves, and Margaret found them in front of the fire and brought them to me....

It was only three days before the new family called on us (a pair of ponies to a basket phaeton—very neat and a nice little groom) and my heart jumped into my mouth when I saw there were two children in with the lady: little girls of eight and twelve, I should say. 'Twas the first carriage callers that ever I'd seen in the place, and Hodges says to me as he goes toward the hall,

"This is something like, eh, Miss Umbleby?"

But I felt odd and uncertain, and when from behind the library door I heard the lady say, "You see I've kept my word and brought my babies, Mrs. Childress—my son is hardly old enough for yours—only four—but Helena and Lou can't wait—they are so impatient to see your little girl!"—when I heard that, I saw what my poor mistress had been at, and the terrible situation we were in (and had been in for years) flashed over me and my hands got cold as ice.

"Where is she?" the lady went on.

At that I went boldly into the library and stood by my mistress's chair—I couldn't desert her then, after all those years.

"Where? where?" my poor lady repeated, vague-like and turning her eyes so piteous at me that I looked the visitor straight in the face and getting between her and my mistress I said very calmly,

"I think Miss Winifred is in the children's garden, madam; shall I take the young ladies there?"

For my thought was to get the children out of the way, before it all came out, you see.

Oh, the look of gratitude she gave me! And yet it was a mad thing to do. But I couldn't desert her —I couldn't.

"There, you see, mamma!" cried the youngest, and the older one said,

"We can find our way, thank you," very civil, to me.

"Children have sharp eyes," said the lady, laughing. "One can't hide them from each other—haven't you found it so?"

"Now what the devil does she mean by that?" Hodges muttered to me as he passed by me with the tray. He always kept the silver perfect, and it did one's heart good to see his tray: urn and sugar and cream just twinkling and the toast in a covered dish—old Chelsea it was—and new cakes and jam and fresh butter, just as they have at home.

I don't know what they talked of, for I couldn't find any excuse to stop in the room, and she wouldn't have had it, anyway. I went around to the front to catch the children when they should come back, and quiet them, but they didn't come, and I was too thankful to think much about it.

After about half an hour I saw the oldest one coming slowly along by herself, looking very sulky.

"Where's your sister, dear?" I said, all in a tremble, for I dreaded how she might put it.

"She's too naughty—I can't get her to leave," she said pettishly, and burst into the library ahead of me. My mistress's face was scarlet and her eyes like two big stars—for the first time I saw that she was a beauty. Her breath came very quick and I knew as well as if I'd been there all the time that she'd been letting herself go, as they say, and talked to her heart's content about what she'd never have a chance to talk again to any guest. She was much excited and the other woman knew it and was puzzled, I could see, from the way she looked at her.

Now the girl burst into the talk.

"Mamma, Lou is so naughty!" she cried. "I saw the ponies coming up the drive, and I told her it was time, but she won't come!"

"Gently, daughter, gently," said the lady, and put her arm around her and smoothed her hair. "Why won't Lou come?"

I can see that room now, as plain as any picture in a frame: the setting sun all yellow on the gilt of the rows of books, the streak of light on the waxed oak floor, the urn shining in the last rays. There was the mother patting the big girl, there was Hodges with his hand on the tray, and there was me standing behind my mistress, with her red cheeks and her poor heaving bosom.

"Why won't Lou come?" she asked the girl again.

"Because," she says, still fretful, and very loud and clear, "because she is taking a pattern of the little girl's hat and trying to twist hers into that shape! I told her you wouldn't like it."

My mistress sprang up and the chair fell down with a crash behind her. I turned (Hodges says) as white as a sheet and moved nearer her.

"Hat!" she gasped. "What hat? *whose hat*?"

There seemed to be a jingling, like sleighbells, all through the air, and I thought I was going crazy till I saw that it came from the tray, where Hodges's hand was shaking so, and yet he couldn't take it off.

"The hat with the rose-coloured ribbon on it," said the girl, "the one we saw as we drove in, you know, mamma. It's so becoming."

"Sarah! Sarah! did you hear? Did you hear?" shrieked my mistress. "She saw, Sarah, *she saw*!"

Then the colour went out of her like when you blow out a candle, and she put her hand to her heart.

"Oh, oh, what pain!" she said very quickly, and Hodges cried, "My God, she's gone!" and I caught her as she fell and we went down together, for my knees were shaking.

When I opened my eyes there was only Margaret there, wetting my forehead, for William had gone for a doctor. Not that it was of any use, for she never breathed. But the smile on her face was lovely.

We got her on her bed and the sight of her there brought the tears to me and I cried out, "Oh, dear, oh, dear! she was all I had in the world, and now——"

"Now you've got me, my girl, and isn't that worth anything to you, Sarah?"

That was William Hodges, and he put his arm over my shoulder, right before Margaret, and looked so kind at me, so kind—I saw in a moment that no one else was anything to him and that he had always cared for me. And that, coming so sudden, when I had given up all hope of it, was too much for me, weak as I was, and I fainted off again and woke up raving hot with fever and half out of my mind, but not quite, for I kept begging them to put off the funeral till I should be able to be up.

But this, of course, was not done, and by the time I was out of hospital the turf was all in place on her dear grave.

William had managed everything and had picked out all the little keepsakes I should have chosen—the heirs were most kind, though Jews. Indeed, I've felt different to that sort of people ever since, for they not caring for the house on account of its being lonely, to their way of thinking, made it into a children's home for those of their belief as were poor and orphaned, and whatever may have been, the old place will never lack for children now.

I never stepped foot in the grounds again, for William Hodges, though the gentlest and fairest of men, never thwarted me but once, and it was in just that direction. Moreover, he forbade me to speak of what only he and I knew for a certainty, and he was one of that sort that when a command is laid, it's best kept.

We've two fine children—girl and boy—and he never murmured at the names I chose for them. Indeed, considering what my mistress's will left me and what his master had done for him, he was as pleased as I.

"They're named after our two best friends, Sarah," he said, looking hard at me, once.

And I nodded my head, but if she saw me, in heaven, she knew who were in my heart when I named them!

THE CRYSTAL

In reviewing the matter dispassionately, it seems difficult to find anybody (anybody, that is to say, to whom her career was or is of the slightest interest) who omits to pronounce Molly Dickett's life an egregious and shameful failure. I should be sorry for any one, for instance, who had the hardihood to address her mother on the subject, for Mrs. Dickett's power of tongue is well known in and beyond local circles; and since Eleanor married young Farwell, who stands in line for cashier of the bank forty or fifty years from now, if all goes well and a series of providential deaths occurs—indeed, ever since Kathryn became assistant-principal at the high-school (because, as her mother points out, a mere teacher's position, even in a high-school, may not be much, but an assistant-principal may be called to consult with the trustees any day and Kathryn has twice refused a college professorship) since these family adjustments, I repeat, Mrs. Dickett's tongue has grown steadily more incisive and her attempts at scaling the fortress of Mr. Dickett's wardrobe more encouraging.

I believe it to be the simple truth to say that she literally never mentions her second daughter, and that Molly sends her letters direct to the factory to be sure that her father gets them—for Mrs. Dickett is Napoleonic in her methods and would really, I am afraid, stop at nothing. Any woman who has borne three children and will learn to drive an electric runabout at the age of forty-five, for the purpose of taking her husband home from his office in it, is to be reckoned with, you will agree.

The last time she is known to have referred to the girl definitely was when she announced the theory that her unfortunate name lay at the bottom of it all.

"Molly," she is reported to have said, "was named by her father—a mistake always, I think. The fact that Eleanor was baptised Ella has little or nothing to do with it; there was never any 'Nellie' or 'Lelie' about it, and at sixteen she began of her own accord to write it Eleanor. Kathryn I named entirely myself—and after all, what can Aunt Ella be said to have done for Eleanor? A silver ring and a bracelet when she graduated! But it was always 'Molly Dickett' all over the town!"

And it must be confessed that this was so, if, indeed, the confession proves anything. Nevertheless Mrs. Dickett cannot deny that for a long time, up to the period of her plunge into outer darkness, Molly was confessedly the flower of the family. Eleanor was rather soggy, a creature of inertia, chocolate caramels and a tendency to ritualism which her mother could not have foreseen when she encouraged her entering the Episcopal communion ("I don't mind candles so much," said Mrs. Dickett, "but I must say I think it's very bad taste to call yourself an American Catholic, when you can't help but feel that Catholics should be foreigners").

Kathryn her mother pronounced "a very ordinary girl, very ordinary indeed," up to the day when she was graduated, head of her class, at the State normal-school. She showed every sign, even after that, of snapping at the bait of a middle-aged widower with three children, simply because his hook was labelled *New York*; but when it became known, as a result of herculean detective efforts on Mrs. Dickett's part, that he employed but one servant, insisted upon the payment of what he termed "spot cash" for every article purchased in his establishment, and disapproved of the theatre, Kathryn yielded to reason and henceforth consulted her mother at each successive stage of her growing career until such consultation was frankly deprecated by the fountain-head itself.

But Molly was neither soggy nor ordinary, being distinctly handsome in a grey-eyed, black-haired, white-skinned way, a clever student, an original conversationalist—in short, a personality. Unlike the usual victim to an older and a younger sister, she managed to get quite her fair share of the family dignities and finances—was in fact accused by her sisters of using undue influence in persuading her father to send her to a woman's college. It is most characteristic of her that at this accusation she refused the favour, interested her teachers in her cause so that they procured her a full scholarship at the college of her choice, and actually completed a four years' course there with no other means than her share of the twenty-five dollars yearly placed to his daughters' bank accounts by their father since the birth of each. On this slender sum, plus the accruing interest, eked out by college journalism, which began to be mentionable in those years—the early 90's—strengthened further in the last terms by tutoring, did Molly Dickett triumphantly assert her independence, and I tell it of her at this length so that none may throw "rolling stones" at her, in what followed. A young woman of eighteen who can set her course in solitude and steer it alone, friendless, except for what friends her qualities can make her, absolutely unaided but for her own exertions, for four years, is not to be called lacking in application, I submit. She got out of that business just what there was in it, *and so*, she insists, *she did at every stage of her subsequent history*. Note this, for it is important.

Here you see her, then, at twenty-two; handsome, accomplished, independent, well-rated on her particular 'Change—one fairly hears Dick Whittington's bells in the air! Her mother, when Molly wrote home the news of her appointment as under-reader in the office of one of the new cheap magazines that began to appear with such frequency at about that time, spoke of her with the typical respect of the dependent woman for the wage-earner, and never dropped that note till the crash came. Mr. Dickett was head clerk by now, with an appreciable advance in salary; and Eleanor's wedding (it was in dressing the Roodscreen at Christmas that young Farwell met his fate), with her sisters as bridesmaids, marked a distinct stage in the family's social career. Old Mr. Farwell, who had long been nursing his only son's bank position, did the handsome thing for the young couple, and stomached, very decently, what must have been his regret at the boy's choice —for we all like our children to "look up and not down," as the motto suggests, in these matters. And he was paid for it, for Eleanor made a man of the boy and a vestryman to boot, and quite won the old man's heart, though he never loved Mrs. Dickett.

By the time Molly had been for two years at her post in *Slater's Monthly*, Kathryn had moved back to her normal-school as instructor—"and they paid well to get her, too," as Mr. Dickett informed his stenographer confidentially. She had been invited to supper more than once, had the stenographer, in the old days, and there had even been a little talk of Kathryn's acquiring this accomplishment, once, but Mr. Dickett was far too wise to suggest her presence at the half-past six dinner now-a-days. He was far too wise, indeed, to do anything that seemed likely to ruffle the increasingly easy currents into which his bark had drifted of late. In a vague way he had always counted on supporting four women until three of them—or two, say, for Kathryn was plain and rather managing—should marry; and lo and behold, all three were off his hands in a twinkle, and there was a pretty little nest-egg growing for little Henry (for Eleanor had been very discreet about the first baby).

So now we arrive at the day when Molly left her desk in the ante-room of Slater's, walked through the book department and the art offices and encountered Miss Spinner, the little dried and spectacled reader of forty-odd years, and centuries (or their equivalent) of magazine experience.

"Miss Spinner," said Molly, "do you mind telling me what they pay you a week?"

"Twenty-five," Miss Spinner replied promptly. "Not at all. Of course I'd been fifteen years at Franklin Square, and it was all that experience that made them offer me the three dollars raise. So I left. But, of course, there are five magazines now where there used to be one. In ten years I think there'll be ten. So does Mr. Slater. That means competition, and that means that experience will always be worth something to the new ones. You started at fifteen, you see, and of course I only got ten ... Gracious, isn't that Mrs. Julia Carter Sykes's voice? Perhaps you'd better step out, my dear—Mr. Slater's talking with that English prison man and said that he wasn't to be disturbed if the Twelve Apostles came!"

Molly went with her swift, unhasty step (she had long legs) and received Mrs. Julia Carter Sykes urbanely, as befitted the best paid woman novelist of her country. Occasionally she had the fancy to "trot around to the office" as she called it: it was believed that she "picked up types" there. And Molly knew how to keep her waiting without offending her, just as she knew how to dispose of the illustrators, from the Great Moguls who came in cabs to scold about the defects in half-tone processes, to the just discovered young genius who waited an hour in the outside hall, his great pasteboard square between his knees.

"You're much too pretty to be here, my child—do you like it?" Mrs. Julia Carter Sykes remarked impertinently (she was supposed to believe that her manner was that of the English Aristocracy, and asked the most embarrassing questions of everybody with an income of less than fifteen thousand a year).

"Not very much," Molly replied placidly. "It's a little dull. I'm thinking of going into journalism. Couldn't you give me some letters to some of the editors? I could do good special article stuff, I'm sure."

"But certainly!" the novelist cried. "You are too delicious! I'll write you a card to Hecht himself this moment—I'm dining with him to-night—and I'll speak of you. I'll tell him to send you to interview me at 'Bonnybraeside.'"

"Thanks," said Molly laconically and rose to show the celebrity to Mr. Slater's sanctum. The English prison man, emerging, took in the contrasted couple at a single glance, supposed them to be the whirlwind editor's wife and daughter, from his greeting ("Come in, come in, my dears, both of you!") and inquired of his wife, eight days later, how she explained a woman of that type, "strung with sapphires, literally," and a daughter like a young duchess, with Irish eyes and a walk like Diana's. His wife could not explain it at all, and said as much.

Molly left Mr. Slater somewhat puzzled. He raised her salary three dollars, might have been pushed to five, but she merely smiled deprecatingly.

"It isn't exactly that," she said, "but there seems no outlook, somehow. I don't think it's a very reasonable profession—if it is a profession."

He exploded into the name of a great English novelist who held precisely that position.

"Yes. But I am not a great novelist, you see," said Molly, and cleared out her desk with the swift thoroughness that characterized her. She put a clean sheet of green blotting paper on it before she left, and washed out the inkwell herself.

"That stenographer spells worse and worse, remember," she remarked. "I'll look in for any mail."

"Why, aren't you going to stay at a hundred-and-three any more?"

Miss Pinner spoke with concern: she knew that the boarding-house recommended highly by Eleanor's rector (his sister had stayed there while studying singing) was very tautly managed, in an unobtrusive way, and that the sisters who directed it had a shrewd idea of the goings and comings of their "guests."

"No," said Molly. "I'll be out at all hours, maybe, and they wouldn't like it. Don't be worried— I'll look in now and then."

And so, for a year, she did, and they were all delighted to see her, for few people likely to enter such offices can talk more amusingly than Molly Dickett. She had always used her material well, when it was limited, and now, when it bumped into the Himalayas at one end (her famous Rajah of Bhutpore interview) and rounded the hitherto speechless promontories of Spud Connors' career, the champion heavyweight of the world (she actually drew vivid metaphors from him and he gave her a tintype of himself at eight years) the entire staff gathered 'round her when she came, and Mr. Slater, under a temporary financial cloud, wept literal tears because he could not afford to buy her back to them. It was, of course, the "Bonnybraeside" interview that did it. So cleverly was this column-and-a-half of chatty sharp-shooting manoeuvred that Mrs. Julia Carter Sykes sent hundreds of copies to her friends, while her fellow celebrities giggled among themselves, and the publishers wondered exactly what the Public really wanted, anyhow. You couldn't tell, any more, they complained.

Just here began the little cloud on Mrs. Dickett's happiness. For two years the family were very proud of Molly, and Eleanor gave a tea for her on one of her infrequent visits to them and got some people she could never have hoped for otherwise on the strength of her sister's celebrityship, for her Sunday morning column-and-a-half got to two-thirds of the town's breakfast tables, and her picture was at the head of it, now. At twenty-five she was called (and probably correctly) the second highest paid woman journalist in the country, and she spoke familiarly of names that are head-lines to most of us and bought evening gowns at "little shops" on Fifth Avenue. She lived with a red-haired friend, a clever illustrator of rising vogue, in a pretty little apartment, and Mrs. Dickett dined there one night with a really great novelist, a tenor from the Metropolitan Opera House and a young Englishman whose brother was a baronet. They had four glasses at their plates and the maid's cap and apron were tremendously interesting to Mrs. Dickett. But when she learned the rental of the apartment, the wages of the maid, the cost of Molly's black evening-frock and the average monthly bill for Molly's hansoms, she no longer wondered that her daughter was always poor. She had never spent seventy-five dollars for a single garment in her life, barring a fur-lined cloak, a Christmas gift from her husband, and to drink crême-de-menthe at a roof garden gave her a very odd sensation. However, there was the baronet's brother...

But at one of the songs at the roof-garden Mrs. Dickett drew the line, and the entire British Peerage, embattled, could not have persuaded her that it could possibly be the duty—not to suggest the pleasure—of any respectable woman to listen to it. As she put it later to the red-haired girl and Molly, no unmarried woman could understand it and no married woman would want to, a simple statement which they persisted in treating as an epigram, to her annoyance.

"But nobody minded it but you, dear Mrs. Dickett," the red-haired girl soothed her, "and it's all in how you take those things, don't you think? Of course, if you find it wrong, why then it is wrong—for you. But really, I assure you, I simply paid no attention to it..."

"Then you must allow me to say that I think you should have!" Mrs. Dickett snapped out.

"Oh, come, mother, a woman of twenty-five is to all intents and purposes as capable of hearing —anything—as a married woman," said Molly lazily. "I'm not a school girl, you know."

"I know that," her mother replied shortly, and might have added that Molly looked Kathryn's age —which she did, and Kathryn was twenty-eight.

She was, however, if anything, handsomer than when her cheek had its fuller curve, for her eyes looked larger and her mouth had more mobility: there was a stimulation in her tenseness. Mrs. Dickett felt a little troubled.

"Although, of course, Molly admitted that the creature had no character and sang that sort of song purposely," she confided to her husband.

Imagine, then, her feelings when Molly's interview with the singer was printed! She began a severe letter to her—and ceased midway of the first paragraph. What possible hold had she over her daughter? What did she know of her friends and associates, and what, had she known and disapproved, would it have mattered to Molly? Since the day she won her college scholarship at eighteen she had been independent, financially speaking, and, though financial independence is not, of course, everything ... but it would almost seem that it is! There must be some mistake here. Mrs. Dickett chewed the end of her pen and thought as hard as she had ever thought in her life. Nonsense! What finally settles the thing is public opinion—Society. If one's world turns the cold shoulder, one retracts, capitulates, acknowledges that the conventions are in the right of it. Well; but Molly's world was not the suburban circle of the Dicketts and her world applauded her; she stood high in it; her interview with the unspeakable one was "a great hit," in their jargon. Molly, in short, applied different standards, was in another class—was it, could it be, a Lower Class? And yet, the baronet!

Mrs. Dickett tore her letter through.

It is quite true that they didn't see her for a year, after that—eighteen months, if you except Kathryn's flying luncheon with her at the time of the Convention of Associated Normal Schools. Kathryn then informed them that the red-haired girl had married her teacher and left the apartment and that Molly lived alone there.

"I'm very glad," said her mother. "I never liked that girl."

"She seems to have been a bad influence," Kathryn agreed conservatively, and there, good, simple people as they were at heart, it would have ended.

But here comes Eleanor upon the scene, Eleanor, with two boys, a probable Warden for husband, and a father-in-law who has become very respectably wealthy from long ago, almost forgotten investments in Southern Railroads. And George is the only son. Eleanor wonders that people can send their children to the public schools, and wishes that Kathryn had married that college professor, even though his salary did barely equal hers.

"Every woman ought to settle, you know—it's nonsense to discuss it."

"But I am settled, my dear," said Kathryn blandly, "and I'm not fond of housekeeping. You don't get any time for anything else."

"!!!" said Eleanor.

Mrs. Dickett here intervened with news of Molly, and Eleanor's eyebrows lifted.

"You don't mean to say she's living alone there?"

Mrs. Dickett nodded uncertainly.

"Really, mother, I must say! She must be crazy. It's not right at all, and I'm sure George wouldn't like it."

"She's nearly twenty-seven," Kathryn put in coldly.

"As if that had anything to do with it! I'm going down to see her."

It was certainly unfortunate that she should have gone unheralded. The first wave of classical dancing had begun to lap the shores of New York society, and Molly's paper had got the first amazing pictures, the first technical chit-chat of "plastique" and "masque" and "flowing line." Behold Mrs. Eleanor then, tired and mussed with shopping, dyspeptic from unassimilated restaurant-lunching (and a little nervous at her task, when actually confronted with it), staring petrified at Molly's darkened dining-room, where, on a platform, against dull velvet backgrounds, an ivory, loose-haired, barely draped intaglio-woman, swayed and whirled and beckoned. A slender spiral of smoke rose from the incense bowl before her: the odour hung heavy in the room. Three or four women (much better gowned than Eleanor) and a dozen men applauded from the drawing-room; a strange-looking youth with a shock of auburn hair drew from a violin sounds which it required no knowledge of technique to feel extraordinarily poignant and moving. All but the dancer were smoking, and Molly sat on the floor (in copper-coloured chiffon, too!) her hands clasped about her knees, a cigarette in an amber holder between her lips and enunciated clearly,

"Bully!"

In describing matters afterward Eleanor referred to Molly's reception of her as brazen. There is no reason to believe that this word has any relation to Molly's state of mind: she saw nothing to be brazen about. When she said, "How lucky you dropped in today, sis!" she unaffectedly meant it.

"Well, rather!" one of the young men replied. "Won't you have something, Mrs. Er—Oh, yes—Farwell? Rhine wine cup, what?"

"No, I thank you," said Eleanor frigidly. "May I have a few minutes' conversation with you, Mary?"

"Not just now, I hope," said some one, "for she's going to dance again."

"In that case I will not trouble you," said Eleanor, rather dramatically, one fears, and backed out to avoid the smoking violinist. It was a little trying, and Eleanor should have had tact enough to let the matter rest, but she was rather inelastic in her methods, and she had come to New York with a Purpose. So Molly disappeared with her into the bedroom, and they had it out, with what result it is unnecessary to say.

It was from that moment that a doubt as to whether Molly were an asset or a liability slipped into the Dickett family. It is improbable that knowledge of the fact that "the disgusting foreign dancing woman" was born and bred in Bangor, Maine, and had never been farther than a stage-length from a vigilant mother, would have greatly affected their judgment. And almost certainly the fact that the baronet's brother had asked her to marry him would only have irritated them the more—and perhaps with reason. Had he ever wanted to marry Molly? Maybe; she never said so.

And here one must pause, to consider the interesting subject of Molly's Relations with Men. It proved singularly lacking in richness. To state that she had lived four years (as she did, ultimately) on the staff of the largest New York daily newspaper, hanging personally over the "forms" many a time, among the printers, from 10 P.M. until 3 A.M., walking home with the milk-carts in the lead-blue morning; sitting in the outer office of one of the greatest city editors for three of these years; studying every "first night," every picturesque slum, every visiting or indigenous notoriety at close range—to catalogue a life like this, add that it was the life of a handsome, well-dressed, high-spirited girl, and pretend that it was an existence unqualified by male adjectives, would be the merest absurdity.

I hear that from the tiniest, most impudent printer's devil up to the Dean of College Presidents, who became so interested in her during his famous interview of "*After Democracy—What?*" that his wife asked her to luncheon and she spent the day with them, every man she encountered "swore by her," as they say. In a novel, the editor-in-chief would have married her and Eleanor would have been delighted; but in a novel the editors-in-chief are handsome, athletic young bachelors (which rarely occurs, as a matter of fact) or magnificent widowers whose first marriages were tragic mistakes, so the emotional field is really clear. Now Molly's editor-in-chief was, so far as is known, quite happy with his wife, and his four daughters were not so much younger than Molly herself. It is true, the art editor of the Sunday edition was supposed to be pretty far gone, but he was married, too, and even his stenographer, who was furiously jealous, admitted that Molly never gave him the slightest encouragement. Such reporters as were free to do so are generally credited with proposals in strict order of income (there had to be some working system), but nothing but continued good feeling ever came of it; and the French portrait-painter who spent three days at the Metropolitan Art Museum with her out of the ten he vouchsafed America, declared openly that she was perfectly cold, a charming, clever boy in temperament—"absolutely insulated." And perhaps she was. She always said that she knew too many men to take them too seriously. And yet when Kathryn remarked once that it was encouraging to observe how women were gradually growing independent of men, Molly laughed consumedly. So there, as the great Anglo-American novelist says, you are!

Living, as she did, alone, utterly unrestricted in her goings, uncensored except by her own common-sense, one readily imagines that there may have been scenes ... how could they have been avoided, mankind being as it is? But if her house was of glass, it was, by its very nature transparent, and I do not see how any one who didn't deserve it could have kept the consistent respect of the entire force of *The Day*.

On her twenty-eighth birthday she came home from a very gay supper at a very gay restaurant with a hard pain at the back of her neck and a deep wrinkle from it between her eyebrows. They had been harder of late, these headaches, and lasted longer, and this one not only failed to yield to the practised massage of her kindly housemaid, but baffled the nearest doctor and left her, finally, a pallid, shaken creature, who saw written on every wall in the little apartment, as she dragged herself about it:

I must not take any coal-tar preparation because my heart simply won't stand it!

"And let me tell you this, Miss Molly Dickett," said the great specialist she had consulted as a matter of course (he ordered Trust Magnates to Egypt and consulted at Presidents' bed-sides, and if Mrs. Dickett had known that he never accepted a cent from Molly, what would she have said?) "let me tell you this. You think you're a very remarkable young woman, don't you?"

"Don't you, Dr. Stanchon?" Molly retorted placidly.

He patted her shoulder and capitulated. "But you ought to be spanked, you know," he said. "Now, listen. For what was all this vitality and endurance given you, my child?"

"If you mean twins," said Molly curtly, "I won't. There are plenty of women to have twins, doctor."

"But there are not plenty of women to have *your* twins," said he.

She grimaced and blew a saucy kiss to him.

"I see why they all want you!" she told him. "But, honestly, do married women never have headaches?"

"There's no good being clever with me, child," he went on, a little wearily (he seemed middle-aged beyond words to her). "You are making a great mistake and when you find it out, it will in all probability be too late to remedy it, worse luck! *That's* the real harm of all this Advanced Woman stuff: if you could only get it over before twenty-five! But when you wake up, you're nearer forty, and then—what's the difference?"

"I'll marry, then, maybe!"

"Dear child, it doesn't matter a continental what you do, then," he said simply.

She gave a little shudder, in spite of herself. He sounded so final, and his eyes were so bright and deep. She stared into them and, somehow, lost herself—the eyes turned to bright points in space, and Time seemed to stop, with a sort of whir like a clock that runs down...

"There, there!" his voice came roughly. "None of that, my girl, none of that! You *are* in a nice state! Now, you march off on a vacation, and take it on a boat of some sort—do you hear? And, listen to me—if I find a nice woman to go with you——"

"Oh!" she interrupted mockingly, "the famous Miss Jessop! Now I *know* you think I'm pretty bad! You forget, doctor, that I've interviewed Miss Jessop—or tried to."

"That's better," he retorted grimly. "You hadn't much of a success, had you, missy? And would you like to know what the famous Miss Jessop said about you?"

"Me?"

"Yes, you. There are two sides to every interview, you know. She said, 'If you don't see Miss Molly Dickett in your office before a year, doctor, I miss my guess. She's a neurasthenic for you, all right.' So what do you think of that, eh?"

"I think she was impertinent," said Molly, weakly, "and you can tell her so."

"Bosh. Now go and lie down," he commanded shortly, and the interview closed.

A vacation seemed a simple remedy, and she started out, bent on one, with the kindest orders to make it long, accompanied by large credit; but the promised renewal of vitality did not come, and the taste seemed gone from everything. The quaint and tiny little fishing hamlet she had fixed upon as a good place for gathering "material" by the way, proved all and more than she had been led to hope for, and when the greatest north-easter that had blown for fifty years bruised and tore the rugged little coast, she "wrote it up" as a matter of course—as a bird-dog points or a carrier pigeon wheels for home. And then Molly Dickett received what was literally her first setback in ten years: the City Editor sent her copy back to her!

"You're too tired, my dear girl," he wrote. "Why not wait a bit? Or pad this out and point it up a little in the middle and send it to one of the magazines. Peterson covered it for us, anyway, at Kennebunkport. The cubs send you an officeful of affection, and we are all yours truly."

But the "cubs" never hung over her desk again, for Molly never returned to it.

"You see," as she explained to them gently, "I lost my nerve—that's all. If I hadn't sent the stuff, it would have been all right, later, I suppose. But I did send it, and I thought it was O.K., and if it was as rotten as you said, why, how could I ever tell, again? Anyway, I'm tired."

They protested, but the City Editor shook his head.

"Let her alone," he said shortly. "It's straight enough. I've seen it happen before. She's gone too far without a check: I don't believe women can stand it. Let her alone."

And when the most talented of the cubs went next to interview Mrs. Julia Carter Sykes as to her recently dramatized novel, he was referred to her secretary—and it was Molly.

"For heaven's sake!" he said angrily. "Are you insane? Wasn't it true that Slater offered——"

"Oh, yes," said Molly negligently, "but I'm tired of offices."

"I suppose you get time for writing your own stuff—on the side?" he suggested awkwardly, but Molly shook her head.

"Writing seems bad for the back of the neck," she said, with a grey flash out of the tail of her eye for the cub.

"We're getting ready for the sanitarium this morning—sun-baths and Swedish Movement Cure and grape diet. Of course you won't mention it," she said. "She can't possibly see you—I do all the interviews now—but if you come around to-morrow, after I get the house closed, I'll give you a good one."

A solemn butler entered.

"If you will be so kind as to cast your eye over the table for the ladies' luncheon, Miss Dickett?" he said weightily.

"There's two orchids short and no time for getting more. And the salt got into the mousse, I'm told by the cook—she wished to know if you could suggest anything. And one of the ladies has been detained and cannot come—by telephone message. Will you take her place, Miss Dickett?"

"Yes," said Molly. "Tell Mrs. Carter not to worry about the orchids, Halsey; I'll arrange something. I must go and dress, now—come to-morrow," she added hastily.

"By George!" the cub gasped, and left, to electrify the office later.

"It's a darned shame," he ended, and the other cubs nodded sagely over their pipes.

"With her talent, too!" they said...

You will have understood, of course, why Eleanor dropped Molly after the unfortunate Greek dancer, but you may be surprised to learn of Kathryn's attitude when she learned of the secretaryship. It wasn't dignified, she said, and she was greatly disappointed in Molly.

Kathryn was Dean of Women, now, in a co-educational college in the middle west, and was spoken of as Dean Dickett in the college journal. Of all her children Mrs. Dickett was proudest of Kathryn, because Molly frightened her and Eleanor patronized her. Eleanor was getting up in the world a little too fast for her mother, nowadays, and knew people Mrs. Dickett would never have dreamed of meeting in the old days—people that she had grown used to the idea of never meeting, even now that Mr. Dickett was in the Firm. Eleanor's little girl went to school with all the little girls on the Hill and was asked to attend their parties. Her name was Penelope, after George's mother, who had never expected it—the name being so old-fashioned—and was correspondingly delighted and had given her much jewelry already.

Eleanor, in so far as she mentioned Molly at all, had expressed her opinion that to live with Mrs. Julia Carter Sykes was the most respectable thing Molly had yet done, and added that there were exceptional opportunities in more ways than one for the woman who held that position—would perhaps even have called on her there, but Molly never asked her to. Kathryn, to her parents' surprise, developed a stodgy but unblinking antagonism to her sister, for what she called Molly's lowering of her sense of what was due to herself, and said coldly that she had no doubt her sister's life was easier now, but that it was un-American.

Un-American it may have been, but easier it assuredly was not. Unlike the factory-girls and clerks for whose benefit Mrs. Julia Carter Sykes gave readings from her unpublished works, Molly's hours were not limited, and her responsibility grew as her executive ability became increasingly manifest. The thousands of women to whom the celebrity's manifold occupations, publicities, hospitalities and charities were an endless wonder and discussion might have marvelled less had they been able to follow Molly's crowded days and nights and peep through the littered desk and scribbled calendar of her study.

To amusement and interest, succeeded fatigue and interest, and to these, fatigue alone. Each hurried, various day became a space of time to be got through, merely, and Mrs. Julia Carter Sykes's heavy sigh as she curled into her wicker-inset Circassian-walnut bed was no more heartfelt than her secretary's. If Molly had ever envied Mrs. Julia, she had long ceased to, and indeed, on that final afternoon when she laid her dark, braided head on her arms and cried on her desk, she felt as sorry for the authoress as for herself.

Mr. Julia Carter Sykes (as many of his friends called him) sat opposite her, biting his nails. He was well dressed, fond of auction-bridge, and travelled abroad in the interests of some vaguely comprehended firm.

"This will just about kill the madam," he said despondently.

"I'm sorry, Mr. Sykes, but I really must—I must," Molly gulped.

"It isn't money, is it?" he asked. "Because though I'm not a popular authoress or anything like that, I could——"

"Oh, goodness, no!" said Molly. "It's not money at all. Only I must get away."

"We've never got on so well with any of the others," he went on jerkily, "and she's certainly awfully fond of you—the madam is. She's taken you everywhere, I know, and all the dinners, and the car whenever you——"

"Mrs. Sykes has been very kind," Molly broke in dully, "but—oh, it's no use, Mr. Sykes. It's got to be done, and putting it off only makes her worse. So I'm going to-morrow. She'll feel better about it later."

"I hope so, I'm sure," Mr. Sykes responded doubtfully. "She was pretty bad when I left her. That brain of hers, you know—it's a great strain, they tell me. Hard on us all, in a way."

Molly always smiled and sighed when she remembered him and the hunched shoulders that leaned drearily over the tonneau.

"Where'll I tell him?" he asked, and she drew tighter the tight line between her brows, sighed, tried to speak, and found her mind quite utterly a blank.

"Where'll I tell him?" Mr. Sykes repeated, looking curiously at her.

To save her life Molly could not have remembered where she had arranged to go! A real horror caught her: was this the beginning of all the dreadful symptoms that few of Julia Carter Sykes's admirers suspected in their idol? She must say something, and there flashed suddenly into her mind, otherwise blank of any image or phrase, an odd occurrence of the afternoon before, an occurrence she had been too tired to try, even, to explain.

"Drive to the docks!" she cried sharply, and the chauffeur touched his visor, and her life poised for twenty minutes on its watershed, although she did not know it.

In the motor it came back to her, that twilight not eighteen hours back, when in clearing out her desk ("the last desk I shall ever clear, I swear!") she had happened on the little transparent glass ball, a paper-weight, she supposed, and fingered it idly, void of thought or feeling, after the last emotional storm with her celebrity.

As she looked into it, staring, her tired mind seemed to sink and sink and submerge in the little clear white sphere till it drowned utterly, and only a rigid body, its eyes turned into its lap, sat in the still, dim room.

Presently, after what might have been hours or seconds, she seemed to gather into herself again, but could not wrench her eyes from the crystal ball, which looked opalescent now, and filmy, so that she shaded her eyes mechanically with the black scarf of her dinner-dress, to shut out the reflections of the room. But they were not reflections, for there was bright blue in the ball, blue and white, and nothing of that sort was in the room.

She peered into the ball, and saw in it, clear and sharp and bright as the little coloured prints that are pasted to the bottom of such things, a tossing sapphire sea with little white-caps on it, a boat with a funnel, and little boats lashed to the side, a white rail, a tilted deck, and herself, Molly Dickett, in a striped blue and white frock and bare head, leaning over the rail on her elbows beside a broad-shouldered man with a cap such as officers on a boat wear. The waves actually danced and glittered in the sun. *But the room was nearly dark*, something whispered in her brain, and just then she had dropped the shielding scarf, and gasped back to a sense of reality and the ball was suddenly empty.

There had been no picture in the bottom of it, after all.

But on the bow of the little boat lashed to the side she had seen, written in tiny, tiny letters just as the Lord's Prayer is written in carved ivory toys of incredible smallness, the letters E-L-L-A, and these letters had fixed themselves in her mind, they had seemed so absurdly real and she had felt so absurdly sure of them.

"Which steamer, Miss Dickett?" the chauffeur inquired respectfully; all the employees of the Julia Carter Sykes establishment respected Molly, as well they might. A sudden, happy irresponsibility flooded Molly's tired mind, and she smiled into the man's face—the old, not-to-be-resisted Molly Dickett smile.

"The name of the boat is *Ella*, Pierce," she said cheerfully, "and it's a small boat, not a liner. Look it up."

And as he disappeared she laughed aloud.

She was still laughing softly when he returned, looking worried.

"I think you must have told me wrong, Miss Dickett, didn't you?" he began hurriedly, lifting out her small, flat trunk. "It's the *Stella* you mean, isn't it? There seems to be a misunderstanding; they said the stateroom was countermanded at the last minute, but the party's name was Richards. It's all right now, but we nearly lost it—they're holding her for you. There don't seem to be any more passengers—are you sure there's no mistake?"

"Perfectly sure," said Molly, sober enough now. "I'm very much indebted to you, Pierce."

She gave him a tip that caught his breath, walked up the gang-plank of the *Stella*, nodded easily to a severe official, and followed a pale, neat stewardess to her state-room.

"Where is this boat going?" she asked of the pale stewardess, who gasped and replied,

"South America, ma'am. Didn't you know?"

"I may have forgotten," said Molly, and then sleep overcame her and the days and nights were one for a long time.

The *Stella* carried hides and fruit and lumber, and, occasionally, two or three passengers, for whose convenience the company had fitted up a stateroom or two, since the demand for these proved steady. People, as Molly learned from the stewardess (whose sole charge she was) for whom a sea-voyage had been recommended for various reasons. There had never been more than five at a time and two was the average; one, very common.

The long, blue days slipped by, she ate and slept and lay in the deck-chair that had been sent by the party named Richards, and spoke to the stewardess alone, who was used to tired and silent charges, and served her meals on a tray.

She was a quiet, refined woman with a hand often at her heart. Molly found her gasping in the companionway once, fed her quickly from the little flask she pointed at in her pocket, and helped her to her berth, as clean and comfortable as Molly's own. This produced confidences, and she learned that Mrs. Cope (every one called her that, she said, and treated her most respectfully) had made her first voyage as children's nurse to an English family bound for Rio, who had turned her off on arriving at that port. The stewardess on that trip proved inclined to drink and sauciness, and at Mrs. Cope's suggestion they had given her the post in her stead and she had kept it for five years. An easy berth, she said, good pay, good board, little to do and pleasant people. She ate alone, was practically her own mistress, and the sea-air had saved her life, she knew.

This Molly could well believe, for she had come to count the days of her ignorance of salt water for days of loss and emptiness. The mornings of wind, the nights of stars and foam, the hot blue moons, sang in her blood and tinted her cheeks: she felt herself born again, the crowded past an ugly nightmare. She says that she had never, till then, been alone with herself for ten years and that she had never had time to find out what she really liked best in the world. We must suppose that she did at last find out, but it cannot be denied that the discovery was unusual.

Mrs. Cope died at Buenos Ayres, suddenly, as she was serving Molly's supper, and Molly, piloted by the first mate, for she knew no Spanish, buried her there and put up a neat headstone over her grave: the possible lack of one had been the poor woman's one terror, and she had sent every cent of her wages to some worthless, mysterious husband whose whereabouts nobody knew. This took all Molly's money but so much as was needed for her return trip, for it has to be confessed of her that she never saved a penny in her extravagant life.

And now we see her speaking, for the first time beyond perfunctory salutations, with the captain, a taciturn recluse of a man, furious just now at some unexpected litigation connected with his cargo and horribly inconvenienced by the loss of his stewardess. Two ladies waiting, literally, on the wharf, have been promised accommodation in the *Stella* by the owners, and there is not a decent, respectable woman to be found on the whole coast of South America, to look after them.

"Suppose you give me the job?" says Molly, quietly.

He looks her up, down and across, with an eye like a gimlet; she takes the scrutiny cheerfully, as her duty and his due, offers him her clear, grey eyes (her only reference for character) and her capable, trim, broad-shouldered figure as security for fitness.

"I suppose you know your own business best," he says brusquely. "You're engaged. What name do you wish to go by?"

"My own," says she, "Molly Dickett."

So now, you see! The secret is out, and you may observe her again piloted by the first mate, scouting through the shops of Buenos Ayres for a blue-and-white striped cotton frock, broad enough through the shoulders. Aprons she purchased and caps (larger caps than Mrs. Cope's, who compromised on white lawn bow-knots) and high-laced, rubber-soled, white canvas boots, only to be procured in English shops for sporting-goods. Their price caused the first mate to whistle.

"What's the idea of all this?" he demanded suddenly. "Of course, you know, you must be up to some game. Your kind doesn't ship as stewardess."

"What game were *you* up to?" Molly replied quickly. "Your kind doesn't ship as first mate, does it?"

"What kind?" he said gruffly.

"The 'Dicky' kind," she answered.

He blurted out some amazed incoherence, and,

"Oh, I've seen Harvard men, before," she assured him pleasantly.

Molly took the best of care of her two ladies and accepted their gratuities with a grave courtesy. They confided to the captain, at New York, that she seemed unusually refined for her position, and he replied that for all he knew, she might be.

"We'll never see *her* again," the first mate grumbled sourly, when she stepped off the gangplank, and the captain shrugged his shoulders non-committally.

They did, nevertheless, but her mother never did. After that one dreadful interview in the Dickett library (it had used to be the sitting-room in her college days) when Eleanor had cried, and

Kathryn's letter had been read aloud, and Mr. Dickett had vainly displayed his bank-book, and her mother had literally trembled with rage, there was nothing for it but oblivion—oblivion, and silence.

"A stewardess! My daughter a stewardess! I believe we could put you in an asylum—you're not decent!"

Mrs. Dickett's cheeks were greyish and mottled.

"Come, come, mother! Come, come!" said Mr. Dickett. "There's some mistake, I'm sure. If you'd only come and live with us, Molly—we're all alone, now, you know, and Lord knows there's plenty for all. It doesn't seem quite the thing, I must say, though. It—it hurts your mother's pride, you see."

"I'm sorry," said Molly, sadly. It is incredible, but she had never anticipated it! She was really very simple and direct, and life seemed so clear and good to her, now.

"To compare yourself with that Englishman is ridiculous, and you know it," sobbed Eleanor. "What if he *was* a cow-boy? He didn't wear a cap and apron—and it was for his health—and George is too angry to come over, even!"

"It's for my health, too," Molly urged, trying to keep her temper. "I never was the same after I went on that vacation to Maine—I told you before. Life isn't worth living, unless you're well."

"But you could have the south chamber for your own sitting-room, as George suggested, and do your writing at your own time," Mr. Dickett began.

"I've told you I'm not a writer," she interrupted shortly.

"George would rather have paid out of his own pocket——"

"We'll leave George out of this, I think," said Molly, her foot tapping dangerously.

"Then you may leave me out, too!" cried George's wife. "I have my children to think of. If you are determined to go and be a chambermaid, this ends it. Come, mother!"

Mrs. Dickett avoided her husband's grasp and went to the door with Eleanor. It is hard to see how these things can be, but the cave-woman and her whelpish brood are far behind us now, and Molly's mother was cut to the dividing of the bone and the marrow. The two women went out of the room and Molly stood alone with her father.

"I'm sorry, father," she said quietly. "I can't see that I should change my way of life when it is perfectly honourable and proper, just to gratify their silly pride. You must realise that I have to be independent—I'm thirty years old and I haven't had a cent that I didn't earn for more than ten years. I have never been so well and so—so contented since I left college, really."

"Really?" Mr. Dickett echoed in dim amazement.

"Really. And mother never liked me—never. Oh, it's no use, father, she never has. I can't waste any more of my life. I've found what suits me—if I ever change, I'll let you know. I'll write you, anyway, now and then. Good-bye, father. Shake hands."

And so it was over, and she jumped into the waiting "hack" ("it was some comfort," Eleanor said, "that she wore that handsome broadcloth and the feather-boa") and left them.

Perhaps you had rather leave her, yourself? Remember, she had dined the brother of a baronet (and dined him well, too)! And George Farwell had never earned her salary on *The Day*. Still, if you will stick by her a little longer, you may feel a little more tolerant of her, and that is much, in this critical civilisation of ours.

She leaned over the rail in her striped blue-and-white, and the first mate leaned beside her. The sapphire sea raced along and the milky froth flew off from their bow. The sun beat down on her dark head, and there was a song in her heart—oh, there's no doubt of it, the girl was disgracefully happy!

"A fine trip, won't it be?" she said contentedly, and drew a deep breath, and washed her lungs clean of all the murk and cobwebs left behind.

"Yes," said the first mate. "My last, by the way."

"Your last?" she repeated vaguely. "Your last?"

He nodded and swallowed in his throat. "Shall I tell you why?"

"Yes, tell me why," she said, and stared at the ship's boat, lashed to the side.

"I've told you about myself," he blurted out roughly, "and my family, and all that. It can't be helped—now. We look at things differently. A man either wants to be an attaché fooling around Baden, or he doesn't. I don't, that's all. And I go bad in offices. And I won't take money from them—or anybody. This suits me well enough. Probably I'm not ambitious."

"Then if it suits you," Molly began, but he put his hand over hers.

"It doesn't suit me to love any woman as much as I've loved you since Buenos Ayres," he said, "and feel that to get her I must give up this and settle down into a smelly office. It doesn't suit me to find that life is just hell without her, but to know that if I know anything about myself I couldn't live any other way but this, and that no decent man could ask a woman to lead the rolling-stone life that I lead—she wouldn't, anyhow."

Molly's eyes were fastened on the bow of the ship's boat; her heart pounded against the rail; she had never felt so frightened in her life.

And suddenly she became aware that she was staring at the letters E-L-L-A, and they looked very tiny, like the letters of the Lord's Prayer written in carved ivory toys, and something she had not thought of since she first left New York flashed into her mind, and she trembled slightly.

Then all the vexed and broken, many-coloured fragments of her life clicked and settled into place, quietly and inevitably, as they do in a child's kaleidoscope, and the final pattern stood out, finished. She smiled slightly and thinks that perhaps she prayed. Then,

"Why don't you give the woman a chance?" said Molly Dickett.

Mr. Dickett pushed little Penelope gently off his knee and stroked a whitening whisker.

"Molly's baby was a boy, mother—I know you'd want to hear," he said.

Mrs. Dickett was silent.

"Her husband's bought a third interest in the boat," he went on firmly, "and she says he'll probably be captain some day."

"Indeed," said Mrs. Dickett.

"They've stopped carrying passengers and the rooms are fitted up for them, quite private, she writes, and the boy weighed nine pounds. I'm thinking of going down to see them, when they get in to this country again, mother. Would you care to see her husband's picture? He's a fine looking chap—six feet, she writes."

"I don't care about it," said Mrs. Dickett, through thin lips. "It is a relief, however, to learn that she is no longer a chambermaid."

"Come, come, mother, the ship's boy did all the emptying, you know," Mr. Dickett urged tolerantly. "It seems a roving sort of life, to us, I know, and unsettled, but if they like it, why I can't see any real harm..."

"Tastes differ," said his wife grimly—and so, God knows, they do!

THE GOSPEL

For the first few days of her stay there, she thought little enough of the strangeness of the situation. To think of it, to marvel at the neat stillness, the quiet precision of all the domestic arrangements, would have been to let her mind dwell on just what she had to avoid. She was sick to her very soul of all that the words "domestic arrangements" implied; sick with an actual spiritual nausea. It was honestly no exaggeration to say that she would gladly have died rather than take the trouble to arrange the details of living.

So every morning she woke when her dreams ended and lay staring idly, through the cross-bars of the primitive window-netting, at the swaying, sinking, tree-tops, and the floating white above them, so white between the blue and green; and then her breakfast came, fresh and chill and shining, with a flaming nasturtium on the snowy linen; and then a dreamy time, when thought ranged among stray lines of poetry and memories of childhood; and then some one rubbed and kneaded and ironed out her tired muscles and she slept again. Sometimes foaming milk came in a beaded brown pitcher that smelt of dairies; sometimes luscious, quartered fruits, smothered in clotting cream, tempted a palate nearly dulled beyond recall; sometimes rich, salted broth steamed in a dim, blue bowl till she regretted to see the bottom of it.

And just at that time she was lifted into a long, basket chair and, propped in lavendered pillows, looked dreamily into the hills and pastures rolling out in front of her. Cows wandered here and there, birds swooped lazily through the June blue, the faintest scent of grapevines hung on the wind. But no human figures blotted the landscape; only the faint, musical clash of distant scythes (a sound as natural as the cawing and lowing and interminable twittering of the busy animal world all around) spoke of men.

Then one day (it might have been a week's time) she caught herself listening for sounds of household labour. Where was the breaking, the slamming, the whistling, the quarrelling, the brushing and the rattling that these thin partitions ought to filter through? Simply, it was not. A little faint, suspicious worry came to her: the house was a tomb, then? Did it have to be? Was she as bad as that?

And when her tray came next, some kind of savoury stew, by now, with fresh picked strawberries on a sea-green grape leaf, she looked directly at the woman who brought it to the bed.

"How still this house is!" she said, and flushed with weakness, for it was her first real sentence, and it occurred to her that only little sighs of fatigue or groans of relief and halting exclamations of, "That feels good," or "No more, thanks," had passed her lips.

The woman smiled. She wore a straight gown of some cool stripe of white and grey and her eyes were grey.

"We live in a quiet place," she said, and lifted the pillows higher.

But it seemed that after that—perhaps it was because she listened—she began to hear faint sounds. The clear falling of poured out water, and the tinkling of dish on dish, now and then, and later, the soft murmur of exchanging women's voices.

Another day she spoke of the freshness of her morning egg, and that afternoon she leaned nearer the casement to catch the cluck of a motherly hen with her brood, and smiled at the scurry of wing and feet as grain was scattered somewhere.

It must have been at that time that the doctor came up to see her, a big brown man, whose beard hid his smile when he chose, but nothing could cover the keen, reading beam of the eye.

"I see you are doing well," he said.

"It is wonderful," she answered him, "but I am sure it is not the world."

"The world is very large," he said, and went away.

"And I never asked about—about anybody," she murmured, her eyes filling, "but I am sure they are all right, or he would have said!"

She was ashamed, afterward, to remember for how long she had thought the woman who attended on her a servant. And yet she did think her so until the morning when it suddenly occurred to her that it was not possible any ordinary servant should be so deft and self-contained at once: servants were not so calm—that was it, so calm. Even the best of them were hurried and anxious, and if they were old and valued, they got on one's nerves the more: one had to consider them. Of course, this was a trained nurse. She had decided suddenly that she felt equal to rising for her bath, and congratulated herself on discerning the nurse in time, for now she could ask for help, if she needed it.

"If you will show me the bathroom," she said, "and will be there to help me over the edge of the tub, in case I feel weak——"

"I will be there," said the woman, "but I must get it ready: the tub is not high."

And when she stepped into the next room she realised, with a little smile, how far she was from white porcelain and tiled walls. On the scrubbed deal floor there stood a white deal tub, clean as new milk, round and copper bound. Towels and soaps and sponges were there in plenty, and great metal ewers full of hot and cold water, and nothing else but one chair in all the scrubbed cleanliness. The woman poured the water over her as she crouched in the fragrant wooden pool and dried her gently and quickly in towels pressed away in lavender, with the deft, sure movements of one well practised in her business; but when she lay, just happily tired from the new exertion, among the fragrant sheets, a tiny shadow seemed about to haunt her sleep. She placed the little discomfort with difficulty, but at length expressed it.

"That tub is very heavy, now," she said drowsily. "Is there a man to lift it?"

For the first time the woman smiled. Till then she had been hands and feet merely, tireless and tactful, but impersonal: now she smiled, and her face was very sweet.

"I shall empty it," she said. "I am quite strong. Go to sleep, now."

Very soon again the doctor came, and at her quiet request gave her news of husband, children and home; all well, it seemed, and smoothly ordered. Days of absolute stillness had broken the habit of insistent speech, and many things that once would have said themselves before she thought, now halted behind her lips and seemed not worth the muscular effort. But one thing she did mention.

"Ought not the nurses here to have more help?" she asked. "Mine lifts out my bath-water every day. Are there not servants enough? I could pay for it..."

"There are no servants here at all," he said, "and there is nobody you could pay more than you are already paying."

"Then they are all nurses?"

"There are no trained nurses here, if you mean that," he said.

"Then who—what is the woman who takes care of me?" she asked, vaguely displeased.

"She is one of the daughters of the house," he said. "She is no more a nurse than her mother is a cook or her sister a laundress. They do what is to be done, that is all. Each has done and can do the others' tasks."

She felt in some way corrected, yet it was hard to say in what she had offended. But Dr. Stanchon was an odd man in many ways. "All the same," she persisted, "I think I had better have a nurse, now. I shall feel more comfortable. Ask Miss Jessop if she could come out to me. I believe I could get along with her, now. I'm afraid I was childish, before."

But he only shook his head. "The time for Miss Jessop has passed, dear friend," he said quietly. "No nurse ever comes here."

"Then this is a private house," she began again, "their own home. And I do not even know their names!"

"It is private because it is their own home—just that," he said. "That is what a home is. It is a simple fact, but one that seems not to have been included in your education."

"Why, Dr. Stanchon, what can you mean?" she cried. "My mother's hospitality——"

"I mean that I do not consider an art museum a home, no matter how highly the chef is paid," he said shortly.

"But there is the place on the Hudson——"

"That is a country club, nothing more," he interrupted. "Your mother dismissed a butler once, because, though he offered eight liqueurs to a guest, the guest asked for a ninth and the butler had neglected to order it. I have attended her there for a really painful attack of sciatica when none of her visitors knew that anything ailed her, though she had been away from them for forty-eight hours."

"But that is mother's house, not mine," she protested, "and I do not pretend to keep up——"

"You do not pretend to, because you could not do it," he interrupted again. "Your father is a multi-millionaire and your husband is not. But it is your constant ideal, nevertheless, and your failures to realise it, even in the degree to which you have tried, have sapped your vitality to a point which even you can understand now, I should suppose."

She looked doubtingly at him.

"Do you really mean, Dr. Stanchon," she began, "that this dreadful attack——"

"'Attack'!" he muttered brusquely, "'attack'! One would imagine I had pulled you through pneumonia or peritonitis! If, after constant sapping and mining and starving-out the garrison, it gives way and falls defeated, you choose to call the day of surrender a yielding to an attack, then you have had an attack."

And again he left her abruptly, a prey to creeping, ugly doubts. For she had been very sorry for herself and the fatality that had stranded her on the dreary coast where so many of her friends had met mysterious wreckage.

"Has the doctor sent patients here before?" she asked her attendant the next morning, when she sat, fresh and fragrant in her invalid ruffles, at the window, watching the poultry yard, which somehow she had not noticed before, and the cow browsing beside the brook where the white ducks paddled, gossiping.

"Oh, yes, often," said the busy sister (she was Hester; the other was Ann). "We are never without some one. So many people are ill in the city. Now I am going to clean your room, and perhaps you will feel like stepping out on the balcony?"

Surprised, for she had not seen any such addition to the simple frame house, she stepped through a window cut down somewhat clumsily, but efficiently enough, and hinged to swing outward, onto a shallow, roofed *loggia* with vines grown from boxes on the sides and two long, low chairs faced to the view of the hills. In one of these sat a woman, slender and motionless, whose glistening white wrapper seemed to melt in the strong sun into the white of the painted wooden balustrade that protected the balcony. Flushed with an invalid's quick irritation and resentful of any other occupant, for her raw nerves were not yet healed, she was about to turn back hastily into the room when a second glance assured her that it was only one of her own white wrappers draped along the chair. The face and hands that her vexed irritation must have supplied amazed her, in retrospect, with their distinctness of outline, and she trembled at her weak nerves.

From inside the room came the swishing of water and the sound of scrubbing; soon the strong clean flavour of soapy boards floated out, and the flick of the drops into the pail; from where she sat she could see out of the corner of her eye the fluff of snowy suds that foamed over the shining bucket as Hester rubbed the milky cake of soap with the bristles. Her strong strokes had a definite rhythm and set the time for the stern old hymn-tune she crooned. The listener on the balcony obeyed her growing interest and turned her chair to face into the room. The kilted Hester, on her knees, her brow bound with a glistening towel, threw her body forward with the regularity of a rower, her strong, muscled arms shot out in a measured curve; on her little island of dry boards she sang amid her clean, damp sea, high-priestess of a lustral service as old as the oldest temple of man, and the odour of her incense, the keen, sweet freshness of her cleansing soap, rose to the heaven of her hymn.

"You sing as if you liked it," said the watcher.

"And so I do," said Hester. "Things must be clean, and I like to make them so."

"Why, you are doing just what we did in the gymnasium the year I went there," cried the invalid, with the first real interest she had felt in anything outside herself. "We kneeled on the floor and swept our arms out just like that!"

"If there were many of you, it must soon have been clean," said Hester, moving the rug she knelt on deftly. "Oh, we were not cleaning it," said the invalid smiling. "It was only the same motion."

"Indeed? Then why were you doing it?" Hester asked, turning her flushed face in surprise toward the ruffled whiteness in the window.

She stared at the worker, but even as she stared she frowned uncomfortably.

"Why, for—for exercise—for strength," she said slowly, and coloured under Hester's smile....

Later in the day she moved out again upon the balcony, regretful for the first time that no one of her own world could be there to talk with her. Hester, wiping bed, chair and mirror with the white cloth that never seemed to soil, whipping the braided rag rugs below her on the green with strong, firm strokes that recalled the scheduled blows she had practised at a swinging leather ball, vexed her, somehow, and she was conscious of a whimsical wish that her delusion of the white wrapper stretched along the reclining chair had proved a reality. The soft grey shadows of early evening covered the little balcony, the chairs were plunged in it, and it was with a cry of apology that she stepped into a grey gown, so soft and thin that she had taken it for a deeper shadow, merely, and had actually started to seat herself in the long chair where the slender woman lay. Her own body appeared so robust beside this delicate creature's that pity smothered the surprise at her quiet presence there, and the swift feeling that she herself was by no means the frailest of the doctor's patients added to her composure as she begged pardon for her clumsiness.

"I thought I was the only patient here," she explained. "Miss Hester and Miss Ann have a wonderful way of getting quiet and privacy in their little house, haven't they?"

"Is it so little?" the stranger asked. She felt embarrassed, suddenly, and tactless, for she had taken it for granted that they were both of the class to which the modest cottage must seem small.

"I only meant," she added hastily, for it seemed that at any cost this gentle, pale creature must not be hurt, "I only meant that to take in strangers, in this way, and to keep the family life entirely separate requires, usually, much more space."

"But do they keep it separate—the family life!"

("Evidently," she thought, "they have not been able to give her a private room, like mine, or perhaps she eats with them.")

"I think that is how they do it," the stranger went on, "by not having any separate life, really. It is all one life, with them."

"All one life..." the other repeated, vaguely, recalling, for some reason, the doctor's words, "but, of course, in a larger establishment that would not be possible. With servants..."

"I suppose that is why they have no servants," said the stranger.

There was a soft assurance in the tone, soft, but undoubtedly there. And yet what assurance should a woman have who did not find this house small? She discovered that she was still a little irritable, for she spoke brusquely.

"People do not employ servants, I imagine, for the very simple reason that they cannot afford to."

"Not always," said the other quietly. "I have known Ann and Hester many years, and there has never been a time when they could not have afforded at the least one servant."

"Tastes differ, I suppose," she answered shortly. "I should have supposed that every woman would take the first opportunity of relieving herself from the strain of household drudgery, which any ignorant person can accomplish."

"Have you found so many of them to accomplish it for you?"

She flushed angrily.

"Dr. Stanchon has been talking about me!" she cried with hot memories of her interminable domestic woes.

"Indeed not," said the grey lady. "I knew nothing.... I only asked if ignorant persons really accomplished their drudgery to any one's satisfaction nowadays? They used not to when—when I employed them...."

So she had been wrecked beyond repair, this shadowy, large-eyed thing! She spoke as of a day long over. The other woman felt ashamed of her suspicion.

"No, indeed," she answered wearily, "that was an exaggeration, naturally. But they might, if they would take pains. They are paid enough for it, heaven knows."

"Ann and Hester are not paid," said the voice from the dim chair. "Perhaps that is why they take pains."

The woman nodded fretfully.

"That is all very well," she said, "and sounds very poetic, but it would be rather impractical for us all to do, on that account."

"Impractical? *Impractical?*"

A hint of gentle laughter from the long chair. "But it seems to me that Ann and Hester are the least impractical of people—are they not? They are surely less harassed than you were?"

("I must have been very sleepy: I don't remember telling her all about it," thought the woman, "but she seems to know.")

"Yes," she said aloud, "I was harassed. Nearly to death, it seems. I am hardly myself yet. I suppose you have been through it all?"

"I have been through a great deal, yes."

The shadows deepened and a thin, new moon sank lower and lower. The grey figure grew less and less distinct to her, and before she knew it, she slept. When she woke, she was alone on the balcony, and the sunlight lay in blue-white pools upon the floor. For the first time in her life she had slept alone under the stars, with no one to settle her into her dreams or to attend on her when she woke from them, and suspicion and displeasure darkened for a moment the freshest awakening she could remember. Had they really forgotten her? No one seemed to be coming, and after a quarter of an hour's impatient waiting she left the long, couch-like chair, opened the door of her room and went with quick determined steps down the narrow hall, down the stairs, straight to the sounds of women's voices in the distance. They led her through a shining kitchen, where a patient, old clock presided, through a cool, dim buttery into a primitive laundry, or washing shed, with deal tubs and big copper cauldrons and a swept stone floor. But no odour of the keen cleanliness she had learned to connect with Hester's soap ruled the wash-house this morning: a breeze from Araby the blest blew through the piles of dewy crimson strawberries that heaped themselves in yellow bowls, in silver-tinted pans, in leaf-lined wicker baskets, and brought all the gardens of June into the bare, stone room. Hester's quick fingers twisted the delicate hulls from the scarlet, scented globes, and near her, measuring mounds of glittering sugar, stood a broader, squarer woman with greying hair, who smiled gravely at her, facing her.

"Here she is, now," said this woman, whom she guessed to be Ann, and Hester, turning to her, added, as one who finishes a sentence, merely,

"And I was just getting ready a dish of strawberries for you. Mother has stepped out for your egg: the brown hen has just laid. The rolls are in the oven and mother has the chocolate ready. I thought you would be early this morning, you were sleeping so soundly."

"Early? early?" she repeated, taken aback by their easy greeting of her. "Why, what do you mean?" And just then the clock struck seven, deliberately.

"Why—why, I thought—then you did not forget—" she began, uncertainly.

"There is nothing like the open air for sleeping, when one is ready for it," said Hester. "Did you not notice the cover I threw over you? You must have gone off before it grew dark, quite."

"Oh, no, because I was with—" then she stopped abruptly. For it dawned on her that the other woman must have been a dream, since she perceived that she was unwilling to ask about her, so faintly did that conversation recall itself to her, so uncertain her memory proved as to how that other came and went, or when.

"It was a dream, of course," she thought, and said, a shade resentful still,

"I never slept—that way—before."

"It seems to suit you," said Ann briskly, "for you have never left your room till now."

Then it dawned on her suddenly.

"Why, I am well!" she said.

"Very nearly, I think," Hester answered her. "Will you have your breakfast under the tree, while sister picks the berries?"

To this she agreed gladly and found herself, still wondering at the new strength that filled her, under a pear-tree, in a pleasant patch of shadow, eating with relish from Hester's morning tray. Ann knelt not far from her in the sun, not too hot at this hour for a hardy worker, and soon her low humming rose like a bee's note from under her broad hat.

"The wash is all ready for you, sister, on the landing," she called. "Tell mother her new towels bleached to a marvel: they are on the currant-bushes now. I'll wet them down and iron them off while the syrup is cooking, I think—I know she's anxious to handle them."

"Are you always busy, Miss Ann?" her guest inquired, for Ann's fingers never stopped even while she looked toward the house-door.

"Always in the morning, of course," she answered, directly. "Every one must be, if things are to get done."

"But in the afternoon you are ironing, and Miss Hester tells me you do a great deal in the garden. When do you rest?"

"In my bed," said Ann briefly.

She was less sweetly grave than her sister, and it was easy to see that her tongue was sharper. She would not have been so soothing to an invalid, but the woman under the pear-tree had her nerves better in hand by now, and felt, somehow, upon her mettle to prove to this broad, curt Ann that there were tasks in the world beyond her sturdy rule-of-thumb.

"But surely every one needs time to think—to consider," she began gently. "Don't you find it so?"

"To plan out the day, do you mean?" said Ann, moving to a new patch. "I generally do that at night before I go to sleep."

"No, no," she explained, "not the day's work—that must be done, of course—but the whole Scheme, life, and one's relation to it..."

"I don't feel any call to study that out," said Ann. "I haven't the headpiece for it."

"No, but some people have, and so——"

"Have you?" said Ann.

She bit her lip.

"It is surely every woman's duty to cultivate herself as far as she can," she began. "Nobody denies that nowadays."

Ann was silent.

"Don't you agree with me?" the woman persisted. "You surely know what I mean?"

"Oh, yes, I know what you mean, well enough," Ann said at last. "I know you have to cultivate strawberries, if you want to get more of 'em—and bigger. The question is, what do you get out of it?"

A flood of explanations pressed to her lips, but just as they brimmed over, some quick surmise of Ann's shrewd replies choked them back. After all, what had she got out of it? What that she could show? She rose slowly and walked back to her room, where the bath, fresh, uncreased clothes, and Hester's deft ministry waited ready for her. Later, she lay again in the balcony chair, not so soothed by her little pile of books as she had looked to be. Beautiful, pellucid thought, deep-flowing philosophies, knife-edged epigrams and measured verse lay to her hand, but they seemed unreal, somehow, and their music echoed like meaningless words shouted, for the echo merely, in empty halls. She drowsed discontentedly and woke from a dream of the grey lady to see her stretched in the companion chair, herself asleep, it seemed, for it was only after a long doubtful stare from the other that she opened her great dark eyes.

"And I almost thought I had dreamed of meeting you before! Wasn't it absurd? I am only now realising how ill I have been—things were all so confused... I find that I can't even reply to Miss Ann as I ought to be able to, when she scorns the effects of culture!"

"Does Ann scorn culture?" the grey lady asked in mild surprise. "I never knew that."

"She scorns the leisure that goes to produce it, anyway."

"Did you give her a concrete instance of any special culture?"

She moved uneasily in her chair.

"Oh—concrete, *concrete*!" she repeated deprecatingly. "Must I be as concrete with you as with her? Surely culture, and all that it implies, need not be forced to defend itself with concrete examples?"

"I'm afraid that I agree with Ann," said the soft voice in the shadow. "I'm afraid that so far as I am concerned, culture needs just that defence."

She tried to smile the superior smile she had mustered for Ann, kneeling in her checked sunbonnet, but this was difficult, with a woman so obviously of her own class and kind. Still the woman was clearly unreasonable, and she was able, at least, to speak forcibly as she replied,

"Aren't you rather severe on the enormous majority of us, in that case? We can't all be great philosophers or productive artists, you know, and yet between us and Ann's preserved strawberries and Hester's scrubbing there's a wide gulf—you must admit that!"

The stranger rose lightly from her chair and walked, with a swaying motion like a long-stemmed wild flower, toward the home-made window-door. At the sill she paused and fixed her great eyes on the stronger woman—stronger, plainly, for the frail white hand on the china knob supported her while she stood, and she seemed to cling to the woodwork and press against it as she sank into the shadow of the eaves.

"A wide gulf, indeed," she said slowly, in her soft, breathless voice, with an intonation almost like a foreigner's, her listener decided suddenly, "a gulf so wide that unless you can cross it with some bridge of honest accomplishment, it will swallow you all very soon—you women of culture!"

She slipped across the sill and presently Hester's clear, firm voice was heard in the narrow hall,

"Yes, yes, I'm coming!" and the balcony was drowned in the dusk, and the woman on it yielded consciously to the great desire for sleep that possessed her. But before she drifted off, not afraid, this time, of night under the sky, it occurred to her dimly that Hester's other patient must come through her own room whenever she used the little *loggia*.

"What is she—an anarchist? a socialist?" she thought. "I must surely ask Hester about her. 'You women of culture,' indeed! What does she call herself, I wonder?"

That next morning as she waited idly for bath and breakfast, the stranger possessed her thoughts more and more. Only in such an absolutely unconventional place, she told herself, could a completely unknown woman appear (in her own apartments, really) and discuss with her so nonchalantly such strange questions. In many ways this delicate creature's words seemed to echo Dr. Stanchon's, and this seemed all the more natural, now, since she was so obviously still his patient. Hester had said that he sent many there—this one was perhaps too frail ever to leave them, and felt so much at home that no one thought to speak of her.

A healthy hunger checked these musings, and more amused than irritated at such unusual desertion, she bathed and dressed unaided and went down to the kitchen.

"They will soon see by the way I keep my temper, now," she thought, "and my strength, that I am quite able to go back. I really must see how the children are getting on."

Following the ways of her last journey through the house she found the kitchen, where an oven-door ajar and a half-dozen small, fragrant loaves in the opening showed her that though empty, the room was deserted only for a housewife's rapid moment. She sat down therefore beneath the patient old clock, and waited. Soon she heard a quick, bustling step, unlike Hester's lithe quietness or the heavier stride of Ann, and knew that the little old lady who entered, fresh and tidy as a clean withered apple, was their mother. She had a pan of new-picked peas in one arm and a saucer of milk balanced in the other hand, plainly the breakfast for the sleek black cat that bounded in beside her. This she set carefully on a flagstone corner before she noticed her visitor, it seemed, and yet she did not appear startled at company, and showed all of the younger women's untroubled ease as she explained that a message from Dr. Stanchon had called them both away suddenly, very early.

"It was perhaps some other patient in the house?" the guest suggested curiously, with a vivid memory of the grey lady's frail white hand and breathless voice.

"Perhaps," said the old woman equably, and tied a checked apron over the white one, the better to attack the peas.

From the shining pan she tossed the fairy green globes into the rich yellow bowl of earthenware at her side, with the quick ease of those veined, old hands that outwork the young ones, and her guest watched her in silence for a few minutes, hypnotised, almost, by the steady pit-pat of the little green balls against the bowl.

"And when do you expect them back?" she asked finally.

"I don't know," said the old lady, "but they'll be back as soon as the work is over, you may depend—they don't lag, my girls, neither of 'em."

"I am sure of that," she assented quickly. "They are the hardest workers I ever saw: I wonder that they never rest, and tell them so."

"Time enough for resting when all's done," said the old lady briskly. "That was my mother's word before me and I've handed it down to Ann and Hester."

"But then, at that rate, none of us would ever rest, would we?" she protested humourously.

"This side o' green grave?" the old lady shot out. "Maybe so. But podding peas is a kind of rest —after picking 'em!"

"And have you really picked all these—and in the sun, too?" she said, surprised. "I trust not for me—I could get along perfectly..."

The old lady jumped briskly after her loaves, tapped the bottoms knowingly, then stood each one on its inverted pan in a fragrant row on the dresser.

"Peas or beans or corn— it makes no odds, my dear," she cried cheerfully. "It's all to be done, one way or another, you see."

An inspiration came to the idler by the window, and before she had quite caught at the humour of it, she spoke.

"Why should you get my breakfast—for I am sure you are going to?" she said. "Why shouldn't I —if you think I could—for I don't like to sit here and have you do it all!"

"Why not, indeed?" the old woman replied, with a shrewd smile at her. "Hester judged you might offer, and left the tray ready set."

"Hester judged?" she repeated wonderingly. "Why, how could she, possibly? How could she know I would come down, even?"

"She judged so," the mother nodded imperturbably. "The kettle's on the boil, now, and I've two of the rusks you relished yesterday on the pantry shelf. Just dip 'em in that bowl of milk in the window and slip 'em in the oven—it makes a tasty crust. She keeps some chocolate grated in a little blue dish in the corner and the butter's in a crock in the well. The brown hen will show you her own egg, I'll warrant that."

Amused, she followed all these directions, and poured herself a cup of steaming chocolate, the first meal of her own preparing since childish banquets filched from an indulgent cook. And then, the breakfast over, she would have left the kitchen, empty just then, for the mistress of it had pottered out on one of her endless little errands, had not a sudden thought sent a flush to her forehead, so that she turned abruptly at the threshold and walking swiftly to the water spigot, sent a stream into a tiny brass-bound tub she took from the deep window seats, frothed it with Hester's herb-scented soap, and rinsed and dipped and dried each dish and cup of her own using before the old woman returned.

"It is surprising how—how *satisfactory* it makes one feel, really," she began hastily at the housewife's friendly returning nod, "to deal with this sort of work. One seems to have accomplished something that—that had to be done... I don't know whether you see what I mean, exactly...."

"Bless you, my dear, and why shouldn't I see?" cried the other, scrubbing the coats of a lapful of brown jacketed potatoes at the spigot. "Every woman knows that feeling, surely?"

"I never did," she said, simply. "I thought it was greasy, thankless work, and felt very sorry for those who did it."

"Did they look sad?" asked the old worker.

In a flash of memory they passed before her, those white-aproned, bare-elbowed girls she had watched idly in many countries and at many seasons; from the nurse that bathed and combed her own children, singing, to the laundry-maids whose laughter and ringing talk had waked her from more than one uneasy afternoon sleep.

"Why, no, I can't say that they did," she answered slowly, "but to do it steadily, I should think..."

"It's the steady work that puts the taste into the holiday, my mother used to say," said the old woman shortly. "Where's the change, else?"

"But of course there are many different forms of work," she began, slowly, as though she were once for all making the matter clear to herself, and not at all explaining obvious distinctions to an uneducated old woman, "and brain workers need rest and change as much, yes, more, than mere labourers."

"So they tell me," said Hester's mother respectfully, "though of course I know next to nothing of it myself. Ann says it's that makes it so dangerous for women folks to worry at their brains too much, for she's taken notice, she says, that mostly they're sickly or cranky that works too much that way. Hard to get on with, she says they are, the best of 'em."

"Indeed!" she cried indignantly, "and I suppose to be 'easy to get on with' is the main business of women, then!"

"Why, Lord above us, child!" answered the old woman briskly, dropping her white potatoes into a brown dish of fresh-drawn water, "if the women are not to be easy got on with, who's to be looked to for it, then; the children—or the men?"

She gathered up the brown peelings and bagged them carefully with the pea pods.

"For the blacksmith's pig," she said. "We don't keep one and he gives us a ham every year.... Not that it's not a different matter with you, of course," she added politely. "There's some, of course, that's needed by the world, for books and music and the like o' that—I don't need Hester to tell me so. There's never an evening in winter, when all's swept and the lamp trimmed and a bowl of apples out, and Ann and I sit with our bit of sewing, that I don't thank God for the books Hester reads out to us. One was written by a woman writer that the doctor sent us here for a long, long time—poor dear, but she was feeble!

"She worked with the girls at everything they did, that she could, by doctor's orders, and it put a little peace into her, she told me. You've a look in the eyes like her—there were thousands read her books."

The guest rose abruptly.

"I never wrote a book—or did anything," she said briefly, and turned to the door.

"You don't tell me!" the old mother stammered. "Why, I made sure by your look—what made ye so mortal tired, then, deary?"

"I must find that out," she said, slowly, her hand on the knob. "I—must—find—that—out!"

And on the balcony she paced and thought for an hour, but there was no calmness in her forehead till the afternoon, when alone with Hester's mother, for the daughters did not return all that day, she worked with pressed lips at their tasks, picking Ann's evening salad, sprinkling cool drops over Hester's fresh-dried linen, brought in by armfuls from the currant-bushes, spreading the supper-table, pressing out the ivory-moulded cottage cheese and ringing its dish with grape-leaves gathered from the well-house.

So intent was she at these tasks, that she heard no footsteps along the grass, and only as she put the fifth chair at the white-spread table (for the old mother had been mysteriously firm in her certainty that they should need it) did she turn to look into the keen brown eyes of the wise physician who had left her weeks ago in the bed above them. He gave her a long, piercing look. Then,

"I thought so," he said quietly. "We will go back to-morrow, you and I—I need your bedroom."

Through the open door she caught a quick glimpse of Ann and Hester half supporting, half carrying up the stairs a woman heavily veiled in black crêpe; Hester did not join them till late in the meal, and went through the room with a glass of milk afterward. No one spoke further of her presence among them; no one thanked her for her services; all was assumed and she blessed them for it.

The doctor passed the evening with his new patient, and when she mounted the stairs for her last night she found her simple luggage in the room next hers: there was no question of helping her to bed, and she undressed thoughtfully alone. The house was very still.

Her window was a deep dormer, and as she leaned out of it, for a breath of the stars, she saw Dr. Stanchon stretched in her chair on the balcony, his face white and tired in the moonlight. In the chair near her, so near that she could touch it, lay the frail creature in the grey dress, black now at night.

"It is his old patient!" she thought contentedly, remembering with vexation that she had absolutely forgotten to ask the house-mother about her and why she had not appeared; and she began to speak, when the other raised her hand warningly, and she saw that Dr. Stanchon slept.

Why she began to whisper she did not know, but she remembered afterward that their conversation, below breath as it was, was the longest they had yet had, though she could recall only the veriest scraps of it. For instance:

"But Mary and Martha?" she had urged, "surely there is a deep meaning in that, too? It was Martha who was reproved...."

"One would imagine that every woman to-day judged herself a Mary—and that is a dangerous judgment to form, one's self," the other whispered.

"But to deliberately assume these tasks—simple because they clear my life and keep me balanced—when I have no need to do them, seems to me an affectation, absurd!"

"How can a thing be absurd if it brings you ease?"

"But I don't need to do them, really, for myself."

"For some one else, then?"

It was then that another veil dropped from before her.

"Then is that why, do you think, people devote themselves to those low, common things—great saints and those that give up their own lives?"

I think so, yes."

"It is a real relief to them?"

"Why not? ..."

She fell asleep on the broad window-seat, her head on her arms, and when she woke and groped for her bed in the dark, the balcony was empty.

There was no bustle of departure: a grave hand-shaking from the daughters, a kiss on the mother's withered, rosy cheek.

"Come back again, do," said the old woman and the doctor commented upon this as they sat in the train.

"That is a great compliment," he said. "I never knew her to say that except to a long-time patient of mine that stayed a long time (more's the pity!) with them. 'Come back,' said Mother to her. 'Come soon, deary, for the house will miss your grey dress so soft on the floor.' They would have cured her if anybody could."

"Then you don't consider her cured?" she said with a shock of disappointment. "I am so sorry. But it is surely a wonderful place—one can't talk about it, but I see you know."

"Oh, yes, I know," he said briefly. "I saw you would pull through in great shape there. This patient I spoke of used to tell me that the duty of her life, here and through Eternity, ought by rights to be the preaching of the gospel she learned there. Well—maybe it is, for all we know. If I could have cured her, she would have been a great—a really great novelist, I think."

"If you could have—" she gasped, seizing his arm, "you mean——"

"I mean that I couldn't," he answered simply. "She died there. I dreamed of her last night."

THE GYPSY

Very early in the last century, while Napoleon still reigned over Europe and the people went journeys in post-chaises through England, John Appleyard, the only son of a thriving Sussex farmer, met, while walking across one of his father's fields, a troup of gypsies camping under a hedge. Among them was a dark young woman, very lovely, with straight, heavy brows and a yard of thick blue-black hair, which she was drying in the wind at the moment, having washed it in the brook. John looked at her hard, walked by, turned, looked again, and stood staring so long that a surly gypsy father slipped a fowling-piece into his elbow and approached him menacingly.

"My daughter, young sir," he said shortly, "may sleep in a wagon and not eat off chayny plates as the like o' you do, but I'll have none eying her like that, be who he may, for she's a good girl, she is, and the best man that walks is none too good to be her husband!"

"Am I good enough?" says John Appleyard, quietly.

And as a matter of fact he married her in the parish church in three weeks' time, and his mother cried herself sick.

It was no use trying to live at the farm, after that, for the neighbours smiled and pointed, and the old farmer was scandalised at his new relatives, and though he had nothing against his handsome daughter-in-law personally, felt himself a marked man and counted the spoons every night. So John, who had never loved farming, compounded for half the outlying land, which he sold very shrewdly, left his only sister the farm, shook hands all 'round and sailed with Lilda, his wife, for the United States of America.

On the voyage he made friends with the captain, who took a great liking to him (and had no dislike, the passengers said, for Mistress Lilda), and put him in the way of business with a thriving grain-merchant of Boston, Massachusetts, whom, after twenty prosperous years, he bought out, and founded the house of Appleyard. He had fondly hoped that this house should outlast the century, but his only son was no merchant, and all for the sea and its constant change and chance, and John was too sensible to blame the lad's roving soul to any one but Nature. So with a sigh and a thrill of how his old father must have felt, he bought a fine trading-packet for young John and established his daughter's husband (she was a steady, prudent girl) as his partner and heir.

John II did wonderfully well and found himself at fifty the owner of the most flourishing packet line in the States, with his only son prize-man at Harvard University and a daughter who nearly whitened his hair by her mad plan for acting in public on the stage. The son went early into buying and selling on 'Change, and was a weighty bank president by the time his daughter had finished her schooling.

This was a trifle more elaborate and thorough-going than most girls of twenty could boast at that time, and for three reasons. First, because she had a brilliant mind and great powers of concentration; next, because John III was not a little vain, in a quiet way, of all his Greek and Latin and historical research; and had plenty of leisure for imparting them; last, because his son

—and only other child—had been a disappointment to him in that line, not only failing to repeat his father's brilliant college record, but proving actually slow at his books and decidedly averse to study, though a steady, competent accountant and investor.

So Lilda, named for her great-grandmother by John III's lady (who, being of Knickerbocker descent, laid great stress on family names), added to the somewhat doubtful accomplishments of a fashionable finishing school a great part of what her own daughter, years later, learned at the then popular woman's college. Nor was other and more practical lore neglected, for her maternal grandmother, a notable *hausfrau* of the old school, taught her, in two long summers at her great country estate on the Hudson River, all the household arts and duties that girls of her own age were beginning to despise. So that when, after a brilliant début in New York and a winter season there in which her wit and beauty, to say nothing of her horsemanship and exquisite dancing had made her the belle of that critical metropolis (not too large, then, for one reigning toast), she married one of the country's most prominent young lawyers, already suggested for high posts abroad, it was felt that America would honour both herself and whatever Court should receive these two young fortunates from her hands.

There is a picture of her in the Court dress in which she made her bow to Queen Victoria, standing at the foot of a Roman stairway of yellowish marble, near a fountain, her baby boy clinging to her hand. Under the blue-black of her heavy hair, her cheeks are tinted like wall-ripened peaches; her strong, curved figure is just the Flora and Juno of the ancient city's statuary.

There is still whispered, in a few old New York houses that have kept their white marble and black walnut, the audacious story of Lilda Appleyard's falling-in-love. It was at the Philadelphia Centennial of '76, whither her father had taken her for a long visit, for its educational influences. He used to say that women had little chance of acquiring practical information of the large and comprehensive order, and that no one would ever know without a trial what of all that sort their brains could or could not take in. The progress of the world, he said, was no greater than the progress of its homes, "and that," he used to wind up, "is no more nor less than the progress of their women."

So Miss Lilda studied the progress of all three at the Centennial, and took sage notes in a little red morocco book, and the proud banker read them in private for years afterward to his friends. But she was not engaged in this interesting occupation by night as well as day, you may rest assured. Many a ball and high tea did Philadelphia's ladies offer their visiting friends, and there was not one of any consequence that failed to beg the honour of Miss Lilda Appleyard's company. And her luggage was by no means limited to the little red morocco book!

A party from New York had come in a special train to Philadelphia for three days at the Centennial, and the occasion was seized by the wife of an army officer to give a large ball in her great house in Germantown. All visiting Knickerbockers who might expect to be asked anywhere were asked to attend this ball, and Lilda's maid assured the hotel chambermaid that she never had known her young lady so hard to suit. And finally, after three different trials, to pick out that strange black mousseline-de-soie! She looked like pictures of foreigners, to tell you the truth, her young lady did! Of course, her grandmamma's pearls would make anything dressy, and there's no denying the black made her arms and neck look like ivory—but to snatch up that flame-coloured scarf her grandpapa had brought from India, and knot it over her shoulder at the last minute! It was downright outlandish. Mrs. Appleyard would never have liked it.

She had a high, staglike carriage of the head, and as she was rather tall, she looked over most of her girl companions. Halfway through the dance she raised this dark head a little higher and stared.

"Who is that man?" she asked abruptly.

"Elliot Lestrange," the girls told her, "but he doesn't care for women. He's very proud."

"I should like to meet him," she said simply.

They tittered and teased her, but after all, she was a belle, and Mr. Lestrange was sent for. The young dancing man who undertook the message told freely how Lestrange had said,

"Oh, hang it all, I'm not dancing to-night!"

"But she's Miss Appleyard, of Boston and New York—she's a beauty!"

"Then she must have plenty of beaux, Clarke, without me!"

So young Mr. Clarke took his little revenge (for after all, he had used his dance with the dark beauty for this stupid errand and resented it), and in presenting the chilly hero, said maliciously,

"Here is Mr. Lestrange, Miss Appleyard—but he says you must have plenty of beaux without him!"

"That is just it," returned the calm Lilda, looking straight at the grey eyes that faced her under the thick honey-coloured hair (Lestrange, though of Huguenot descent, was curiously blonde). "I have *not* enough beaux—without Mr. Lestrange! Will you have the next waltz, Mr. Lestrange—Mr. Clarke's, I believe it is?"

"Thank you, yes, and this schottische, too, if I may," says Lestrange. The young people standing about said that they never took their eyes off each other from the moment she spoke to him, and that they swung into the dance like automatons, leaving her lawful squire, a young Philadelphian, irate and ridiculous.

"These may be New York manners," he said sourly, "but they would never do in a *civilized city*!"

His opinion was a matter of indifference to the couple.

They are supposed to have talked very little, but danced frequently together. As the young ladies were putting on their capes and cloaks, just before the dawn, one among them shrieked suddenly across the room.

"Why, Lilda! where is your flame-coloured scarf! You've lost it!"

"I gave it away," she said briefly.

They gasped.

"Good heavens!" said another. "He'll be proposing before you know it!"

"He proposed at twelve," Miss Appleyard said placidly, "and I accepted him. Will you be maid-of-honour, Evelyn?"

No one had ever told her of John I and his gypsy.

They had a wonderful wedding-tour among the Italian lakes and came back after a three months' honeymoon to the solid "brown stone front" of the period, which, furnished from cellar to attic, had been John's wedding gift to his daughter.

"Well!" some gossip had cried, "it's big enough, in all conscience! But I suppose Mr. Appleyard was thinking of the size of Elliot's family." (He was one of eight children and had nine uncles and aunts.)

"None of us has ever had but two," said Lilda calmly, "and the Appleyards don't change, papa says."

And as a matter of fact little Elliot Lestrange never had but one contestant for nursery rights—his fair-haired, gentle sister.

"I wonder which of the children will be the 'wild one'?" Lilda asked her husband one night, as they sat opposite each other in the great, high-ceilinged dining-room. They were, for a marvel, alone, and unlike the ordinary quiet jog-trot couple who welcome any casual stranger to break the monotony of five years of table tête-à-tête, they delighted in this happy chance that recalled their honeymoon meals together. They were so much sought after, and Lestrange's position required so much and such varied entertaining, that they could not remember when, before, the attentive coloured butler had had but two glasses to fill.

Lestrange looked admiringly at his handsome wife. Never had he ceased to bless the day he married her. He was a proud man, conventional and ambitious to a degree, and at moments during his short betrothal period he had felt threatening chills of doubt when away from his enchantress as to the wisdom of such a feverishly short acquaintance, such a sudden, almost dramatic alliance. Never for a moment would he have been satisfied with the standing of an ordinary lawyer; the career he had set before himself needed a larger background than any one city, even his country's metropolis, could offer, and in his future the position and qualities of his wife would count enormously. Money, breeding and beauty he had always told himself he must marry, but to win brains and a loving heart into the bargain was more than even he could have expected, and he admitted the justice of his friends' half-earnest jealousy.

To-night he raised his glass gallantly and drank to her bright dark eyes, noting with pleasure that she had remembered to have her new gown of the filmy black material he fancied so much!

"Why should either of them be 'wild,' dearest?" he asked.

"Papa told me once, when I was a child, that every Appleyard that he had ever heard of had two children, a son and a daughter," she said thoughtfully, "and one of them was always staid and steady and—oh, well, looked up to in the community, you know, and the other always flighty and ... unusual, to put it mildly. And certainly, as far back as *I* can remember, it has been so.

"There was Aunt Adelaide. Grandpapa found her one day acting in a play in the town hall in the little village where they went for the summer—right on the stage with all those travelling actors. She actually wanted to go with them!"

"Absurd!" said her husband, selecting and peeling for her a specially fine peach.

"But grandpapa himself," she went on thoughtfully, "threatened to go as a common sailor before the mast, rather than be tied down to business—papa showed me a letter he wrote once; he said it was sickening to him to think of putting up the shutters every night and heaping up money in a strong-box."

"How about your great-grandfather?" he asked idly. "I don't know about him," she said, "except that I am named for my great-grandmother. They were the first Appleyards to come to this country, you know."

"I know," he said politely. He himself traced his ancestry to a cousin of Henry of Navarre, and was furiously proud of it, though wild horses could not have dragged from him an allusion to it.

They dipped into the heavy crystal finger bowls in silence. Then, as a sudden curious idea struck him,

"But how do you account, on that theory, for your own generation?" he asked. "Certainly no one could call Johnny wild?"

"Poor old Johnny!" she said, laughing, "no, indeed! The wildest step he ever took was to put type-writing machines in the bank!"

"Then, is it you?" he demanded, and smiled gravely, for her dignified young matronhood was his pride.

"It may come out in me later," she threatened, "for Appleyards don't change, you know."

But old Mr. Appleyard, who perhaps knew more instances of the tradition than he imparted to his daughter, died peacefully at seventy-two, the accepted Appleyard age for that process, convinced that he, at last, had produced two steady children: he was a little worried about his grandson, young Elliot, who displayed a freakish talent for composing and performing music for the violin, and an unfortunate preference for the society of professional musicians, of which his mother seemed almost culpably tolerant, not to say proud. The arts were rising, socially, in that generation, and Elliot was actually excused from an examination in ethics for the purpose of attending a concert by the Boston Symphony Society.

By this time, of course, they had returned from their European period. It had been a brilliant ten years, and Mrs. Lestrange had met most royalties and all travelling Americans of any consequence—all with the same gracious dignity, the same delicate balance of charm and reserve that delighted foreigner and compatriot alike. Her portrait was painted by a great German, her bust was modelled by a great Frenchman, the words of a little lullaby she had composed for her baby girl was set to music and made famous through Europe by a great Italian. Queen Victoria complimented her on her devoted personal care of her children, and sent her an autographed *carte de visite*, as they were still called then, framed in brilliants. The silver trowel with which she laid the foundation stone of her school for instructing the peasant-girls of her adopted country in the simple household arts is still a bone of contention between her two proud children. A duke stood godfather to her little Wilhelmina and Royalty herself embroidered at least one frill of the baby's christening robe.

When the children were twelve and fourteen, however, the family returned; papered, painted and decorated the house anew from top to bottom, and settled down to the task that had brought them back—the bringing up of their boy and girl in an American tradition. If Mrs. Lestrange ever missed the polish and variety of European social life, if she found the "Anglo-mania" (just then so fashionable in New York) a little shallow and unconvincing, she never showed it. Handsome and serene, a trifle more matronly than women of her age appear to-day, perhaps, but none the less admired for it, she moved through her duties of household, nursery, ballroom and *salon*, omitting nothing, excelling in all.

No charity bazaar, no educational exhibition, no welcoming of distinguished foreigners, no celebration of the arts, was complete without Mrs. Elliot Lestrange. For her son's sake she patronized music extensively, for her daughter's, she sat through endless balls and garden parties. By the time they were both married, her dark hair was powdered with silver.

"What a beautiful old lady mamma is going to make," Wilhelmina said to her brother, who had made a flying visit across the Atlantic and left the old Italian villa where he made music all day among the birds and orange-trees, to see his sister's baby son.

"You think so?" he answered quickly, with his darting, foreign air. "I am myself far from certain."

"Why, Elly, what do you mean?" she cried, looking up a moment from the lace-trimmed bassinet. "What a thing to say!"

He laughed indulgently.

"Oh, you know everything I say always shocked you, Sister Mina," he said. "What a joy it must have been to you and father when I left these Puritan shores for good!"

"No, no," she began, but he tapped her lips.

"Yes, yes!" he contradicted. "Even to marry an opera singer, you were glad to see me go! But about mamma: I suppose you mean that she will sit in a Mechlin cap and knit, with a blue Angora cat on the rug beside her, and hear this little lady in the bassinet here say her lessons?"

Something very like this had been in Wilhelmina's mind and she admitted it.

"Well," young Elliot said, reflectively, "all I can say is, I don't think so. There's something about mamma that you can't be sure of."

"Why, Elly, what do you mean?"

"I can't explain it exactly," he said, "but she's very deep—mamma. Father doesn't understand her, you know."

"Now, Elliot, that is rank nonsense!" his sister contradicted. "You remind me of that nurse Dr. Stanchon sent up when mamma had that fit of not sleeping last year. She and mamma got on famously, from the first; she stayed out of doors all night with her till mamma got to sleeping again. She was used to it—the nurse, I mean—and didn't mind, she said, she'd been doing it in the Adirondacks.

"I remember asking her why she thought mamma should have insomnia—for there was nothing whatever on her mind, and they say that's the cause, you know. She gave me the strangest look.

"'Are you sure your mother has nothing on her mind?' she asked me, 'your mother's very deep, you know!'

"'What nonsense, Miss Jessop!' I told her. 'Mamma's as open as the day!'"

Elliot laughed.

"Sensible woman, your Miss Jessop," he said.

"Oh, I don't know. She was very decided, certainly, and easy in her ways. More so than I quite like in a trained nurse. I will say for her, though, that the out-of-doors idea was hers. Though father was quite alarmed about it."

"That's what I say. Father doesn't understand her."

"Oh, Elly, how can you? Every one says there never were two people so suited to each other. There's not one wish of father's she doesn't carry out, and never has been."

"I don't say not," he agreed, "but that merely shows what a good, clever wife she is. That doesn't say he understands her. He certainly never understood me, I know; Uncle John didn't either."

"But you were always—always—*queer*, you know, Elly," she explained deprecatingly.

"Was I?" he questioned lightly. "Mamma understood me, all the same. So perhaps she's 'queer,' too."

"Nonsense," Wilhelmina said briefly. "Mamma is like anybody else, only a great deal cleverer."

"Maybe, maybe," he repeated thoughtfully. "But she always gives me the impression of having something up her sleeve. She said a strange thing to me after my little girls—the twins, you know—were born. She was holding them out in the orange grove, and saying such sweet things to Maddelina, and then she turned to me suddenly and said,

"'Have I been a good mother to you, Elliot?'

"'Why, madre, you've been perfect,' I said.

"'Is there anything more you think I could ever do for you?' she asked.

"'Honestly, dear, I don't think there is,' I said.

"'That's all I wanted to know,' she said, and sailed the next day.... What's the matter? How strange you look!"

"It's only that she said just that to me, last week," Wilhelmina told him, "and left the next day for New York. But I supposed it was to get back to father. She depends so on him."

"Do you really think so?" he asked curiously.

But every one agreed with Wilhelmina—perhaps because Wilhelmina very seldom said anything that any one was likely to disagree with—and so every one was much surprised at the comparatively short time that Mrs. Lestrange spent in retirement after her husband's sudden death. He had not the Appleyard habit of living to be seventy-two, it appeared, and succumbed to pneumonia, following fatigue and exposure.

His wife's hair turned quickly to an iron-grey, soon after, but she moved steadily on among the many educational and philanthropic schemes with which she had begun to fill her time after her daughter's marriage. Organized charity was developing rapidly, just then, and Mrs. Lestrange's clear common sense, executive ability and knowledge of European institutions of the sort made her, with her wealth and leisure, a leader on New York boards and councils.

It was noted that the year after her widowhood found her less frequently in the public meetings, less willing to organise new centres of work, more determined to avoid presidencies and chairmanships. For this she gave as an excuse the frequent trips abroad, which seemed to have no special purpose and displeased Wilhelmina, who frequently offered her a home in Boston.

"I cannot understand why she refuses," said Wilhelmina, on the occasion of Elliot's last flying trip to America. "The children would love their granny to be with us, and she could have her own sitting-room. Can't you persuade her, Elly?"

"I'm afraid not," he answered absently. "You know she's winding up all those boards and trade-schools and hospitals and things?"

"And a good thing, too," said his sister. "Mamma's done enough for the community. She ought to settle down. And you see she's going to."

"So that's the way it looks to you, Mina?" he asked, looking searchingly into her pale blue eyes, and shrugging his shoulders slightly.

"Gracious, Elliot, if you know so much more about mamma than I do, why don't you ask her to live with you and Maddelina?" she suggested sharply.

"It wouldn't do any good—she'd never think of it," he answered simply.

"Well, of course, she and Maddelina..."

"Exactly," he agreed with his teasing foreign smile.

"And I'll tell you another thing," she went on; "all these sudden trips about the country and to Europe—what is the sense? Mamma will be fifty in a few days, and anything might happen ——"

"Oh, nonsense, Mina," he laughed at her. "Mamma is stronger than either of us, and you know it."

"Of course she's never been ill," his sister admitted. "But all this travel makes her nervous, just the same. She's not like herself. Why, yesterday, we drove out through the suburbs—she seems to want to be out doors all the time, you know—and under a big tree there was a camp of those horrid gypsies. The horses were unhitched, and the dirtiest children playing all about, and they were cooking over a fire. Nothing would do but we must stop the horses—the new bays, you know, and they hate anything queer—and mamma actually made quite a visit among them! They were English gypsies, from Sussex, they said. One of the women ladled out some mess or other from the great pot and mamma actually ate it. And it was odd, too, but they wouldn't take any money.

"'Not from you, lady, not from you!' they said. The woman put her hands behind her back."

"That *was* odd," said Elliot.

"Yes. And as we drove off she looked after them and said the strangest things. 'Could any one be happier, do you think?' she said, and afterward: 'Life seems so unwrinkled, somehow, when one sees it lived that way!'"

"And what did you say to that?" asked her brother.

"Why, of course, there was nothing to say. I only said that I couldn't conceive how any educated woman could be happy without a bath-tub."

He chuckled.

"Of course you did," he murmured.

"That's what mamma said," she sighed.

"What?"

"Why, she looked at me so queerly and said, 'Of course you would say that, Mina!'"

"Do you know what I've come over for?" he asked abruptly.

"On business, I suppose," she answered idly.

"Yes. Uncle John sent for me, to ask if I had any idea of mamma's intentions. And then there were papers to sign."

"Papers?" she looked alarmed.

"Yes. I think you might as well know. But we're not to discuss it with her, understand. She's disposing of all her property."

"Why, Elly!"

"It's divided into thirds. One-third to me, one-third to you, and the other third cut up into servants' legacies, one or two charities and enough for herself to give her a hundred pounds a year."

"Pounds?"

"It's in English securities. It looks as if she meant to live in England. Uncle John asked if he might tell us, and she said only on condition that we didn't discuss it. She meant to travel for some years, she said, and she had arranged to have us notified immediately in case of any accident or difficulty. She expected to write occasionally, too, she said. You know how mamma is—she simply hypnotised the old gentleman."

"Why, Elly! you don't think her mind..."

"Bosh! Her mind's better than ours will ever be! Uncle John went to Dr. Stanchon about it and he said that mamma was in perfect health, good for twenty-five years more——"

"She always says 'twenty-two,'" Wilhelmina interrupted.

"——And that she was not to be bothered or crossed in any way. He said that at her age women often took odd fancies, and that with a woman so capable and determined as mamma, the best thing was to give her her way. 'Mind you, now, Appleyard,' he said, 'your sister consulted me long before you did, and whatever she does I justify in every way!'"

"Well, of course, with mamma, there's nothing else to do," sighed Wilhelmina, "but—five hundred dollars a year! Why, it's impossible! She can't travel on that!"

"No, but she can't starve, either," said Elliot, philosophically, "and everybody was always telling her she could have earned her own living in a dozen ways—perhaps she's going to do that."

"Oh, Elly!" cried poor Wilhelmina. He turned to go, then picked up a small blue-print from the top of a pile on a camera.

"What's all this?"

"Oh, that's one of the photographs the children are always taking nowadays. That one—why, that's one of mamma and the gypsies, that I told you about! See, there's the gypsy woman handing her out the soup. They get very clear prints, now, don't they?"

"But what an extraordinary likeness!" he exclaimed. "Isn't it remarkable!"

"Oh, you mean mamma and the gypsy," she said indifferently. "Yes, the children both noticed it at once. The other gypsies did, too, I'm sure, from the way they pointed and stared. Well, she always was that dark type, you know. Would you like to keep it?"

"Thanks, if you don't mind," he said, and put it carefully in his pocketbook. "It's better of mamma than any of the professional ones."

Nobody who attended the great dinner-party given for Mrs. Elliot Lestrange on the occasion of her fiftieth birthday will forget it readily. It was as much a public as a private function, and around the great hotel dining-room used for the occasion stood many different tables for many different classes of people. Between the party of girls trained years ago in her trade-school and the long table of boards of directors of different movements in which she had long been prominent, sat the entire cast of one of the theatrical successes of the season, the play being openly founded on one of the dramatic incidents of her life as a diplomat's wife, a generation ago, in Europe. The old composer of her famous cradle-song shared with the publisher of her "Letters from an Attaché's Wife," and the prima-donna she had discovered and educated, a merry little Italian table where her musician son made the proud fourth. A party of old pupils from the convent school where she had spent a year surprised the room with the valedictory verses she had written for the class, and at her bridesmaid's table only one was lacking—the saucy maid-of-honour, Evelyn, of thirty years ago!

A goodly fraction of what was just about to be known as the famous "Four Hundred" of New York society chattered and stared at the poets and novelists from Boston; and, for the sake of future memories, Wilhelmina's children and the olive twins from Florence gazed curiously from under their governesses' wings at the lights and roses and jewels and tinted glass that made the great room a scented fairyland to their round eyes.

At every table was a vacant chair, and to each of these she moved in turn for the space of one of the courses of the elaborate dinners of the end of the nineteenth century, a majestic figure in black velvet, frosted to the waist with her grandmother's wonderful point-lace, her shoulders, firm and creamy still, twinkling with her father's wedding diamonds, her neck soft under her husband's birthday pearls.

It was said of her on that night that she was the one person in the big room who could have been perfectly at ease at every table there, and the pride of the children as she took her nuts and coffee among them was delightful to witness.

"You have, indeed, lived every moment of a rich life, Signora," said the composer to her, in Italian, as he sat again after their graceful bows on the rendering of his now almost classic lullaby by the great singer. "Is it not so?"

"It may be, *Maestro*, but there is, after all things, and for all people, a rest at last," she answered gravely.

Her son, who was dressing them one of his inimitable salads, looked up sharply at this, though the others only smiled.

"And you start on your travels, it appears, after this triumph?" the *Maestro* inquired.

"To-morrow," she said.

"And may we know..."

"I go alone," she answered, smiling.

About each of her ecstatic granddaughters' necks she gravely clasped her pearl or diamond chains, as they stood at the foot of the stairs in her brownstone house long after midnight; in each grandson's hot, astonished palm lay a glittering ring or bracelet, "For your wife, some day!"

"How strangely mamma is acting," Wilhelmina complained to her brother. "I suppose she is excited by all this?"

"She appears perfectly calm to me," he answered. "I have always told you, Mina, that you have a tendency to call any one excited who does anything that you don't expect."

Their mother sat in silence in her room while her maid, a faithful mulattress of many years' service, undressed her.

"Is that little tin box where I can get it?" she asked at last, when all was done.

"Yes, madam."

"Are the house-keys here?"

"Yes, madam."

"Then I shall not want you any more. You have always been all that I could wish, Ella, and I shall miss you. Take this, to remember me by," and the woman stared at the watch and chain in her hand.

"But—but—when you come back, Mrs. Lestrange, shan't I—shan't I——"

"If ever I come back, yes. But Miss Wilhelmina will make a good home for you. Good-night."

Amazed, the woman closed the door, and the house lay in darkness, but for one lighted room—the room of its mistress.

Mrs. Lestrange went to a wardrobe, dragged out a small tin trunk, no larger than a leather case, opened it with a key from a private drawer, and turned out the contents.

These were two sets of plain, warm underclothing, some stout boots, a heavy skirt and jacket of coarse dark blue stuff, a mackintosh, a cheap wooden brush and rubber comb. A sensible wallet for her hand and a canvas bag on a belt under the clothes which she put on quickly, held some notes and gold. She fingered the coarse, plain handkerchiefs, the brown Windsor soap, the stout cotton umbrella, lovingly. Over her thick iron-grey hair, twisted firmly into a plain knot behind the ears, she pinned a small round hat with a twist of cheap ribbon around it, slipped her hands into a pair of new cotton gloves, took a seat by her window overlooking the Central Park, and sat silently for an hour. Her eyes were fixed on the shadowy bulk of the trees in the park; her hands were still on her lap: she waited.

Soon the air grew vaguely grey, then white, then a pearly pink. The trees came out clear, the city sparrows and robins chirped. The milk carts rumbled loud, and here and there, even in that wealthy quarter, a few early workers crossed the park paths. It was day. She rose, tied a thick green veil over her hat and face, lifted the tin box by its handle and opened her door softly. In that house it was still midnight. She went quietly down the corridor, through a service hall, down some narrow stairs, through the warm kitchen, clean for the new labour of the day, then took out a key from her wallet, turned it gently and stepped into the area-way. This had an iron gate and a second key opened it: once through and the last gate locked, she put her hand through the bars and slipped both keys under the metal frame laid out ready for the milk bottles. No one was in sight. Alone in the street, she gave one comprehensive, quick glance at the great sleeping house, and drew a long, deep breath that seemed to stretch the very depths of her lungs—one would have almost thought she had not really breathed for a long time.

Then she turned her back, and grasping the box and umbrella strongly, a plain, sturdy, middle-class figure of a travelling working-woman, she walked to a car-line, lifted her box beside her, and sitting between a negress with three children and a plumber's bag with a kit of tools, made her way to the downtown wharves.

Here all was activity: the day was well along for these labourers, and she had to push her way to reach the officer who would let her board the steamer.

"Second class," she said briefly, producing her ticket.

He ran down a list quickly. "Number sixty-three," he said, "Mrs. Stranger."

"Yes," she answered, and still carrying her box, went in the direction he indicated.

It was not a large steamer and not very swift, and for ten days the sturdy figure lay inert on her chair, silent and absorbed. She had no book, no friend, no knitting. Silently she sat and stared at the purple horizon-line, silently she ate, silently she bestowed the modest gratuities that brought her what little assistance she needed. Her only social act was the nursing of the two sisters who shared her cabin, and this was done so quietly and competently that they were certain she was a professional nurse on her vacation.

One of the sisters, a head clerk in a great department store, offered her a newspaper on the third day out.

"It's old," she said, "but you may like to look it over. That's Mrs. Elliot Lestrange in the picture. That was a grand banquet she had. I'll bet she was proud, with all that fuss made of her! Isn't she a lovely lady?"

"It is handsome lace," Mrs. Stranger agreed.

"My, it's a fortune! I've waited on her. She's fine—so aristocratic, but no airs. I'd never have been here, but for her, maybe. She and the other League ladies got us our vacations, they say, at our place, and she started the lending fund so those that need it can get the third week, by borrowing. That gives us the trip both ways, you see. She must have a grand life—Sister says there's no house she couldn't go into here or the other side, and every hour of the day is planned out for her by a secretary she keeps. Sister says she wonders when she ever has a moment to herself."

"Perhaps she will have—some day," said the other woman quickly. "I agree with your sister, that she needs it."

"Sister says you look like her," the clerk went on, with a laugh. "The hair and eyes, she says. Of course, I see what she means, but, gracious—if you could have seen her the day she came in last winter! A sable wrap to her knees, and her hair all waved, and besides, her figure was different —much taller."

"All dark women with thick grey hair resemble each other, more or less, I think," said Mrs. Stranger.

When she walked down the landing plank to the Tilbury dock, Mrs. Stranger stood for a moment, scanning the little crowd that waited on the water's edge. She appeared to expect some one, for her tin box lay at her feet, and she stood negligently by it, her head raised rather haughtily for a woman of her general appearance. Suddenly she smiled oddly, drew again that deep-lunged breath of relief, stooped and picked up the box, and carried it unassisted to the great train-shed.

From London she travelled south and west, and beyond purchasing at Salisbury a warm red-hooded cape bought nothing and transacted no business except for a brief cablegram to New York despatched from London, signed with initials only, and a telegram to a small town in the south of England. On arriving at this town, she waited fully an hour at the little station, but if the time were wasted, she did not seem to feel the waste annoying, for she sat comfortably on a bench, her box and umbrella at her stout-shod feet, her eyes placidly on the distance. A stray dog attached himself to her and laid his black head on her umbrella; she made no motion to drive him away.

About noon a red-faced teamster drove into the square before the station, looked about inquiringly, caught her eye and dismounted.

"Name o' Stranger?" he asked gruffly; she nodded.

"Have you the wagon?" she asked.

"Horse ain't none too fond o' they engines," he responded. "He's waiting by the Crown and Stirrup—will you step across?"

By the little sleepy inn stood a roomy, covered cart drawn by a solid middle-aged bay, with heavy brass tips on his high collar. The vehicle had evidently been freshly painted, for the red and black twinkled in the sunlight and the harness looked strong and new. As Mrs. Stranger lifted the back curtain and threw a quick, keen glance around the interior she smiled briefly. Rows of tins, coppers and kettles hung there; bales of cotton prints, notions and such lay on narrow, fenced-in shelves on the sides; a sort of bunk filled one-half, covered with a neat patch-work quilt, and thick waterproof curtains' were rolled in readiness all around.

"There's oats in the box and a nose-bag," said the carter, "but there's good cropping all about. Will that be your pup, Missis?"

"If no one else claims him," she said brusquely, and examined the horse carefully, foot by foot. All seeming to suit her, she took a small canvas bag from her wallet and handed it to him.

"Count it, please," she said and the carter with much biting and inspection of each gold piece, signed a receipt and handed her, formally, a new stout whip.

"You'll wet the bargain, I hope," the interested landlord suggested, and Mrs. Stranger having ordered a quart of his best ale, and gravely taken a glass, the carter finished the rest with due ceremony.

She mounted the seat deftly, nodded all 'round, and drove off at a steady jog through the village, the dog under the cart.

"*That's* no new hand," said the landlord. "It's well you provided a good animal, carter!"

"First letter showed me I'd best do so," said the carter briefly. "A tidy bit of savings she had, for a woman."

"She'll earn as much more, *I'll* lay. There's money on the road, as much as ever there was, for them as knows the business and don't drink," said the landlord. "She'll be one of that gypsy sort, by her looks."

Mrs. Stranger drove steadily along through the countryside. The road lay clear before her, the emerald grass and the white may of the hedges smelled sweet from a week's rain, the clap-clap of the big bay's feet and the birds' twitter were the only sounds. She was between two villages, and only a straggling farm or two at either side broke the distant view; a grey church tower caught the sun far away. The driver's eyes never left the road, as became a good driver, but they seemed to be turned inward, too, and to see more—or less—than that empty road offered to the ordinary sight. One would have said that something other than the present unrolled before those absorbed brown eyes under the straight, dark brows, but whether it was the past or the future was not shown. Either was full enough, probably, in the case of Mrs. Stranger.

Shortly after noon she began to study the roadside more carefully and soon, pausing by a particularly lush, green spot, she dismounted, led the horse off from the road and quickly traced the green area back to a tiny bubbling spring. Unharnessing the horse deftly, she fastened him to a pointed iron picket she took from the cart and drove firmly into the ground, lifted out a little portable tin oven which she propped between two rocks, kindled a fire from some dried fagots tied below the axle-tree, and taking a slice of fresh beef from a stone crock on the seat, cut it slowly into small pieces with an onion and a yellow turnip from the crock. She filled a small iron pot at the spring, dropped in the meat and vegetables, set a potato to bake in the ashes and measured out a little coffee from a cannister. While the stew simmered, she watered and fed the horse, threw a bone to the dog, and then spread her red cloak on the ground, sat on it, and resumed her inward contemplation. When the savoury fumes smelled rich enough, she threw a pinch of pepper and salt into the pot from another small cannister, poured boiling water from her kettle over the coffee, cut a slice from a fresh cottage loaf, ladled her stew out on a new tin plate, and ate and drank with a sort of eager deliberation, inhaling at intervals the aroma of the coffee and the cooking food. When a generous plateful had vanished, she gave the anxious dog the rest, cut herself a block of orange-coloured dairy cheese and ate it with a handful of small biscuits from a square tin. Then, leaning against the great rock from under which the spring gushed, she took from her ample pocket a small worn volume, opened it at random, filled and emptied her lungs with a third great breath, like only two others in her life, and began to read.

The book's title page read, "Compensation, and Other Essays, by R. W. Emerson," and on the fly leaf was written in a firm, masculine hand, "L. L. from her father, Boston, 1870."

The horse grazed quietly, the dog rested a grateful head on her skirt, the spring trickled on, and the woman read—if that can be called reading where the eyes wander inward after every sentence.

After a little of this she was disturbed by a thick-set, middle-aged farmer rattling by in a springless cart. At sight of her he stopped, stared, but not too curiously, got out and addressed her:

"Peddler's goods, I see," he said.

She nodded.

"Had you any thoughts o' going up Endover way?" he inquired, "it's out o' way, somewhat, but my wife was wishing only yesterday for some cooking ware, and but that you need to make village by dark——"

"I do not need to, unless I choose," she assured him; "my time is my own."

"Ay, is it?" he said. "There's few trades can say that, these days,—is that why you gypsies take to this one, maybe?"

"Maybe," she said, smiling gravely.

"You're new to these parts, I think," he went on, "though there'll be plenty o' your kind before summer's gone—few as thrifty to look at, though. I'll lay your cloth's not rotten."

"That's true," she said, rising and beginning to wash her simple cooking pots. "Which turn for Endover, farmer?"

"First to the left after Appleyard's woods," he began, and at her start and cry of "Appleyard?" he explained, "Why, yes, it's hard to change old names. Appleyards ran out when I was a boy, but the name sticks. Hundred years ago, an old farmer Appleyard owned most o' what you'll see from here. My granny knowed one of 'em well; a well-to-do woman she was, and her husband got all the land, or near it, account o' the brother's running away to foreign parts."

Her brown eyes held him and he warmed to his tale.

"You've heard all this, maybe?" he hazarded.

She shook her head.

"I knew there was such a family, once, somewhere about these parts," she said, "but I did not know just where——"

"Why, it was just here," he went on slowly, looking around, "here and no other spot, whatever, Mrs. Peddler. Here's what granny called 'Gypsy's Spring,' 'account of their always searching the best water, you see—like yourself. Gypsy Spring in Appleyard Lower Field, she'd tell us, and there was where he met the gypsy and the land changed hands and the name ran out."

"Who met the gypsy?" she asked, her eyes large and mellow on him.

"Who? Why, young John Appleyard, Mrs. Peddler, and married her, and off with them both! They're all for roaming, you see—*you* know. 'But she'll be back, sooner or later,' my granny used to say: 'Come spring, back she'll be, if not him; for there's two things certain and they won't change, my time or yours,' she said. 'An Appleyard must own a good horse, and a gypsy woman must come back.' But, you see, for once my granny was in the wrong of it, for 'twas a full hundred years ago, what I'm telling ye, and they never came."

A slow, satisfied smile crept over the peddler woman's firm lips. Her eyes rested on the great, browsing bay; her strong sea-browned hand caressed the watchful dog's head; the odour of the may in the hedge filled her nostrils. Life spread before her.

"No, farmer, your granny was right," she said gravely, "gypsy women always come back."

THE WARNING

Weldon leaned forward slightly in his chair, his hands loose between his knees, and faced the president steadily. The moment had come. All his rehearsals of it, all his tremours, all his incredulities must end here. He felt a distinct surprise at his collected coolness, his almost amused grasp of the situation. Except for the tense, guarded muscles that a month's racking, overworked strain had left conscious of their possible trickiness, he was absolutely himself.

And yet, what had the doctor warned him? To be very cautious when he felt so especially clear-headed and calm, after days of strain—yes, just that. And when he had expostulated, "But, my dear Stanchon, how foolish!" had not the doctor replied, "All right, old man, but didn't you tell me that it was always after such little exaltations"—he had shrugged impatiently at the phrase —"that you were subject to these strange dozes you describe?"

"Not exactly dozes," he had objected. Dozes, indeed! Those months and years of experiences that raced by—and one woke with a start, to realise that the clock was still striking! It was this, too often repeated, that had sent him against his will to the rising specialist: he remembered so well the dark, sympathetic eyes of the office nurse who had brought him the much-needed stimulant after he had yielded to one of the curious fits at his very first consultation.

After he had passed out from the inner office with echoes of that futile order to cease all business for six weeks (to stop, *now!* to leave with the fruit almost in his hand!) and commands as to a southern sea-trip stimulating his taut, trembling nerves, he had sunk for a moment into a chair near the door, just to rest his head in his hands a bit and dream of the future, and the nurse had appeared from a misty somewhere and stood beside him.

"I wouldn't be discouraged, Mr. Weldon," she had said kindly. "Your case is not so uncommon —really. He has cured much worse."

"You're very kind, Miss—Miss Jessop," he had answered gratefully (her rich, brown colouring was so restful, her hand on his shoulder so firm and deftly powerful).

He had thought of her all the way home.

Now, curiously enough, perhaps because the president's desk was placed in the same position as Dr. Stanchon's desk had been, he thought of her again, irrelevantly. That was the trouble—not to be irrelevant!

The president's careless glance conveyed just such a tinge of critical surprise as the occasion called for: he toyed with a slender tortoise-shell paper-cutter. The pendulum of the sombre, costly grandfather clock behind him swung tolerantly, silently; the murmur of the bank beyond them was utterly lost behind the heavy double doors and forgotten behind the bronze velvet curtains. The president's voice sounded on—he seemed to Weldon to have been uttering pompous platitudes since time began. His voice was as meaningless as a cardboard mask: how could people pay attention to him? Weldon wondered irritably.

"...Nor has it ever been my policy to render myself inaccessible to my—my corps of assistants. No. Not in the slightest degree. Our interests..."

Here Weldon's mind slipped softly from its moorings and drifted off on seas that soon grew tropic: should it be Bermuda, after all? Oleanders and a turquoise bay—what a relief to pavement-gritted eyes!

"Nevertheless, trivial, inconsequent interviews between one in my position and those of my— my corps of assistants who may so far forget themselves as to seek them, must always be deplored. They tend only to weaken..."

And yet this man had a reputation for cleverness—nay, it was no empty reputation. Did not Weldon know what he could do, know better than any living man? And yet, how he babbled! Hark, here was his own name.

"You inform me, Mr. Weldon, that you have been ten years in the employ of the bank, a gratifying but by no means unusual record. Our cashier, you know, is now in his twenty-third year, if I am not mistaken. Yes. Was it to inform me of this only that you requested this interview?"

"No," said Weldon wearily, for the president's voice hit like a dull hammer on his ear. "No, it was not for that."

"I trust, Mr. Weldon, that your mention of the fact that your salary is two thousand dollars was not intended in any way ... was not, in short, to be regarded in the light of..."

"No, no, no," Weldon murmured impatiently, trying to shake off a compelling drowsiness that threatened him.

"Because in that case ... in that case ... it was, I remember, only upon Mr. Bingham's urgent recommendation that it was made two thousand. The post has never carried but eighteen hundred. But your exceptional work, according to Mr. Bingham ... I am glad to hear it is not a question of salary. I never discuss..."

Again Weldon's mind slipped off, and this time groves of palms hovered between the grooved Corinthian pillars of the president's office, palms and frosty coral wreaths. To breathe that languid, blue-stained air!

"... May I ask, then, Mr. Weldon, for what purpose you have requested this interview?"

Consciousness returned with a flash and Weldon straightened in his red leather chair.

"I have been waiting for some time the opportunity to tell you, sir," he said coolly, and the angry start that greeted this positively strengthened him. It was a natural start, at least.

"Mr. Deeping," he continued, with only a little catch of the breath, "what you describe as my 'exceptional work' has led me to request this interview. I believe it to be in many ways exceptional. During Mr. Russell's illness I assisted Mr. Bingham, and after his recovery I continued this assistance in other ways. Mr. Bingham has perhaps intrusted me with more responsibility than was in every respect wise—certainly with more than he realised. I was enabled to give him some opportune help on the occasion of the last inspection, and this gave me a fairly general survey——"

"One moment, Mr. Weldon."

The president glanced at the clock and laid the paper-cutter down with a decisive motion.

"Let me suggest to you that whatever assistance you may have rendered Mr. Bingham (for which, by the way, I consider you have received ample compensation), you rendered it entirely of your own volition and on your own responsibility. It is quite your own personal affair. I could not for a moment consider——"

Weldon's taut control snapped short under these booming syllables.

"Damn it all!" he cried fiercely, "shall we talk here all night? This should have been over long ago. Listen to me, if you can. I have been for a month convinced that there is something vitally wrong in this bank. In the beginning I couldn't tell why. Some men have an instinct for false figures, a sort of scent for rotten conditions, I suppose. I'm one of them. I've been working at it for a month. And now I know."

The president laid the paper-cutter gently down again, and Weldon realised that he must have picked it up. As it touched the polished desk one half of it was seen to be at the least angle from the other: it was in two parts.

"And now you know, Mr. Weldon?" he repeated quietly. "You surprise me. What do you know?"

Weldon smiled approvingly at him. There was stuff in this babbler, this hypnotist, this phrase-maker.

"I know that one of the cleverest frauds in the history of banking has been accomplished in this bank, Mr. Deeping, and I know by whom and how it has been accomplished. I know how Mr. Bingham has been used in the matter and how ignorant he is of the tool he has been. I know how completely the directors have been deceived and how ably the books have been doctored. I know precisely where the discrepancies are and how great they are."

"You have been very diligent, Mr. Weldon," said the president gently. "I presume you to have the proofs of all you assert?"

Weldon put his hand into an inner pocket and drew out a slip—a small slip—of paper.

"You must, of course, have a memorandum by which to check this," he said a little huskily, but meeting the older man's eyes steadily, "so I made it as condensed as possible. You will understand it, however, I am sure."

Without a moment's hesitation the president put out his hand and took the slip. Weldon touched his thumb and it was like an icicle. For a brief space he studied the close, tiny figures, then he raised his eyes from them.

"You are to be congratulated, young man," he said, pausing slightly between his words, "on the possession of a very keen mind and abilities far from ordinary. I believe you said you had no assistance in all this?"

"I did not say so," Weldon replied, "but it is true."

"And no confidants, I infer?"

"Absolutely none."

"It would be idle," said the president, "to assume ignorance of your motive in obtaining this interview."

Weldon bowed in silence.

"I will merely inquire of you what guaranty I have, in case I arrange for the purchase of this slip from you, that the terms will be final?"

"Only my word to that effect," said Weldon composedly, "which I do not think I have broken since I was eighteen. Also the fact that I intend to leave the country—finally, to the best of my belief."

"But you must have a duplicate of this slip?"

"None. I have a mass of rough memoranda, from which I could after some trouble reconstruct it, but this I should destroy. After that, unless I had free access to the bank, I should be helpless. And in six months, barring accidents, you will be able to set everything straight: you have left the way open admirably."

The president folded the list small, and pushing aside the tail of his frock-coat, put the square of paper into his hip pocket—an odd selection, it seemed to Weldon.

"And where did you say you were going?" he inquired, in his perfunctory voice.

"I did not say," Weldon returned, marvelling at the man's control, "but I am going south somewhere."

"No," said the president quickly, still pushing the list deep into his hip pocket, "you are not. You are going to die, Mr. Weldon," and something shone in his hand on the flap of the pocket.

His elbow was crooked back; his muscles were those of an elderly man, not quite coordinated with his tongue. In a breath, a space too short for thought, Weldon flung himself across the gap between them and drove his head and shoulders straight at the rounded, broadcloth vest: under his impact the elaborate swivel-chair slipped, swayed, crashed to the ground, and they went down together, Weldon's weight on the bent arm.

He raised himself cautiously, hands pressed on the fat shoulder under him.

"The old fox! The old fox!" he muttered aggrievedly. "Shoot me, would he? Murdering old fox!"

There was no heaving in the heavy body under him, but he was not to be easily hoodwinked now —he had had a taste of the man's mettle. He held his breath and listened: the clock ticked tolerantly, wealthily; the flames flickered in the open, sea-coal fire; there were no other sounds at all.

Reaching with infinite care around the relaxed, portly body he felt for the hip pocket and drew out the small revolver, then sprang quickly backward.

"Get up, Mr. Deeping!" he said softly, "get up, sir, some one may come."

But it seemed that for once the president was indifferent to appearances, for he did not move, but lay as he had fallen, with one bent arm. Weldon walked over to him and lifted the coat-tail from his face. Then he perceived that it was improbable that Mr. Deeping would ever get up again. His face had long been a mask, but never had it been coloured in this way, and Weldon knew that the artist responsible for that tinting never worked on any subject but once.

Between two ticks of the clock, it might be, Weldon saw himself leaping to the window, pouring water from the inner lavatory, calling for brandy, loosening the collar. So vivid was this vision that it seemed he must be doing all this, actually, and he stood vacant-eyed, staring at the dead man. Once he tried to take a step, but his very muscles seemed paralysed, and a voice, steady as the clock, seemed to tell him:

"How senseless! The man is dead. Dead. You know it. Let him alone. Think what to do. How can you escape? Think! Think!"

Suddenly his mind cleared and he laughed shortly, with relief. He had felt literally guilty. But he had not killed the president. It was the president who would have killed him. What had he done but protect himself? If the shock of his defensive lunge had done for Mr. Deeping, how could he help that? The man's time had come, that was all. And it was a quick death, a good way. He moved toward the body again and tried to lift it, but had not the strength. He could not do it decently. The revolver was still in his hand, and with a quick exclamation he pushed it into the hip pocket again, considered a moment, took it out, felt for his folded list at the bottom of the pocket, got it, and restored the revolver. Moving toward the little mirror in the lavatory, he straightened his tie, wiped his face, then stood, thinking, between the body and the door.

Curiously enough, the figure on the floor hardly disturbed his consciousness. It was difficult for him to take Mr. Deeping seriously, even in death. He had, always been an absurdity; posturing, phrase-making, repellant. Death conferred a dignity, he had supposed, but death had not done this for the president. Another time-worn superstition, that: humanity had invented so many. Suppose all those old ideas should turn out, on the event, to be as threadbare, and empty? Remorse, for instance? Would one dishonesty, one violent break with the canons of honour, never repeated, *oh, surely never repeated!*tincture all the future with a slow, spreading black drop? If so ... but why imagine it? It was unlikely. A whip in the closet to frighten the timid children....

He shook himself briskly. A clever business, to stand philosophising, with a dead man in the room, and all his work to do! Now, what was the next step? To see the directors? There was Webb; would he be clever enough for Webb? And yet, if Webb had not been able to detect the frauds that juggled along under his nose, how should Webb be a match for him, who had thus detected them? It would certainly be to Webb's interest to keep this quiet till they could straighten it all out. Then they could divide what the president would have got. And nobody would be a penny the poorer. It was absurd to call it a crime—if the event proved successful. And it would be more than absurd to refuse him the reasonable amount he would ask for: their gain would far exceed his, even if five of them should divide the whole.

Stop a moment! Suppose he could confront them with Deeping's own memoranda? Suppose he should control the material the president must have had ready, in case ... why, he must have an incredible sum by him, all ready at a moment's notice, something he could convert in an hour into cash, before he fled. He kept the revolver: he would have kept this. He was ready for anything. His pockets...

Weldon pushed aside the coat flap, but his hands refused the further motions. To go through another man's pockets! And yet Deeping had done worse than this: what sums had he not twisted and turned, added and subtracted, borrowed and replaced? But not an actual pocket. No, no. He cursed himself for a weak fool, but the pockets he could not touch. The spirit indeed was willing, but the flesh, tyrant after years of honest, deep-indenting habit, travelled its accustomed grooves and would none of such muscular innovations. Well, he must take his chance with the Board. He flung open the door and seized a brass-buttoned official of many years' inferior but faithful service.

"Run," he muttered, "run, Henry, for Mr. Dupont! Mr. Deeping has had some sort of stroke. Get him and call a doctor quickly—don't make any row now about it, you understand. I'll stay here."

The man touched his cap and hurried off and Weldon stood nervously by the door. A minute passed, two minutes. Suddenly he turned, slipped the ornate brass bolt above the Yale lock, stepped quickly to the dead man's side, and went with rapid, tactful fingers from one pocket to another. The clock ticked leisurely, and unconsciously he muttered, counting the strokes,

"Seven, eight, nine ... he must have them here...."

A low knock at the door caught his strained ear. His hand held a thick time-table; *New York, New Haven and Hartford* stared him in the face. The leaves fell apart as his hand for the first time shook, and between them—ah! there they were! "Memoranda, etc.," was written on the top paper. Thrusting the slender sheaf into his pocket, he threw the time-table on the desk and drew the bolt slowly, peering out between the bronze curtains with caution.

"How is he—gone?" whispered Dupont, the dead man's brother-in-law, tiptoeing across the room. "Heart, I suppose. Henry's called the doctor, but he said he guessed it was no good, from your face. Nobody has an idea of it—you managed very well, Mr. Weldon."

He glanced at the body and said a few perfunctory words.

"Well, well, we all have to go. Sixty-one, I think. Has any one sent for Webb? I think Webb should be sent for."

Weldon glanced curiously at the mild, unimportant brother-in-law. He was always thought of and mentioned in his capacity of brother-in-law. Why should he think of Webb? Common-sense answered, why not? Webb was immeasurably the head of them all. Opening the door to discover if there were yet any disturbance in the bank, he confronted Potter, a fat, red-faced, many-millioned man, who puffed excitedly by him.

"Terrible thing, isn't it, Dupont? Great shock to you. Naturally. Has—has Webb been informed? Quite right, quite right."

He dropped into a chair and wiped his pink, fat forehead, looked once sharply at the body on the floor, then obstinately at his knees. He appeared very excited to Weldon; more so than the death of his associate could properly explain, perhaps? No, no: what folly! Probably it made them all feel rather shaky—overfed, weak-hearted old fellows, all of them. They saw their end.

A soft tap on the door followed, and as the two older men looked with one accord at Weldon, he pushed aside the portières and admitted Mr. Fayles, a thin, aristocratic, iron-grey man, who made himself one of them without a word. Stepping to the body he looked a moment, then sank into the chair Weldon had occupied during his interview, fitted his gloves into his top hat, dropped it beside him, and with an extraordinary convulsion of countenance buried his face in his hands. After a moment's annoyed contemplation of his motionless figure, Weldon met Dupont's eyes inquiringly. The brother-in-law shook his head, no wiser, evidently. Weldon gestured imperiously toward the fat man, and Dupont tiptoed over to him, whispering hoarsely, "I didn't know he was so attached to Edward, did you, Potter?"

Potter pressed his puffy hands together till they streaked red and white.

"Good heavens! Good heavens!" he burst out, "this is awful! Where can Webb be?"

Dupont stared, then shrugged his shoulders vaguely and returned to his seat. "I really didn't know he was so attached to Edward," he murmured to Weldon confidentially.

They sat in silence. The president's great bulk stretched among them like some sleeping, foreign animal in a zoological garden. It was like a funeral; the funeral of some associate, attended with perfunctory punctiliousness. The blow was financial, not human: it was the death of so much bank stock.

Another knock. Again Weldon, recognised master of ceremonies now, opened the door, this time for the doctor. It was the president's own doctor; Weldon wondered why it was that important men's doctors were always to be got so quickly. Did they have a secret call in the event of a bank president's death? What would happen in case one were called from the birth, say, of another bank president's son? Imagine the doctor's state of mind ... he shook himself to dissipate such idiotic thoughts: his mind worked as the mind of one in a worried, hurried dream.

"Good-day, gentlemen, a sad errand for me," said the doctor gravely. "Ah, yes, a little more light, please? Ah, yes. Instantaneous, of course. Half an hour, forty minutes, I should say? Ah, yes. I supposed so. Any one present ... any shock or excitement?"

Weldon spoke briefly. He had been discussing bank matters with Mr. Deeping. He had mentioned a few of the matters in discussion when Mr. Deeping had put his hand into his pocket, appeared to sustain some stroke, slipped back in his chair, and fallen dead-weight on the bent arm. Just as they saw him. It was impossible to move him, except to free him from the chair. He appeared to have died instantly. It had been made known immediately.

"Ah, yes," said the doctor. "Just as I expected. I warned him of it. Not a month ago. A great loss to the community, gentlemen. All the arrangements, now ... Mr. Dupont, I suppose you ... or if you had rather that I...."

"If you would, please," said the brother-in-law gratefully, "I am bad at that sort of thing—I—my head——"

"Ah, yes. Perfectly natural. I will have the body removed, then, as soon as possible——"

"Not till Webb gets here!" Potter broke out, twisting his hands convulsively, "wait for Webb. I insist on Webb!"

The doctor stared.

"Mr. Potter, I believe?" he inquired courteously. Then turning to the others generally, "Do I understand that there is any reason——"

"No reason at all," Dupont interrupted irritably, "not the least. Webb will be informed, fast enough. If you are kind enough, doctor——"

It was obvious that he dreaded the chance of any personal responsibility. What a rabbit of a man he was! Weldon remembered suddenly that a night watchman had been dismissed for saying that Mrs. Dupont blew her husband's nose for him! One could almost believe it. Hear him, now.

"Mr. Fayles will, I am sure, agree with me——"

"With you? With *you*?"

Mr. Fayles's voice was hollow, tortured. His face was wet. He turned his red-rimmed eyes on the man before him.

"What in God's name are you?" he said ferociously. "Wait for Webb, of course."

His head went back in his hands and they stared at one another. Fayles, the cold aristocrat. Fayles, the unruffled! The doctor's glance settled finally on Weldon, as a possible clew to the situation.

"This is—this is—we make every allowance, of course," he began, "for such an unsettling occurrence. Of course. Mr. Webb, of course, would naturally ... and yet I hardly like the idea ... it seems..."

There was a strange sense of tension in the room, not to be accounted for by that dead creature on the floor. No, there was something else. Weldon with difficulty repressed a smile. That fool of a brother-in-law knew nothing, clearly. Potter was merely irritable and at sea generally, he was sure. He could swear that whatever alarmed Potter alarmed him only through Fayles, whose collapse was unprecedented. Did Fayles know? Impossible. Fayles stood for old-fashioned, delicate scruples, finical standards. "As straight as Joseph Fayles," they said. And yet, why.... He remembered that he had not yet answered the doctor. How his thoughts ran away with him!

"Mr. Webb's connection, of course," he murmured, "principal director, you might say, made it natural to lean on him ... to depend ... undoubtedly he would have been notified. Probably if the doctor were to send for the body, Mr. Webb would have got there before, and his colleagues be satisfied. They depended on his judgment to such an extent..."

The air of the room seemed to tighten round them. That doctor was no fool. He must feel something—what, how much? He pursed his lips.

"Just as you like, of course," he said briefly. "It would seem that there can be very little difference in judgment as to the expediency of burying a dead man, however. If that is what you mean. I will do as this young man suggests. These matters, of course, have a certain formality. There are precedents.... Ah, yes. Good-day, gentlemen."

He looked toward the door, which Weldon, in his capacity of master of ceremonies, opened for him, and passed out, drawing a deep breath as he crossed the threshold and hurrying, it seemed to Weldon, down the corridor. Did he want to be rid of them? It seemed so.

There they were. All the directors but Webb. All that counted, that is. One would imagine it a meeting of the board. Then why was he here? Suddenly he lost himself in a great yawn, and realized that he was dying of sleepiness. Neither last night nor the night before had he closed his eyes.

"As there seems nothing more for me to do, gentlemen," he said abruptly, "I think I will go now. There is no more assistance——"

"Wait for Webb," cried Potter nervously, "wait, won't you? I—I insist on it!"

One felt really sorry for this rich, fat man. How ludicrously he resembled his caricatures!

"I really wish you would wait for Mr. Webb, Mr. Weldon," Dupont assured him, "it would be a great convenience. You could tell him just how it happened, you know. Just. You see, your being there, you know...."

"Of course I will stay, if you desire it," Weldon answered gravely, wondering if he could keep awake. His eyeballs fairly dragged down. The tall clock's tick confused itself with his thoughts: *one, two! one, two! one, two!* Suppose he were to run now, with the "memoranda, etc.," and take whatever Mr. Deeping had been going to take? That was folly, if the rest didn't know. Then he would be a common criminal. If they did know, then he could leave his memoranda slip and they would understand and make up the sum amongst them. Let Webb and Potter fork out, for once. Let them bleed the depositors. *One, two! one, two! one, two!* Why not? why not? why not? His eyes fairly closed for a second.

But a soft click of the door opened them. There was no knocking here. The curtain moved and Mr. Webb was in the room. Involuntarily they rose to meet him, and Fayles for the first time took his hands down. Tall and unnaturally thin, his sallow cheeks framed in lank, sandy hair, his eyes turned down, it was hard to realise that this almost slouching fellow held the attention of the shrewd in these matters as the certain head of them all, when the present great leader should have dropped his sceptre. But this was the Webb in whose labyrinthine meshes the cartoonists delighted to picture the unhappy flies of their country's financial system; this was the weaver whose warp was of railroads and his woof the unhappy populace, in yet other pictorial fancies. This was that Webb before which many patient Penelopes had sat through many Sunday editions, dressed in stars and stripes, a sorrowing, perplexed America, and gaped to find it unwoven by day, though thick patterned with rich promises in the evening.

"All over, is it?" he said in his dry, sceptical voice, "too bad, too bad."

His eye shot out from its heavy lid and took them all in. It lingered on Weldon.

"This the young man with him at the time? Sudden shock, eh?"

Weldon told his story again. They had talked of business. The president had put his hand in his pocket. Handkerchief, probably. Had experienced some shock and fallen, dead-weight, on his bent arm. As you see him now. Unable to lift him. Notified Mr. Dupont immediately. Nothing more.

"Dear, dear!" said Mr. Webb. "As quickly as that! Hard on you. Nothing handy, I suppose; only window up and water and such things?"

For the life of him Weldon could not help the slow red in his face. He glanced at the window: it was locked. For Heaven's sake, why lie? He was no murderer. And yet—any one, *any one* would have opened that window.

"I did what I could," he said in a low voice, "but it was plain that Mr. Deeping was dead. He never drew another breath."

"No brandy about, I suppose?" pursued Webb.

But Potter interrupted.

"For Heaven's sake, Webb," he implored, "let all that go! He's gone. You know he never touched a drop of anything. Of course there was no brandy."

"Of course," Weldon interrupted, relieved. Every one knew the president's views on that subject; he had forgotten them.

"Of course," repeated Mr. Webb softly and glanced again at the window. An intense irritation flared up in Weldon: this man flicked him on the raw with every syllable.

"If you have no further use for me, gentlemen," he began, but Webb waved his thin, small-boned hand negligently.

"One moment, Mr.—Mr. Weldon, I think? What business did you say you were discussing with my poor friend?"

Mr. Fayles took a quick step and grasped his colleague's arm.

"For God's sake, Webb," he muttered huskily, "look at us! Where are we? What's to be done? They've sent for the body by now."

Potter seized the other arm.

"Will you tell me what all this means, Webb?" he blustered, "what's the matter with Joe Fayles? Is it possible that—is anything——"

Webb's lids lifted and the snake-like swiftness of his glance at Fayles was not lost on the others.

"If Mr. Fayles," he began slowly, "has occupied himself in spreading the disquiet he has endured since he discovered (and imparted to me) the fact that my poor friend here carried a revolver about with him, he has done a mighty foolish job. That's all I have to say."

Even Dupont was alarmed now. It was with a grim amusement that Weldon watched them all. Dupont suspected Potter, was staring malevolently at him and chewing his slight moustache nervously. Potter never took his eyes from Fayles, whose clutch on Webb was the anguished clutch of the drowning man that has caught at sea-weeds. They seemed to Weldon like actors in a play, and he was the spectator. He observed them from his red plush seat, almost despising them for the entertainment they gave him. How absurd they were, with their dead president and their suspicions. They were mad to get at the pockets—he knew! But they hadn't the nerve. And Webb, crafty old Webb, was holding them in like dogs on a leash.

"Did he really carry a pistol?" he said gently, "let's see."

He leaned over the body.

"I wonder why he wanted the pistol pocket?" he went on casually, "any idea, Mr. Weldon?"

A tiny, fine chill tingled at Weldon's heels and flew up to his hair. He had a sudden flashing sense of being in a net that was softly tightening. In an agony of regret he wished that he had not that sheaf of "memoranda, etc." It was suddenly clear to him that he had stolen them.

"I have no idea, sir," his tongue answered stolidly.

"No, ... of course not," said Mr. Webb thoughtfully. "Well, gentlemen, I can't see the need for any more discussion. This is very deplorable—a great shock. He was very methodical and no doubt everything is in easy shape...."

They drew close to him and Weldon, though he caught the murmur of voices, distinguished nothing but the steady notes of the clock: *one, two! one, two!* His head nodded a trifle and for one blissful second his eyelids fell. The clock began to strike eleven. *One!* he struggled, but it was too sweet. *Two!* He became dimly conscious of a rustling and movement by him. *Three!* there was a light touch on his arm and Webb stood near the chair he had dropped into. The others must have gone.

"You seem exhausted, Mr. Weldon," he said quietly.

"I—I have missed my sleep lately," Weldon stammered, trying to control the motions of his mouth, his voice striking his own ear as mechanical, far away, laboured.

"Exactly," said Webb suavely. "And now, Mr. Weldon, *how much do you expect for those papers?*"

Weldon drew his chair across the broad verandah in an aimless, leisurely way, anchored it in the shadow of a wicker table laden with cool glass pitchers and iced fruits, and sank into it, sighing restlessly. The pillars of coral that supported the verandah roof framed, each pair of them, an oblong of sapphire bay; vivid masses of pink oleanders hedged the foreground; the tremulous sapphire crawled softly over a creamy crescent beach. In the pleasant noon stillness the mild whine of a patient puppy, broken by the chuckles of some young human thing, rose on the air. Jars of sweet flowers sent out their almost tropical odours with each tiny, invisible wind current: they seemed to puff it into his face.

A great green and flame-coloured parrot, hung head downward in his yellow cage, began suddenly a mechanical, dry litany:

"*Mañana! mañana! mañana!*" It was like a clock—passionless, regular, meditative. Weldon shrugged his shoulders distastefully; he had never been able to conquer his dislike of steady, measured sounds. It was an unreasonable weakness, but incurable. He twisted uneasily in his white flannels as the bird droned on,

"*Mañana! mañana! mañana!*"

"Be still, Chico, be still, sir!"

A fair, finely grown boy took the coral steps two at a bound and threatened the parrot.

"Daddy, keep him quiet, won't you? He frightens my white mice awfully. Why do mice hate parrots? Do you know, daddy?"

Weldon's face cleared and he threw his arm over the slender shoulders.

"I don't know, Pippo, I can't guess," he said. "Where's your mother?"

"Just beyond you," and the boy slipped away to his pets, grudging the time for her kiss in passing.

She stood softly behind the wicker chair and laid her hand on his forehead. Her lips were only a little smoother.

"Still troubled, dearest?" she asked him in her pleasant voice. "Still dreaming?"

She was very dark, with reddish lights in her thick, low-growing hair, and brown, broad eyebrows. Under them her eyes shone, a frank, dark brown; she bore a curious likeness to that nurse he had seen in the doctor's office, so many years ago. How strange that a passing fate should have set his ideal of dear and loving women forever! She had even the same small dimple at the left of her mouth.

She slipped to the floor beside him and laid her head in her wifely way against his knee.

"I'm so sorry it bothers you, Phil," she murmured, her cheek against his hand. "One would think you were a superstitious boy, you silly! Hear baby—he's playing so dearly with those puppies! He pats them and then pinches their tails so slyly! Oh, Ted! Oh, baby! Call to mummy!"

From the balcony above a shrill crow drowned the complaint of the puppies.

"Doesn't he say it plainly!" she cried, flushing a beautiful mother-rose. "And he is so strong, Phil!"

He caressed her absently. Ten years gone, and a dream had swept those years to one side as one would draw a bronze curtain, had opened the past as one would open a heavy mahogany door! All night a tall, carved clock had ticked, ticked through his dreams, *one, two! one, two! one, two!* A sinister, sandy face had mocked and probed him, a fat, animal face had irritated him, a pale, haunted face had pleaded with him. He had tossed himself awake, had listened thankfully to the soft breathing beside him, had kissed the fragrant braid across his face, and sunk again into heavy, sultry nightmare, doomed to live that shameful day through every clock-tick. And now his brain was cloudy with it. His hand lay listless on her shoulder.

A five-year-old girl, lovely as a tea rose, stood doubtfully in the cedar-wood door, poised for flight either way, sucking in the dimple at the left of her mouth. Running at his call she flew into his arms and dropped her buttercup head on his shoulder. For the first time he smiled, and the wise wife slipped quietly away and watched them from the door, guessing at their murmurs, counting their kisses. Later she disturbed them reluctantly.

"I want to say you are not at home," she said, "but I daren't quite do that, for he is from the States, dear, and it is important business. His name," dropping her eyes to the white rectangle in her hand, "is Webb. Shall I send him out here?"

Weldon put the child down from his knees and half rose.

"Yes," he said, clearing his throat, "send him out here. And keep the children away."

So this was it. It had not been for nothing, that dream.

The tall, lank figure was before him, the ironical smile drooped on the tight lips. Ten years had left him as they found him, but for a thought of grey in the sandy hair.

"Sit down," said Weldon briefly, "what is it?"

"You've put on a little weight, I see," said Webb, nodding at the proffered chair, "but that's only proper in the president of a bank, I suppose. You've done well, Mr. Weldon."

Weldon bowed.

"You did not come to Bermuda to tell me this, Mr. Webb, I think?"

"No," said Webb, "I didn't. Ten years ago, Mr. Weldon, you called me a mind-reader when I had put two and two together once or twice, put myself in your place for ten minutes, complimented you by assuming that your course had been what mine would have been, and spoken to you accordingly. Can't you do a little mind-reading on your own account, now?"

"I confess myself unequal to it," Weldon said coldly.

Webb nodded indulgently.

"All right," he returned, "we'll take it that way, if you want to. Mr. Weldon, I don't know if you read our papers down here at all?"

"I have never opened an American newspaper since I left the country," said Weldon briefly.

"I see. I suppose you know that Blickenstern's dying, though?"

"Yes," Weldon answered indifferently, "we all know that, of course."

"Yes. Well, Mr. Weldon, I'm supposed to inherit his shoes. It's not much to you, of course, but a lot to me—and to a lot of other people, too. Now for something you don't know. In just about five days, Mr. Weldon, we're going to break through the crust and drop into the biggest panic since '93. That and Blickenstern's death—he must go soon, now—and this fearful railroad business—I won't bore you—will put me into a bad hole. A worse hole, I don't mind telling you, Mr. Weldon, than Blick's successor can afford to get into. It's all a matter of balance now; pretty fine balancing, too, for the next week. In six weeks there'll be enough for most of us, but just now—well, there'll be dozens of us in the Street who'll be grateful for ten thousand in cash around the corner. Think of it—ten thousand! Now I'll be short. I need some money—not stage money, Mr. Weldon, real money! I wouldn't take Blick's name on paper for what I want this week—and getting it or not getting it means the top of the heap for me, or three years' fight for it. I can't afford three years. I wasn't a bank president at forty, you know."

"You mean you want the ten thousand pounds you gave me?"

"Just so. I want fifty thousand dollars, Mr. Weldon—for six weeks. I hate to do it, honestly. Nothing but this infernal panic could have driven me to this. But I'm helpless. And it's worth millions to me to have no one suspect it. I can't touch a penny elsewhere—it's all tied up. I must be able to produce it without any fuss, or disturbing the jack-straws a particle. There's no use in going into the details."

"No use at all," said Weldon stiffly, "for it will be impossible for me to lend you such a sum, Mr. Webb, impossible. I have paid well for my position here."

"And a good move, too," said the other heartily. "You stand well, Weldon; none better."

"I have never been what you would call ambitious," Weldon went on, more passionately, now. "When you yourself asked me why I demanded no more than the ten—the fifty thousand, you remember my answer. I knew that it would buy me a good, respectable interest out here, assure me of a position I had every capacity to sustain honourably and efficiently, and give me the leisure and climate that I wanted. I shall never be a rich man—by your standards. I don't care. I thought my brains and initiative were worth what I asked, and you agreed with me. I promised utter silence and have kept my word. You promised the same and have broken yours. I can do nothing for you, even if I wished to. I'd rather not discuss it further."

"*Mañana! mañana! mañana!*" the parrot shrilled. It still hung head down in the shining cage. Weldon could have wrung its neck. It was worse than a clock. Webb sighed regretfully and raised his heavy lids. As the old snakish glance reached him Weldon felt the old net-like sensation, the old baffled rage.

"I'm sorry, Weldon, but I can't let it go. It's no use—you can't afford it. It's all like a house you build out of cards, you see, and you can't slip out one without the whole thing caving in. Whatever I pull out I have to explain. How do you suppose I got you your fifty thousand, back there? You know I've never had much money—to call money. It's brains—what you call mind-reading, you other fellows—that I've matched against the rest of them. And I've got them where they're afraid of me. I can't drop back. Listen to me, Weldon!"

He drew his chair close and talked low and steadily for five minutes. The air seemed to grow dense; the rustling hiss of the foam on the creamy beach was the hiss and flicker of a sea-coal fire; the grotesque shadow of the wicker chair, black on the white verandah floor, was the spread, silent bulk of a dead man.

The low voice ceased.

"How about it, Weldon?" it added abruptly, "can you afford that?"

Weldon pushed away his chair roughly. "Come down to my room at the bank," he said.

Hours afterward he dragged himself into his bedroom, an older man by ten years than when he had quitted it. His body seemed heavier, his face hollower, with pinched lips and sunken eyes. The man who waited on him stared openly and mentioned the doctor, only to receive a curse for his pains—the first he had ever heard from his master.

In the late dusk his wife found him asleep in a long chair with an empty decanter beside him and heavy rugs dragged up to his chin. They tried, both of them, to make that nervous chill account for the change in him, but she watched him narrowly and he felt her eyes day and night.

Something tolled like a bell in him and never stopped for a moment:*six weeks! six weeks! six weeks!* all his waking movements went to that intolerable rhythm; he was like a man under a gallows, with a reprieve coming to him, at the mercy of all the elements. It was observed at the bank that he worked harder and longer and much alone: they said the American blood was coming out at last, and smiled at each other.

"Only mind you don't engage us in speculations, old man," said one of his colleagues jocosely, "'safe and sound,' you know! Look at the States—a pretty mess that!"

Weldon turned on him in a fury of anger.

"Speculation! speculation!" he cried harshly, "you know that I hate it like hell!"

They were genuinely anxious about him.

One morning he found his wife in his dressing-room, white-faced over something in her hand.

"Philip! Philip!" she whispered and clung to him.

He put the shining little steel-eyed thing behind him.

"My dear, don't be foolish," he said quietly, "if I have my reasons for wishing a certain sort of protection for a few days, will you make me regret my sparing you?"

"You—you mean the bank?" she gasped.

"What else could I mean?" he said steadily, and in some quaint woman's reasoning she was appeased.

At the end of three weeks the strain eased a little. He read a letter from Webb with a grim smile, bought an American newspaper, and passed an entire day away from the bank. His wife held her breath as she watched him, but affected not to notice the change, and he blessed her for it: his nerves were raw. Two days, three days went by. He sent out for another newspaper and later in the day raised the tiny salary of the page who had brought it to him. In the cool of the afternoon he rode with his wife, the boy on a shaggy pony beside them, and kissed her as she turned in the saddle in the shadow of the dusk.

"You are the best wife a man ever had," he said, looking deep into her honest brown eyes, and she galloped away from him to hide her happy tears.

The next day he told the servant to bring the parrot cage back to the verandah, where the little daughter liked to have it, and grimaced tolerantly at its strident cry:

"*Mañana! mañana!*"

Life is as it is, he thought, and can we hope to change it because we change? Surely not. Everything had its price, and he had really never paid the price of that ten-years-old bargain till now—he acknowledged it. Out of that blue-stained air the messenger of fate had dropped and taken his toll of youth and candour and elasticity, and departed again, and now the weight was slackening from his chest and there were but fourteen days to wait. The next day he found a second letter from Webb on his desk. To relieve him from needless anxiety, said the great financier, he wrote to inform Mr. Weldon that six weeks had proved too wide a margin and he promised himself the pleasure of a complete settlement six days from the date of writing. Weldon stared at the letter head: it had been three days on the way—that meant in three days— by the next boat! The letter was grave, but subtly jubilant. The railroads were subdued. Blickenstern was dead, the country hailed his successor. A foundation of millions lay firm beneath his feet.

The president left his bank early and went home on horseback to luncheon. His wife saw the husband of many days ago and asked no more of life, but sang among her flower jars.

"Will you come up to Government House this afternoon, dear? It's weeks since you've been," she said, and he smiled and promised. "I've a new frock," she confided shyly, like a girl, "and I think you'll like to see it—now."

"I'll be back before four," he told her, "a little late, but I promised one of our young fellows an appointment."

She pouted as she had done in her courtship days.

"A young man!"

"I can't disappoint him, sweetheart. Youngsters feel those things. He wants more money, and I really believe he's worth it."

As he entered his private room something struck him disagreeably. He glanced about—a sea-coal fire burned in the tiny English grate. He scowled and touched a bell. Asked to explain, the page confessed that he had promised Mrs. Weldon to put a fire there whenever any dampness should threaten, and that to-day being noticeably damp he had kept his word. The president nodded and the lad made his escape.

In another moment a slender young man entered, with a discreet knock, and faced him. He seemed unaccountably excited—even blustering, for a young man in his position.

The president took out his watch and counted the ticks to quiet his irritation. We must be kind to the young ones—promotion means so much to them.

"Let us look at all this a little quietly," he said, softened already, "believe me, I want to satisfy every reasonable claim. It is to my interest——"

He caught his breath. Something in the young man's attitude as he faced him, level eyed, hands between his knees, a contemptuous smile on his hard young face, smote him to the very marrow.

"What is he thinking of me?" flashed through him. The answer came like the shot from a cannon.

"Is it to your interest to satisfy every reasonable claim on the ten thousand pounds you borrowed from the bank last month, Mr. Weldon?"

The soft lines faded from his face and two grey streaks grew around his mouth. The ticking of the watch in his hand rose and swelled and filled the room—*one, two! one, two! one, two!*

So this was the end. Never a night of honest sleep again. Never a free swell of the chest. To go down in sight of land, to drop just outside the fort! *All over! All over! All over!*

The young man was still talking, quickly, definitely enough, but it grew blurred as it reached his brain. He found his tongue, dry and stiff in his mouth, asking questions mechanically?

Did any one know of this?

No, only the young man. He was not inclined to be rapacious. He had an interest in a bank in Gibraltar, and two thousand pounds would establish him there. He had thought it might be worth the president's while to put him in the way of two thousand pounds—considering everything. Promotion was slow in Bermuda ... dead men's shoes....

The tongue in Weldon's mouth asked, calmly enough, how he was to be protected against further demands. The young man explained very clearly. The president had managed thoroughly well: in a few days the recent transaction would be a ripple under water. But during those few days ... he smiled disagreeably.

The fire whistled in the grate; the bank was utterly still. They were alone in it. In one second of time, years and the future itself wheeled before Philip Weldon's sunken eyes. So the black drop *had* lasted, after all, and would tint his life as long as that life lasted on earth ... and longer? Anything was possible. Must the sordid drama play itself eternally, through the years and countries, till the final ripple hit the southern-most port of refuge? Would this young man sit before a sea-coal fire in Gibraltar, one day, frozen, his life and honour nipped at the root by the triumphant hound who had tracked down his one fault? Before God, it was *his* only one! He was white beside some others who lived and died respected. Prove the contrary, any one!

One, two! one, two! one, two! That watch. Either he was going mad or it could be heard in the street outside, it shouted so. Who was he, anyway—Deeping or himself? Who was that young man?

Suddenly his head cleared. He moistened his lips and leaned forward, the watch crystal shivered in his grasp.

"And you are going——"

"To Gibraltar," said the young man briskly. "I am glad that you——"

"No," said Weldon thoughtfully, "I am afraid you are not going to Gibraltar. You are going to die."

He pushed his hand back into his pocket and felt the precious hard little object there. His finger clasped it, when a heavy blow sent him reeling in his chair. A pain like a knife cut through his heart and he fell heavily backward on his bent arm.

His eyes opened. He drew a deep breath. A tall, carved clock in the corner struck, and a man, a lank, sandy man beside him, seemed to have said something, for his voice was in the air.

"He must have had some papers—if there is anything wrong—good God, Webb, what shall we do?"

This was a slender, foppish man, iron-grey. Weldon sprang to his feet, pulling his right arm from behind him, wide, wide awake now. He was free! He was free!

The clock struck again.

Thrusting his hand in his coat he drew out a sheaf of papers and pressed them upon Webb.

"Here, gentlemen," he cried breathlessly, "are the papers you want! And here," he threw a small folded slip on the floor, "is an explanation that may help you with them. I wish you good-day."

To get out! To get out! He burst through the portières and the door, as four men, uniformed, with a black stretcher between them, entered it from without. In the moment of his withdrawal from them he saw, as one sees a stage group from his red plush seat, Potter, panting and terrified, Fayles, anguished, Dupont dazed and suspicious, their eyes fixed on Webb, who, calm as in his own office, ran over the sheaf with his snake-like eye. Even as he nodded shrewdly, the stretcher was in the room and the group dissolved.

Weldon found his hat in his hand; he polished it furiously as he strode down the corridor. He threw himself on the outside door and as he opened it, he heard through the unclosed door of the private room the great clock strike eleven. With a shudder he plunged across the threshold, out, out into the clean, free air.

THE LEGACY

Of course, it doesn't make any difference to me whether anybody believes this or not. It's only because Dr. Stanchon asked me to, that I'm writing it, anyway. And nobody needs to get the idea that I think I'm a writer, either: I'm not such a fool as all that. But there's not a nurse in the place who wouldn't lie down and let the doctor walk over her, if he wanted to—and he knows it, too. Not that he's cocky about it, though.

"You know I'm no magazine muck-rake, doctor," I said as I got out of the motor (he had taken me up through the Park to Morningside and back, while I was telling him), "and I'll probably be a little shy on style."

"Style be damned," he said. "You're long on facts, and that's all I want, my dear. And don't for heaven's sake work in any of that C——r's rot on me!"

I had to laugh, really, at that, because he was so funny about it. I took care of Mr. C——r, the novelist, when he had his appendix removed, and he used to dictate a lot to me, and Dr. Stanchon always insisted that my charts were made out in his style, after that. But of course they weren't.

"Just tell it as it happened, you know," he said, "and in your own language. I'd like to keep it."

And of course anybody can do that. Although Mr. C——r told me once that that was the hardest job he ever tackled. He said he could write like his heroes easy enough, but not like himself. But he was always joshing, that man.

"Why, Miss Jessop," he used to say to me, "if I could write like myself, I'd have won the Nobel prize any time this last ten years!"

But he wrote awfully well, I always thought. Hardly a patient I had that year, but if I offered to read, they'd say:

"Oh, well, what's the last C——r's?" and when I got to the parts I'd taken for him (I learned stenography before I took up nursing) it used to give me a queer sort of feeling, really!

It was Dr. Stanchon that got me the case. He 'phoned me to drop in at the office, and a patient of mine took me around in her car: I'd been shopping with her all the morning. She had just invited me to go out to her country place for a few days, and I was quite pleased with the idea, for I was a little tired: I was just off a hard pneumonia case that had been pretty sad in lots of ways, and I felt a little blue. It's an awfully funny thing, but nurses aren't supposed to have any feelings: when that poor girl died, I felt as bad as if it had been my own sister, almost. She was lovely.

But when the doctor asked if I was free, of course I had to say yes, though my suit-case was all packed for the country.

"That's good," he said, "for I specially want you. It's nothing to do, really, and you'll enjoy it, you're such a motor-fiend. There's a family I'm looking after wants a nurse to go along on a tour through the country—New England, I believe. They've got a big, dressy car, and they expect to be gone anywhere from two weeks to a month, if the weather's reasonably good."

"What do they want of a nurse?" I said.

"Oh, they just want one along, in case of anything happening," he said. "They can afford it, so why shouldn't they have it?"

Well, that sounded all right, and yet I got the idea that it wasn't the real reason, somehow. I don't know why. Those things are queer.

Of course, there was no reason why it shouldn't be so: I spent a month on a private yacht, one summer, just to be there in case of sickness, and nobody wanted me all the time we were gone, for a minute. As a matter of fact, the lady's maid took care of me the first three days out!

But I never happened to be asked on a motor-trip in that way, and it seemed a little different. For of course you could pick up a nurse almost anywhere, if you wanted one, on that sort of a tour, and every place in the tonneau counts.

"Isn't there anything the matter with any of them?" I asked.

"What a suspicious lot you nurses are!" he said, with his queer little chuckle (all the young doctors try to imitate it in the hospital). "The daughter's a little nervous, that's all. It's for her they're taking the trip, to give her a change."

"Now look here, Dr. Stanchon," I said, "I'm here to tell you that I don't want any of your old dope cases, and I might just as well say so first as last. That last young man of yours was about all I wanted. He was a sweet creature, wasn't he?"

This probably sounds very fresh to you, but everybody knows me: I speak right out, and if you want me, you have to stand it! And the way I slaved over that boy, and he getting morphine from his valet right along—it was simply disgusting.

"It's nothing like that—nothing at all," said he; "don't get so excited!"

"Oh, very well," I said, "then I suppose it's melancholia. Not for mine, if you please. Perhaps you remember that charming woman that jumped out of the window? I'm no clairvoyant, and that was enough for me, thank you."

"You're getting saucy, Jessop," he said, "but it's not melancholia. But you certainly had a hard time with that one."

And I should say I did. The foxy thing was as good as gold for three weeks, minded everything I said, fairly ate out of my hand, and got us so that we all believed she did better for me alone than when I had help handy. Of course I kept my eye on her, but nevertheless, the other nurse just above gave up the job, and used to be off learning French from the governess they had, most of the time. So when madam got us where she wanted us, she tied me to the door knob and jumped out of the window before my eyes! And I can tell you, the thirty dollars a week that would get me on a case like that again, never left the Treasury!

"I assure you it's not that at all," he said. "It's a case of nerves, that's all."

"Nerves! nerves!" I repeated (I *was* pretty snippy, I suppose). "That's all right for the family, doctor, but what's the matter with her? I've got to know, haven't I, some time?"

"Well, I must say you nurses are getting to be the limit," he said. "The truth is, I spoil you. But there's something in what you say, of course. Now here's the whole business. This girl, and she's a sweet, lovely girl, too, had a maid, that was a sort of nurse, I believe, when she was a child, and had seen her grow up, and was very much attached to her, and all that. Like all those old servants she was pretty well spoilt, I imagine, and seems to have had the girl under her thumb. She always slept in the room with her. Now; the maid had bad headaches and used to take all sorts of proprietary remedies for them—coal-tar, of course, and probably had weakened her heart with them. Anyway, she waked the girl up one night with her troubles and the girl gets up and gives her an overdose in the dark, and the maid's dead in her bed in the morning."

"Oh, I see," I said, trying to make up for my nasty attitude about that suicidal woman. "So she's blue about it, and thinks she's to blame. An automobile trip will certainly do her a lot of good."

"Well, there's a little more to it than that," he said. "As a matter of fact, she's a very sensible sort of girl and she knows she's not to blame, really. Of course it was pretty rough, but then, the maid had no business to expect her to wait on her, and she ought to have given careful directions about the dose, anyhow. She might have gone off any time, and the girl knows it. But the night of the funeral, after the girl was in bed, what does she see but the maid sitting on the foot of the bed, looking at her! Of course she was overwrought nervously. Only the trouble is, this was three months ago, and she swears the woman comes every night. She knows it's hallucination, optical delusion, anything you like, and she tries to treat it as such, but she's beginning to break down under it, and I don't know what to do. They've travelled, they've had her in a sanitarium, they've tried auto-suggestion—no use. She's all right through the day, but at night, in any bedroom, under any circumstances, this thing appears and she just has to go through with it till morning."

"Why doesn't she have some one sleep with her?" I asked.

"It doesn't make the slightest difference," he said. "One week she had a bed between her father's and mother's, but it was just the same, and of course they got pretty bad, out of sympathy. They'd spend two or three ordinary fortunes to cure her—but it's one of the cases where money doesn't talk, unfortunately. So there we are. It came over me last night that I'd like to have you try what you can do with her."

"But, heavens and earth, what good will I be?" I said. "Am I a ghost-catcher? I never knew it."

"No," says he, "but I'm sorry for the ghost that would run up against you, Jessop—honestly, I am!"

"Much obliged, I'm sure," I said, "but why doesn't she take her sleep in the daytime? That would fool the ghost from her point of view—wouldn't it?"

I'll never forget the look he gave me. "Listen to me, my girl," he said, running out his jaw in the way he does when he's in dead earnest and means you to know it, "listen to me, now. If that young woman ever takes to living by night and sleeping by day, on that account, *she's a gone goose!*"

"What do you mean?" said I.

"I mean it's all up with her, and she might as well engage a permanent suite in Jarvyse's little hotel up the river," he says, very sharp and gruff. "I've staved that off for a month now, but they can't see it and they're bound to try it: Jarvyse himself half advises it. And I'll risk my entire reputation on the result. If she can't fight it out—she's gone."

He waited a moment and put out his jaw.

"*She's gone,*" he said again, and I felt creepy when he said it, and I tell you I believed him.

"Well, I'll try my best," I said, and I went on the case the next morning.

As soon as I saw her I got the idea of her I've always had since: that's me, all over. I went to a palmist's once with a lot of the other nurses and that's the first thing he said to me.

"It's first impressions with you, young woman," he said. "Take care to trust 'em and act on 'em, and you'll never need to count on the old ladies' home!"

Well, as soon as I saw Miss Elton she put me in mind of one of Mr. C——r's heroines, looks and clothes and ways, and all, and I've never changed my mind. Her things were all plain, but they had the loveliest lines, and she always looked as if she'd been born in them, they suited her so! Her hair was that heavy, smooth blond kind that makes a Marcel wave look too vulgar to think about, and her eyes and complexion went with it. And with all her education she was as simple as a child: there were any number of things she didn't seem to know. She took to me directly, her mother said, and I could see she liked me, though she hardly spoke. She had big rings under her eyes and seemed very tired.

She got a nap after lunch—only two hours, by the doctor's orders—and it did seem a shame to wake her, she was off so sound, but of course I did, and then we walked for an hour in the park. I didn't talk much at first, but I saw that she liked it, and so gradually we got on to different subjects, and I think she was entertained. She seemed interested to hear about the nurses at the hospital and some of the funny things that happen there, and I could see that she was trying to keep her end up—oh, she was all right, Anne Elton was, and no mistake! There was nothing morbid about her: she was trying to help all she could.

When I came down for dinner there was a young man with them, a handsome, dark fellow, and he talked a great deal with me—I could see he was trying to size me up, and it was easy to see that he was pretty far gone as far as Miss Elton was concerned, and didn't care who knew it. We must have seemed a strange party to any one who didn't know the ins and outs of the thing—only the five of us in that big dining-room with the conservatory opening into it; the mother, one of those stringy, grey New York women, that always wear diamond dog-collars, worried to death and nervous as a witch; Mr. Elton—he was Commodore of the New York Yacht Club at that time—fat and healthy and reddish-purple in the face; young Mr. Ferrau (he was from an old French family and looked it, though a born New Yorker) and me in my white uniform and cap next to Miss Elton, all in white with a big rope of pearls and pearls on her fingers. She could wear a lower cut gown and look more decent in it than any woman I ever saw. All her evening dresses were like that, perfectly plain, just draped around her, with long trains and no trimmings: her skin was like cream-coloured marble, not a mark or line or vein on it, but just one brown mole on the right shoulder blade, and that, as her mother said, was really an addition.

Nobody talked much but Mr. Ferrau and the old gentleman—there's no doubt he had been a gay old boy in his day!—for I never do talk when I dine with the family, and the mother was too nervous for anything but complaining of the food. The Lord knows why, for it beat any French restaurant I ever ate in, or Delmonico's either, and Mr. Ferrau and I got quite jolly over how they put soft-boiled eggs into those round, *soufflée* sort of things with tomato sauce over them, without spilling the yolks. Then they asked if I'd play bridge a bit, and though I don't care for games much, I learned to play pretty well with my morphine-fiend and his mother, so of course I did, and the old gentleman and I played the young couple, and Madam Elton crocheted, sitting up straight as a poker on a gold sofa.

It always makes me laugh when I read what some persons' ideas are of how rich people amuse themselves. The nurses are always jollying me about my rich friends and playing the races and champagne suppers and high-flying generally, and I often wish they could have seen us those evenings at the Eltons, playing bridge—no money, mind you, and Apollinaris at ten! The Commodore had to have ginger-ale, the ladies hardly ever drank, and I never take anything but water when I'm on a case, so Mr. Ferrau had all the champagne there was at that dinner. At ten the masseuse came and rubbed Miss Elton to sleep, and I got into my bed next hers before she went off, not to risk disturbing her. There was a night lamp in her bath and I could just make out her long braid on the pillow—the pillow cases had real lace insertions and the monograms on the sheets were the most beautiful I ever saw.

I went off myself about eleven, for I was determined to act perfectly natural: I knew I'd wake if anything was wrong. And sure enough: all of a sudden I began to dream, a thing I seldom if ever do, and I dreamed that my suicidal case was clambering over me to jump out of the window, and woke with a start.

Miss Elton was sitting up in bed staring at me, breathing short.

"Can I do anything for you?" I asked quietly and she gave a sort of gasp and said,

"No—I think not, thank you. I'm sorry to bother you, but the doctor told me to."

"Why, of course," said I, "that's what I'm here for. Do you see anybody?"

I didn't say, "Do you think you see anybody?" for I never put things that way.

"Yes," she said, "she's there—Janet." I glanced about, and of course there was no one, and I tell you, I felt awfully sorry for her. It was all the worse that she was so pretty and calm and decent about it: I didn't like that a bit.

"Where is she?" said I.

"Right on the foot of the bed," she answered, in that grim, edgy kind of way they always talk when they're holding on to themselves. Oh, how that morphine boy of mine used to begin!

"Excuse me, Miss Jessop, but would you mind assuring me that there's nobody crouching under the bed?" he used to say. "Of course I know there's not, but there appears to be, and I'd be obliged if you'd look!"

If I went under that bed once, I went fifty times.

"Why, to tell you the truth, Miss Elton, I don't see a thing," I said. "Shall I turn on the light?"

"No—not yet," she said. "The doctor said to hold out as long as I could. Would you mind putting your hand there?"

"Not a bit," said I, and I pawed all over the foot of her bed. Finally I got up and sat there.

"What happens now?" I asked her.

"She just moves up and sits farther out," said she.

I couldn't think of much to say to that, she was so quiet and hopeless, so I waited awhile and finally I said,

"Would it help you any to talk about it?"

"Oh, if you didn't *mind*!" she cried out, and then the poor thing began. It makes me tired, the way people treat a patient like that. There was that girl just bottled up, you might as well say, because they all thought it would make her worse to talk about it. Her father pooh-poohed it, and her mother cried and asked her to send for their rector, and even Dr. Stanchon slipped up there, it seemed to me, for he advised her not to dwell on it. Not dwell on it! Why, how could she help it, I'd like to know?

"What I can't understand," she'd say, over and over, "is her coming, when it hurts me so. Why, Janet loved me, Miss Jessop, she loved the ground I walked on, everybody said! And she knows —she must know—that I wouldn't have hurt her for the world. Why should I? She took care of me since I was six years old—sixteen years! She said to put in those powders in the box and I put them in. How could I know?"

"Of course you couldn't know," I said, "she knows that."

"Then why does she do this?" she asked me, so pitifully, just like a child. "Why does she, Miss Jessop?"

"Well, you know, Miss Elton," I said, "you wouldn't believe me if I lied to you, now, would you? And so I must tell you that I don't think she *does* do it: none of us do. It's just your idea. If Janet's there, why don't I see her? You're overstrained and excited and you feel that she might not have died——"

"Ah, but I didn't feel that the night she came!" she broke out, "truly I didn't. Dr. Stanchon and all of them said I was very brave and sensible. He talked to me and made me see: if Janet had been sleeping with one of the maids and waked her up and told her not to turn on the light because it hurt her head, but just to give her the powders in the box, that maid would have done it. I can see that."

"Of course," said I.

"I didn't blame myself—really," she went on, and suddenly she looked straight to the foot of the bed.

"Janet," she said, "the doctor said never to speak to you, and I never will again, but I must, this once. Janet, *do* you blame me? Are you really there? Why do you come this way? You're killing me, you know. I can't sleep. You shouldn't have taken that strong medicine, and the doctor told you not to, you know, yourself. Won't you go, Janet? Not to please Nannie?"

Really, it would have melted a stone to hear her.

She was still a moment and then she began to cry and whimper, and I knew that it had made no difference.

"She won't go—she won't go," she said, crying, "not even for Nannie!"

Well, I talked to her and read to her and stroked her head, and by two o'clock or so she was off for an hour, and I got a nap myself. But from three till nearly five she was awake again, and I had to light up the room; she said she hardly saw her then—only felt her, and that wasn't so bad.

I don't know that anything different took place for a week after that. We went through the same business every night, and I took a nap every afternoon when she did. She told me, what I wasn't much surprised to hear, that she and Mr. Ferrau were engaged—or just about—when this precious Janet died, and that now she wouldn't hear of it and had refused to marry him till she was well again. And I must say I think she was right. Of course the old gentleman didn't see it that way, and we had many a discussion about it, he and I.

"God Almighty, Miss Jessop, my dear," he used to say to me, "you know as well as I do—I'm speaking, of course, to a woman of practical sense and experience, and therefore I speak plainly —you know as well as I do that the day after the wedding all this will be done for! We'll never hear of that damned Janet nonsense again. Now, would we?"

"Well, Commodore, maybe not, but you can't tell," I'd say. "It's a good bet, but—it's a bet, after all. It would be awkward if it didn't work out, you know."

"Oh, bosh, bosh!" he'd burst out, and roll off to the Yacht Club. People that live in big houses like that, I've noticed, always have to go out to get a little peace, they say, and privacy. It's funny.

The weather was bad, so we didn't go on the motor trip at all, and that was just as well, for if we had, I should never have gone up to the hospital that day and never seen old Margaret. She was an old darky woman that used to come in to clean the wards when they were short of help, and all the nurses knew her, because she used to tell fortunes with cards and a glass ball she looked into—pretty fair fortunes, too. I've known of some awfully queer things she told different nurses that were only too true. She always liked me because I used to jolly her up, and I stopped to speak to her, and she asked me where I was working.

"Oh, a grand place on the Avenue, Margaret," I told her, "marble stairs and a fountain in the hall."

"What's the sickness, honey?" she asked, for those darkies are always curious.

"The patient's got a ghost, Margaret," I said, just to see what she'd say, "and I'm sorry to say we can't seem to cure her."

"Co'se you cayn't cure her," says she, "no stuff in bottles for that, honey! What the ghos' want?"

"Nothing at all," said I. "It just sits on the bed and looks."

"Laws, honey, Miss Jessop, but that yer kine's the wors' of all," says she, staring at me. "She'll jes' have ter leave it onto somebody else, that's all."

"Why, can you do that?" I asked.

"Sure you can do it," she says. "Was it one that loved her?"

"They all say so," said I.

She struck her hands together.

"I knew it—I knew it!" she cried out. "It's always that-a-way. My ole mudder she had that ha'nt fer ten years, and it was her half-sister that brung her up from three years ole! She'll jes' have ter leave it onto some one."

"Well, I'll tell her so," said I, just in joke, of course.

"You do," says she, solemn as the grave, "you do, Miss Jessop, honey, an' she'll bless you all her life. You get some one ter say they'll take that ha'nt off her *right w'ile it's there, so it hears 'em,* and w'ile there's a witness there ter hear bofe sides, an' you hear to me, now, she'll go free!"

"I'll certainly tell her, Margaret," I said, and I went on and never gave it another thought, of course.

We went up to the Elton's camp in Maine all of a sudden, for Miss Elton got the idea she'd feel better there, and though it was cold as Greenland, it did seem for a little as if she got a bit more sleep. But not for long. We slept out on pine-bough beds around a big fire, for that made more light, and that precious Janet seemed to be fainter, but she was there, just the same, and the poor girl had lost eighteen pounds and I felt pretty blue about it. It didn't really look as if we got ahead any, as I told the doctor, and she hardly spoke all day. I'm not much for the country, as a rule, it always smells so damp at night, but the Lord knows I'd have lived there a year if it would have helped her any.

Then came the night when Mr. Ferrau ran up to see how she was getting along. It was too cold for Madam and the Commodore, so we were there alone except for a gang of guides and servants and chauffeurs and masseuses. She had a bad night that night, for she got the idea that this lovely Janet was sitting up nearer and nearer to her, and she had it in her head that when she got to a certain point it would be all up with her. And when I told the doctor that, over the telephone, all he said was:

"Too bad, too bad!" So I knew how *he* felt.

Well, she got talking rather hysterically for her, and I began to wish somebody else was around, when Mr. Ferrau jumps out of his door in the bachelor quarters and dashes over to us in a heavy bathrobe, white as a sheet.

"For God's sake, Miss Jessop, *do* something!" he said, but I just shrugged my shoulders. There was nothing to *do*, you see. She was all bundled up in a seal-skin sleeping-bag with a wool helmet over her head; her eyes certainly looked bad. I just about gave up hope, then. The moon made everything a sort of bluish-white and we all must have looked pretty ghastly.

"I think I'll give her a little codeine," I said. "Just stay here a moment, will you?"

He knelt down by her bunk while I began to unwind myself from all the stuff you have to get into up there.

"Oh, Anne, my dearest, dearest girl," he said, "if only I could take this instead of you! If only I could see her, and you not!"

"Would you—would you, really, Louis?" I heard her say. "You *do* love me, don't you? But that would be too dreadful. I couldn't allow that to happen."

"Heavens, my dear girl, I'd take it in a minute, if I could!" he cried. "Oh, Anne, do try to look at it in that way—try to give it to me! Perhaps if you used your will-power enough for that——"

"That can't be, Louis," she said, "this is just my fate. I must bear it—till it kills me. But if it could be, I'll tell you this: I *would* give it to you, dearest, for you are stronger, and maybe a man could fight it better."

I was off to the main camp then, but when I got back with the codeine she was asleep with her head on his shoulder, and he kneeled there till four without moving—he was game, that Mr. Ferrau, and no mistake!

She slept right through till eight, and I left them together all day, as much as I could, and I let her off her nap, she begged so. I could see from the solemn way she talked that she was saying good-bye to him, as much as he'd let her. She told me that as soon as it began to get on her brain, really, and she got worse (we always called it "getting worse"), she was going up to Dr. Jarvyse's place, and he wasn't to see her at all.

"I want him to remember me—as I was," she said. It certainly was tough. I used to cry about it, when I was alone, sometimes. You get awfully fond of some patients.

He stayed the next night, too, and I took my regular nap from ten to one. I could nearly always count on that, and I'd got so I woke the moment she did. I was fast asleep when I felt her touch me, and I woke, feeling scared, for she almost never did that.

"What is it?" I said, half awake. "Is she coming nearer?"

"Miss Jessop, dear Miss Jessop, she isn't here at all!" she said, shaking and crying. "I've been awake an hour, and she hasn't come to-night! Oh, *do* you think, *do* you——"

"Yes, I do," I said, though I was pretty excited myself, I can tell you. "I believe you're getting better, Miss Elton, and now I think I'll have Miss Avidson rub you, and see if we can get through the night all right."

The Swedish woman put her right to sleep, working over her head, and we never opened our eyes till nine. One of the guides told me that Mr. Ferrau had been called to the city early, and had left quietly, not to disturb us, but we were both so delighted and yet so anxious not to be delighted too soon, that we didn't notice his going much. She ate three good meals that day, besides her tea, and we walked five or six miles—I wanted to wear her out. And that night she slept right through!

We waited one night more, to be certain, and then I 'phoned the doctor.

"Hurray!" he yelled, so I nearly dropped the receiver. "Bully for you! Keep out for a week and then move in—with a light. Drop the light in another week. Then I'll send 'em all off to Beachmount." This was their Long Island place.

Well, it all worked out perfectly. She gained nine pounds in three weeks, and I don't know when I've been so pleased. The old people came up to see her, and I spent most of my time convincing them that it was no case for tiaras and sunbursts, as I never wore them. Mrs. Elton really looked almost human. She cried so that I finally had to take a little string of pearls. They were small, but all matched, and she said I could wear them under my blouse and I could always sell them. You'd have thought that I'd cured the girl, when, as I told them, the thing had just run its natural course, and her youth and good sense and the outdoor life had done the rest.

Of course, there was no more use for me, and I went right off on a big operation case—a very interesting one, indeed. I promised to come to the wedding, if I possibly could; she told me she would be married just as soon as Mr. Ferrau wished, she felt she'd made him go through so much in the last four months. And it seemed that he *had* felt the strain more than they thought, for her mother told me that just as Anne recovered, he seemed to give way and got very nervous and had gone off on a yacht with some of his college friends to the south somewhere. I was rather surprised not to see him at the house, and so was Miss Anne, I thought; but he sent the loveliest flowers every day and telegrams, and of course they were working on the trousseau and pretty busy, anyway.

I couldn't get to the wedding, after all, for my patient was taken to Lakewood and simply refused to let me off, which was rather mean of her, for I could have run up for the afternoon as well as not. But that's what you have to expect, if you go into nursing, and you get used to it.

Mrs. Elton called me up once at the hotel, to see if I couldn't get away (they were going to send the car for me if I could), and I asked if Mr. Ferrau was all right again.

"Really, Miss Jessop," said she—and I could just see how she must have looked, from her voice —"really, my dear, I am terribly, *terribly*worried about Louis. He looks frightfully, so pale and nervous and run down. And he simply *won't* see a doctor, and when I earnestly begged him to consult Dr. Stanchon, he flew out at me—he really flew out!"

"What can it be?" said I. "What does Miss Elton think?"

"Why, how can she know, my dear?" says the old lady. "Only he assures her that it will be all right once they're married, and begs her so not to put it off, that she won't, though I don't entirely approve, myself. Really, you'd scarcely know Louis, Miss Jessop."

It did seem too bad, but then, those things will happen, and I just thought to myself that probably there was more to that southern trip than the old lady knew, and let it go at that. The doctor says that all the nurses have dime-novel imaginations—but where do we get them, I'd like to know, if not from what we see and hear? The Lord knows we don't have to invent things.

Miss Elton was dreadfully disappointed that I couldn't be there for the wedding, and promised me they'd stop a minute at the hotel on their wedding journey and see me. They were going on a motor trip, nobody knew just where, and Lakewood would only be a few miles out of their way. Wasn't that nice of them? But it was just like both of them. So I was quite excited, of course, and when it poured rain all day, and got worse and worse, I did feel so sorry for them and never expected they'd leave town. But, lo and behold, about five o'clock didn't the boy bring up their cards, and for a wonder my patient was decent and said she wouldn't want me till next morning —she had her own maid with her and really didn't need me but once a day.

I ran down to one of the little reception rooms—I must say I like those big hotels—and when I saw them I nearly collapsed, for though she was looking perfectly beautiful and well as could be, poor Mr. Ferrau certainly did give me a shock. He was all tanned, well enough, but as thin as a rail, and dreadful around the eyes. And yet he looked very happy and seemed quite glad to see me.

"Isn't she looking magnificent?" he asked me, and I said—I just have to say right out what I think—"Yes, she is, but I can't say the same for you."

"Oh, I shall be all right—after a bit," he said, turning red and not meeting my eyes. "Just let me get away with Anne for a while, and you'll see."

They insisted on my having tea with them, and I couldn't help but think that she didn't realise how bad he looked and acted: his hand shook so that his tea-spoon jingled. And yet he was as straight as a string, I was sure.

It kept on pouring so dreadfully that they gave up the idea of going on anywhere, and he engaged a suite at the hotel for that night, and I said good-bye to them, then, for they were to have their dinner served by themselves and I knew they'd want to get off quietly in the morning. My patient kept her word and didn't bother me, and I listened to the music for a while and then went up to my room and wrote some letters. About ten I put my boots outside the door and happened to notice the boots opposite and saw that they were Mr. Ferrau's—they were patent leather, with rather queer cloth tops. So I knew that they had the suite opposite ours; there were only those two for the one little hall.

I couldn't seem to sleep that night at all. I kept dreaming about that suicide of mine, even when I did sleep, and finally I put on my wrapper and decided to take a few turns up and down the corridor. I opened the door softly and stepped out—and ran right into Mr. Ferrau! He was stalking along in a bathrobe, his arms spread out, and tears rolling down his cheeks, and he was chattering to himself like a monkey. His eyes rolled, and I could see he was just on the verge of a regular smash-up.

"Why, Mr. Ferrau, what's the matter?" I asked.

He stared at me like a crazy man. "You here!" he said. "For God's sake! Go up to her—go to Anne—I'm all in," he said. "Oh, Miss Jessop, it didn't work! It didn't work!"

He pointed to his door, and I went through the private dining-room and the sitting-room and a dressing-room and a big marble bath, and there she was, crying like a baby in one of the beds.

"Why, Miss Elton—I beg your pardon, Mrs. Ferrau—what *is* the matter?" I said, running up to her and taking hold of her hand. "Are you ill?"

She only sobbed and held on to me and suddenly something struck me and I said, "You haven't seen Janet again, have you?"

"No, no—but I wish I had! I wish I'd never stopped!" she gulped at me. "Oh, Miss Jessop, *Louis sees her*! He sees her all the time; that's what makes him look so ill! Ever since she stopped coming to me, he's seen her, and he never told."

"For heaven's sake!" said I.

"She sits on the bed, but she doesn't look at him—he only sees her profile. He walked twenty miles a day—he did boxing and fencing and riding—it was no use—he thought when we—when —he hoped if we were married—oh, Miss Jessop, she came just the same!"

"For heaven's sake!" I said again. It wasn't very helpful, but I simply couldn't think of anything else. She was so pretty and sweet, and he was so plucky, and who would have supposed it would have got on his nerves so!

Her night gown was solid real lace, and the front of it was sopping wet where she'd cried, and the top of the sheet, too.

"I gave her to him, and he won't give her back—I can't make him!" she went on, gasping and sobbing. "I begged him on my knees, but he wouldn't."

"And don't you see her?" I asked.

"No, no, I can't!" she cried. "I try, but I can't."

"Well, that's something, anyway," I said. "You wait till I go and speak to him again, and put some cold water on your eyes, why don't you?"

For it just occurred to me that maybe I could do something with him, after all. He was leaning against the window at the end of the corridor, and I never like to see excited people near windows, after my suicide woman, so I sprinted along till I got to him. But I really don't believe there was any need for it—he wasn't that kind.

"See here, Mr. Ferrau," I said, "do you really believe that Miss Elton—I beg your pardon, Mrs. Ferrau—really gave that old Janet ghost to you?"

"Believe it? *believe it*?" he said, staring at me out of his red eyes. "No, I don't believe it, Miss Jessop—I know it! I tell you I see the damned thing, in a brown dress, on the edge of my bed every night!"

"Well, then," I said, "do you think you could give it to anybody else?"

And just at that moment, and not before, I remembered old Margaret!

"Why—why, I never thought of that," he said. "I—I wouldn't put any one else through such a hell, though——"

"Oh, come, now," I said. "Maybe they wouldn't think it was so bad as you do, Mr. Ferrau."

"But who would—oh, it's too crazy!" he said, half angry, but all broken up, so he didn't much care how it sounded.

"Oh, lots of people," I told him. "Why, you might easily find some one with an incurable disease, you know, that hadn't long to live and wanted money——"

Of course, this was all nonsense, but anything to humour people in his condition—it's the only way. And what do you think? He turned around like a shot and stared at me as if I'd been a ghost, myself.

"That might be possible," he said, very slowly; "it's just possible I know ... excuse me, I'll go in and speak to my wife a moment!"

He left me there and in a few minutes he came for me again, and I went into their parlour. She had on a beautiful pale rose negligée all covered with lace and her braids were wound around her head: she'd wiped her eyes.

"Would you perhaps play a little bridge with us, Miss Jessop?" says he, trying to keep calm. "We think we'd better have some one with us."

So there we sat till four in the morning, playing three-handed bridge, and if anybody knows of a funnier wedding-night, I'd like to hear of it!

I suppose anybody would have thought us all crazy if they could have seen us, the next night, sitting, all three of us, by the bed of that queer old man that lived in old Greenwich Village. (My patient let me off, for I told her it was a case of a young bride and groom, and she was delighted to oblige the Eltons. She told me she should call on them after that! She was a climber, if there ever was one, that woman.)

He was an old valet of Mr. Ferrau's father, and Mr. Ferrau was supporting him till he died in a little cottage there. He had angina and was likely to go off any minute, and the Lord knows what Master Louis paid the old monkey—I'll bet it was no thirty cents! He only talked French, but I could see he thought Mr. Ferrau was crazy—he looked at me so queerly out of his little wrinkled eyes and nodded his head as if to say, "What a pity all this is! But we must humour him."

Mrs. Ferrau told me afterward that her husband promised him solemnly to take Janet back if he couldn't stand her—and he would have, too, and don't forget it! He was a game one. But the old fellow just kept saying:

"*Bon, m'sieu, bon, bon!*" and kept reaching for his envelope. He was only afraid they'd change their mind, you see.

Then Mr. Ferrau lay down on a cot next the old fellow's—he was kept very clean and neat by the woman that boarded him—and I stayed in the room while Master Louis gave that darned old Janet away. He insisted that I should witness it, and to tell you the truth, when I remembered what black Margaret had said about having a witness, I *did* feel rather queer, for a moment. But of course they were all crazy—as crazy as loons—so far as that one thing went. You see, it was what Dr. Stanchon calls an *idée fixe*. They had to be humoured.

Mrs. Ferrau and I went out, then, and walked up and down for an hour through the village with the chauffeur behind us, a little way, and I really thought I'd be dippy myself, before long, if I had to pretend to be serious about it much longer. It's no wonder to me the doctors in asylums get touched themselves, after what I went through with those two.

In just about an hour he came dashing out and pushed us into the car. We didn't need to ask him —he looked ashamed, but oh, so different!

"Let's get back to town," was all he said, and I never mentioned it to him again, any of it. Of course, a sensible fellow like him *would* feel too ridiculous; knowing he had that silly idea in his head, yet not being able to get over it without such childishness—I felt sorry for him.

I know that they didn't go back to Lakewood, for her maid packed up there, and a week after that the old lady wrote me from Long Island that they'd gone for a honeymoon tour in the car through Southern France, so I knew that father-in-law's valet hadn't gone back on his bargain. I never knew what that old monkey made on it, but Mrs. Ferrau told me he was going to leave it to the Catholic church in Normandy, where he was born. I hope it did some good.

I went up to Greenwich that summer with a little boy who had tuberculosis of the spine (the sweetest little fellow, and so clever!) and on one of my afternoons out with him I stopped at the old cottage where the valet lived, just to ask after him. The woman there told me he had passed away about ten days after I was there before.

"In the night?" I asked, more for something to say than any real reason.

"No, in his sleep, in the afternoon," she said. "He didn't sleep much at night, after his young gentleman came, I noticed. He seemed to have bad dreams. He'd be praying away and clicking those rosary beads half the night, sometimes. But he went out easy, at the last. I learned a little French when I was lady's maid to a party, once, so I could get along pretty well with him. But I couldn't make out about those dreams, exactly; they seemed to be about something brown, with its back to him, on the bed. But he was pretty contented by day, when he was awake; he kept telling me of all he was leaving to his church."

... When you think about it, it was queer, wasn't it?

THE MIRACLE

"And are they all really insane?"

He looked at me curiously.

"'Insane'?" he repeated, "'really'?"

He was very young, but very clever, and I had known his mother well and listened to his letters from school many a time; she was intensely proud of him.

"I tell you what it is, aunty," he began, selecting a cigarette with the deft manual gesture of a born surgeon (he was only twelve years younger than I, and his phenomenal record of almost impossible accomplishment made him seem far older than his years; but we kept to the habits of his perambulator days, when I had been tremendously pleased with the title). "I tell you what it is, aunty—I'm hanged if I know!"

He peered slit-eyed through the clouds of smoke, and I waited eagerly for what would come; when his eyes took on that look the boy seemed to me, frankly, inspired. Twenty-three years (he had finished Harvard at nineteen) appeared so pitifully inadequate to account for him! One was forced to the belief that he had directly inherited that marvelous "intuition" of his: that it was actually part of his famous father's experience—for he was Richard Stanchon's only son.

"Of course, you know," he said quietly, "I see what they mean—most of 'em. I always do, somehow. And the more you do that, the less insane they get to seem to you. It's only you and I, a little warped, a little exaggerated. My idea is that fewer and fewer of them will be sent to places like this, and more and more put out among families—oh, don't shiver, aunty, there's nothing to shiver at, I assure you.

"Look here—do you see that tall girl in the blue silk shirtwaist?"

I saw her—she was reading *Punch* before the big library fire (it was furnished like a wealthy private club, the library), and just because she was so calm and high bred and Madonna-faced, I flattered myself that I could jump in the right direction.

"Does she murder babies?" I asked resignedly.

"Not at all," he replied, with a tiny grin for my cleverness, "not a bit of it. She only insists on taking five baths a day and never touching any washable thing that's been handled. She wears five changes a day and cleans the piano keys before she plays—plays very well, too."

"But—but, is that all?"

"Every bit."

"Then why must she come here?"

"Oh, well, there are practical complications, of course. She thinks most people are pigs, and says so. Then her family is nervous—I notice most of them come from very nervous families—and they simply couldn't rub on. She shampoos her head every day. It's my firm belief, aunty, that if some steady-going German-American family without any nerves would give her two rooms and a bath and put up with her for a few months, she'd be all right. Honestly, as it is, she's fretting herself crazy. She's no fool, you know."

"Heavens, Will! Why, I can perfectly understand——"

"Of course you can. Not mother, though. Mother won't hear about her—and the joke of it is, you know, aunty, mother takes her three tubs a day all summer and never shakes hands in warm weather!"

I gasped.

"But, Will, this is awful! Why, we're all on the verge, if you look at it that way!"

He shrugged and put out his hand to a heavy-faced, ordinary woman of the well-groomed New York type.

"Good afternoon, Miss Vint—let me present you to my aunt, Mrs. Ba—oh, come, now, aunty's a woman of the world and she's married, too. There's no reason on earth why you shouldn't."

"But, doctor, you know what I am——"

"I know," he said kindly, and the real sympathy in his boy's eyes struck moisture into my own, "I know. But you're living it down—no woman could do more."

"Really?" she begged, her features working, "really, doctor? Heaven knows I try!"

"And you never slip back. *You never slip back!*" he said slowly and emphatically. "Just think what that: means, Miss Vint!"

We nodded at each other and she hurried off, almost smiling.

"She looks no more insane than I do," I suggested, and again he shrugged.

"There's where it is," he answered quietly; "she's just a little over the line, that's all. She's Levi B. Vint's daughter, you know."

"Really!"

"I'd hate to think what she pays a week. What she's really worrying about, I believe, is the old man's money. She insists he was all right, you know, and all this exposure business, though it couldn't shake her trust in the old scoundrel, got on her nerves and she got worrying over herself. Everybody argued with her—the whole Vint gang are a set of bronze mules, you know—and finally she arrived at a definite *idée fixe*: I'm sure it could have been prevented. Anyway, she thinks she's—she's all sorts of a bad lot, you know. She won't speak to the girls here—not even to the maids. She says she might corrupt them."

"How absurd—I mean how sad! But she's so healthy; she'll soon recover?"

"I don't know," he said briefly, and something scared me in his voice. "She's a very hard case. A bad age."

We walked in silence through a long glass-walled hall, a sort of conservatory, with palms and caged canaries chirping and trilling.

"I hate those birds!" I cried nervously; he stopped and looked thoughtfully into me—it was no less than that.

"That's interesting," he said abruptly, "I don't like 'em, either. And you're one of the best-balanced women I know. Mother, too—she doesn't care for them. No—nor Beatrix."

Beatrix was the hardy young woman who contemplated marrying him—a tremendous venture, it seemed to me!

"But they seem to like 'em here. The crazier they are (there's nobody bad here, you know) the more they like 'em, ... Did you know mediums and spiritualists and all that sort can't live without 'em? I never heard anybody mention it, but it's so. When I went over to Lourdes, last year, I made a point of looking up the families of the people that had the visions, and they all kept larks in cages——"

I saw he was following some train of thought and kept silence. At length he shrugged his shoulders.

"But that isn't what I asked you out for," he began. "I thought you'd be interested in seeing—Oh, Mrs. Leeth, how are you?"

"Very well, thank you, doctor."

A busy, quiet, elderly woman, plainly dressed, cut across our path through the long conservatory.

"Everything all right to-day?"

"Everything, I think, thank you, doctor."

There was nothing to remark about her until she lifted her eyes, and then the curious, intense depth of them (like a dog who could speak, I thought), held me almost breathless with sympathy. She looked, somehow, as if she had gone through more than would be right for her to tell.

"Poor creature," I said as she disappeared through a baize door. "Tell me about her. What is her trouble?"

"She has none that I know of," he replied quietly. "She's the housekeeper."

"Good Heavens, Will! I think I should go mad myself, if I lived here! How does one tell them apart?"

"I don't think one does, always," he remarked placidly. "I sometimes think that accounts for a good deal! There's a man, now—see that fussy little fellow getting out of his motor coat? That's Jarvyse."

"*The* Jarvyse? The great specialist?"

"That's it," he grunted with a disrespectful grin. "From my point of view, you know, aunty, he might about as well stay in, now he's here. I wouldn't go too near him, if I were you—he'll say you're a paranoiac, if you mention your prejudice against free silver or thick soup at dinner or steam heat. Everything's been paranoia with him since 1902. It's just as much an *idée fixe* as anybody's here. If you object to anything he says, he diagnoses you immediately. You couldn't build asylums fast enough to hold all Jarvyse's paranoiacs! That's why I'm here, by the way; the case I want you to see is really father's. But he loses his temper so, when he meets Jarvyse, that he sends me up, instead. The old boy doesn't bother me—'Morning, doctor."

We stepped into a noiseless lift and he ran it to the fourth floor. At the end of the corridor an open door showed a pleasant little interior; a window full of red geraniums, goldfish in a globe, an immense grey cat by a little Franklin stove with brass balls atop, and in the centre a round old-fashioned mahogany table piled high with various household linen. We walked directly into this little home-like picture—a great relief after the lavish publicity of the immense halls—and as I greeted the housekeeper, who stood by the heaped table (with an actual note of apology in my voice for having mistaken her!) I noticed a little elderly man, a vague pepper-and-salt effect, sitting by a business-like desk in the corner, his hat and stick on the chair beside him, a book and pencil on his knee.

"Good morning, Mr. Vail, I rather hoped you might be here; let me present you to my aunt, Mrs. _____"

"Good heavens!" I almost said it aloud, for the vague pepper-and-salt took on familiar lines suddenly, and the matter-of-fact little features scattered so indistinguishably, as it were, though the boyishly round face became obviously one with the much-photographed trader-prince; it was Absolom Vail, the multimillionaire! When had he...

"Mrs. Leeth used to be Mr. Vail's housekeeper for many years," my young doctor's voice sounded reprovingly (had my jaw dropped?) "and he often looks in on her like this."

"Oh!" I recalled the hat and stick and breathed again. Not that I had any interest in the old gentleman, but he seemed a sort of public character, he and his "old stocking savings-bank," his "millions for deposit, but not a cent for speculation," his "every penny earned in honest trade," and all the rest of it.

"Never forgot an old friend yet," he chirruped, and the housekeeper smiled gravely. It was very decent and kindly and quite what one would have expected; I remembered that every employee always received a personally selected gift at Christmas and that he had stood godfather for seventeen (or was it twenty-seven?) children of labourers, born on the great eight thousand acre estate on the Hudson.

My boy listened a moment to a call from the house-telephone, turned on his heel and swung hurriedly down the corridor. I appeared to have been abandoned.

The housekeeper's lips moved silently as she fingered the napkins on the further corner of the table; it was unnecessary, evidently, to include her in the social situation, though she would be perfectly capable of the inclusion if it should be thought best.

"I had the pleasure of meeting your daughter in London last spring, Mr. Vail," I said.

"Minnie?" he inquired, his shrewd little eyes on me.

"I think so—the Countess of Barkington."

"Yes, that's Minnie. Well, Minnie's a good girl, I guess. I haven't seen her much lately. Not for some years, but once or twice. Ever see Irene?"

"I don't think so. She married——"

"She took an Italian. She's a countess, too—contessa they call it over there. The Contessa di Abbriglia. Hannibal, her husband's name is—always seemed like a Newfoundland dog's name, to me. He hasn't any such amount of land as Barkington, but the family's older, I believe. Hannibal's old enough, anyhow. How old was the count, Mrs. Leeth, when Irene married him?"

"Miss Irene was twenty-one, Mr. Vail, and Count Hannibal was forty."

"You knew them both?" I asked her, caught by a sudden curiosity to see those deep, secret brown eyes once more. The famous Absolom was just what I had supposed he would be, neither more nor less; the most interesting thing I could see in him was this simple, friendly kindness to an old retainer.

"I dressed both the young ladies for their weddings," she replied quietly.

"It must be very pleasant to you—these talks of old times," I hazarded.

"It is," she answered.

I thought of a number of remarks suitable to one or both of my old companions, but they all, somehow, seemed banal and excessive as I marshalled them to my lips. A quaint, almost hypnotic quiet rose like the tide around us: all seemed said and agreed to. A tiny fire flickered on the Franklin hearth; the iridescent fan-tailed fish bent and flattened and glided in the translucent globe; an old clock ticked restfully somewhere. The two elderly friends there—for they were friends; one felt it. And why not? They were from the same class, undoubtedly, the hardware king and the housekeeper, the solid bourgeoisie that is essentially alike in all countries and centuries—these two friends exhaled an atmosphere of contented trust in each other and what life had left for them that spread like a visible cloud, a sort of sunset autumn haze, quite through the little, homely room, and took me under it, with them. No wonder he liked to come there: it did not require much imaginative faculty to infer that neither Barkington nor di Abbriglia had been able to offer such an asylum to their father-in-law....

Asylum! How unconsciously I had fitted the original sense of the kindly old word to its technical uses! Asylum: that was what it was, a refuge, a shelter, a little back-water in the great whirlpool of overstrained, nervous modern life. And Absolom Vail had found one here, it seemed. For he was unmistakably at home here; this was not the first nor the second visit, that was plain. Such atmospheres do not grow from casual encounters.

We exchanged comfortable, old commonplaces from time to time, while Mrs. Leeth sorted, and the hardware lord actually jotted down her notes as to necessary darning and replacing, in a worn red account book—it was almost too quaint for belief! He chuckled at it a little, but not much; it was, after all, such a practical, sane sort of interlude in all the horrid, morbid confusion that the place, with all its conservatories and old mahogany and spacious vistas, necessarily included. They were more than common normal, this simple, middle-class pair, on their friendly little housekeeping island, with this treacherous sea of pain and revolt forever lapping at the edges.

I don't remember how he got to telling me of his early life, but I believe it is a habit of all that sort, and Absolom was no exception to his class and stratum. I was particularly impressed by one little incident, the foundation, really, of his fortune—if any event can be selected in those lives which seem destined to exhibit the farthest possibilities of accumulation.

"I had just exactly one hundred dollars," he said (he had the characteristic superstitious reverence for set sums, even decimal multiples of the national symbol) "that I'd saved up as carpenter's assistant in Greenwich, Connecticut. I took it out of the savings-bank and I came to New York with a clean shirt and a tooth brush and my old mother's Bible, packed in a little basket with some boiled ham and bread. I looked out a verse just as I stepped onto the train— what do you think it was?"

"I have no idea, Mr. Vail."

"No. You wouldn't have. Well, it was this: *Blessed shall be thy basket and thy store. D'you see— basket*! And I always intended to keep a store."

He fixed me triumphantly with his twinkling Santa Claus eyes.

"It's in Deuteronomy," he said.

"The coincidence must have seemed very comforting to you," I suggested gravely.

"It did. It did," he answered, "and from that moment on, I never had a doubt. Barkington didn't care much for that story, though—he says that the old fellows that translated the Bible away back in some king's time—King——"

"King James," said the housekeeper quietly.

"Yes, King James. Well, he says that they didn't mean that kind of a store. Maybe not. But it did the job for me, that verse, just the same."

The whole incident seemed very characteristic, very national, somehow, and I reflected gently upon it as we sat in silence, broken only by Mrs. Leeth's practical, dry voice as she announced:

"Greek Key, Irish weave, spring, 1908, six dozen, fair order.

"Thistle pattern, fall, 1906, four dozen, eight darned, ten badly worn."

It seemed that I had been there a long time....

At length I heard Will's quick, nervous step, and as it neared the door I rose, really reluctantly, and met him.

"I am quite in the doctor's hands," I said, "and I see that he thinks it time for me to leave. Good-bye, Mr. Vail"—he put his hand out for his gloves and cane—"if you are going, too, perhaps, can I take you back in town with me? I motored out."

"I'm afraid you can't," he replied, with his twinkling smile, "because I'm one of the ones that don't get out!"

I stared at him blankly.

"'That don't get out'!" I repeated stupidly. "*That don't get out*? Why?"

"Because I'm insane," he said placidly.

I don't pretend to any unusual share of equanimity, and it was not till we were back in the shelter of my own home, with the comfort of my own tea-tray before me and my own little applewood fire snapping on the hearth, that I brought myself to discuss the matter with Emily's boy. He had come back with me and we were going to the opera together later.

"I suppose that was what you wanted me to see?" I said abruptly.

He nodded.

"Just that. I wanted your idea. It's one of the most interesting cases—with all its complications—I ever knew. Father's turned it over to me, practically. He knows all about it."

"But, Will, the man's as sane as I am!"

"How much did you talk with him?"

"Quite as much as with hundreds of other people!"

He smiled thoughtfully.

"Talk much with Mrs. Leeth?"

"Oh, yes—she seems much more ordinary than her eyes, doesn't she?"

"What did she say?"

"Oh, just commonplaces—I don't recall anything special...."

"Well, try, won't you? What *were* the commonplaces?"

I applied myself to recollection. What, after all, *had* she said? As a matter of fact, beyond her linen tabulation I could not recall more than a dozen words.

"Anyway," I remonstrated, "she makes you feel as if she talked! She doesn't seem silent."

"No," he admitted thoughtfully, "that's true. But she never talks. She hardly speaks to the servants—they're all under her, you know—but they all seem to know what she wants. I've tested lots of them: the cook, the laundresses, the furnace man, the steward—and when they come to consider, they can't recall a dozen words a day. But they always insist, at first, that she gives them detailed orders and criticises them constantly. It's funny."

"Oh, well," I broke in impatiently, "never mind her! Tell me about Mr. Vail—how long has he been there?"

"He's been there six months!" Will announced triumphantly, suppressing a delighted smile at my amazement.

"Six months! And nobody knows?"

"Nobody but the family. Oh, he gets out, now and then: I or one of the doctors goes with him and he puts in a day at the office. Everybody thinks he's travelling or taking electric light baths for his liver or Roentgen rays for his lungs or osteopathy for a cold in the head—Lord knows what!"

"A day at the office? But how can he, if he's insane?"

"He's not too insane to make money." His smile was deliberately intended to intrigue me, I thought.

"He's no more insane than I am!" I cried. "Who put him there?"

"The Countess of Barkington—primarily. Abbriglia agreed, but *they'd* never have done it alone —Irene's too fond of the old fellow."

"Do you mean to say——"

"Oh, don't get excited, aunty—he committed himself. Nobody roped and gagged him."

"But what doctor——"

"Two besides me."

"Besides you? Why, Will!"

"Oh, I didn't say that I recommended him to an asylum. Not at all. If he had fought it, I could have found reasons on the other side."

"Like a corporation lawyer!"

"Oh, well...."

He began rolling cigarettes; they were his one weakness.

"The question is," he said slowly, "what is insanity? Medical insanity's one job, legal insanity's another.... Suppose your butler was convinced of the fact that he was Napoleon: would you care a continental, provided he buttlered as per contract? So long as he didn't shout, '*Tête d'armée!*' as he passed the salad, what would you care? It's quite possible that he has some such delusion, for all you know."

"Of course, I see that."

"There was that old nurse of ours—Esther, you know? To the day of her death she swore that the druggist on the corner of Hartwell Street was Charley Ross—the child that was abducted long ago. You couldn't argue her out of it nor laugh her out of it—she said she had a feeling. She brought us up in it, you know, and for years I believed that he was Charley Ross and regarded him with veneration. She was a perfectly good nurse, just the same. But that idiotic fancy was part of her life—strengthened with every year of her life. It was an *idée fixe*."

"Well?"

THE STRANGE CASES OF DR. STANCHON

"Well. Esther died a poor woman, but if she had left fifty thousand to—to a home for blind mulattoes, say, the first thing her nephews would have brought forward was that idea of Charley Ross."

"Brought forward?"

"To break her will. They would have said that it proved her mentally incapable."

"But it doesn't, Will, does it?"

"That's just as you see it. She wasn't incapable of looking after us and dressing mother and doing the marketing and keeping the accounts and making all her own clothes and some of ours. But if you ask me if she had a perfectly normal mind, I should have to say no."

"I see, Will."

I was extremely interested: I seemed to see, glimmering far off, what we were getting to, and it was gripping, absorbing. But I had no idea what we really were getting to—not then.

"Now, we'll take another case," he said, at another cigarette.

"I was at Lourdes last year, as you know, studying the Pilgrimage. Curious thing. Not an atom of proof, you see, that anybody was ever cured of a headache there. Not even sense enough to use the immense suggestive power that's massed there to do real good to neurasthenics and hysterics —in fact, they try to bar them. They prefer goitre, which is *not* cured by dirty baths, unfortunately. The people who go away from there think they were cured from this, that and the other; whole business founded on a perfectly authenticated case of *dementia praecox*—as much a pathological condition as gout or insomnia. I interviewed a prize case; she appeared before their bluff at a scientific council and presented affidavits of cure from consumption, a year previous. I examined her later. It was—as the man said—interesting if true, but the trouble was, it wasn't true, for she was nearly gone, then. I gave her three months, and she died, I took pains to learn, in ten weeks. Well: that was her delusion. Was she sane?"

"She was misinformed—mistaken."

"Quite so—but she *knew* she was cured, remember. She felt it. The rest of us didn't.

"Now let's go a step farther, if you don't mind. Beatrix tells me that the Almighty God, the creator of the universe, is the father of the son of a young Jewess, and sacrificed his son in order to save the world. This seems to me fantastic, frankly. But mind you, aunty, though I know that druggist wasn't Charley Ross, and though I know that the miraculous baths of Lourdes didn't cure poor Marie Tremplin of her tuberculosis, I can't say that what Beatrix assures me she knows about the Deity isn't so! It appears to me quite incapable of demonstration, but maybe it all happened as she says. Only I don't believe with her that she *knows* it. I say she *believes* it. If it helps her, as she says it does, to be the good and lovely girl she is, all right. It might help Parrott to stand straight to think he was Napoleon. All right."

"That's pragmatism," I suggested.

"Oh, well," he said, with one of his curious old smiles, "they call it different things different years, I suppose."

He drew himself up, and I could see something was coming.

"Now, aunty, attend to me. I couldn't put Beatrix in an asylum for what I and many, many others consider *her* delusion, could I?"

"Why, Will, of course not!"

"No, nor Marie Tremplin."

"Equally of course not. She has a right to her miracle, legally, I suppose, as well as Beatrix."

"Precisely. Well, here comes along Absolom Vail, and says *he's* had a miracle, too. He hasn't millions of people behind him, like Beatrix, nor thousands like Marie, nor even half a dozen, as our old Esther had—she converted all the servants and us children. He has only one—himself. A poor miracle, perhaps, but his own. And Barkington lands him in an asylum. The day of miracles is over."

"Why, Will! Why, Will..." I murmured. I seemed to feel myself on the edge of something very big and cloudy and confusing, but very necessary, somehow, to be understood. The trap he had led me into so neatly had fastened softly, but with almost an actual click, upon me.

"What—what *is* his miracle?" I inquired, in a subdued voice. I was beginning to feel a little afraid of this boy of ours.

"I had hoped he'd tell you himself. He will, if you ask him.... We ought to go and dress, oughtn't we?"

There was no more to be got out of him that night: he was passionately fond of music and had no mind to lose the prelude to *Tristan*.

But through all that evening the big, shadowy something he had stirred up in my mind grew and grew and troubled me increasingly.

"A poor miracle, but his own..." it haunted me. I went up with him again in two days' time, as he had expected me to, I have no doubt.

In the little room with the gold fish and the Franklin grate everything was the same except that the piled linen on the table was new: it was being listed and stamped. And at the little desk in the corner, his gloves and stick beside him on the floor, sat Absolom Vail, the hardware king, in a pepper-and-salt suit.

"I brought my nephew up with me and thought I'd look in for another little chat, Mr. Vail," I said. The housekeeper lifted her unfathomable eyes to mine for a moment, then dropped them.

"Six dozen snow-drop twenty-eight inch breakfast napkins," she said quietly, but my mind received—I cannot explain how—a totally different impression from what the sound of these words conveyed. Afterward, I realized that I thought suddenly of the sea, great clouds, unheard of, enormous fish, and myself driving like the wind across high, tumbling waves ... it was extraordinary. I had been literally lost in her eyes.

"Always glad to see the doctor's friends," he chirped, and soon, as Will had said, he was talking.

It was all very simple—simple and pathetic and typical enough. The hall bedroom, the rising clerk, the new branch in Kansas City, the young, fresh wife, the little story-and-a-half frame house, the bigger one on a better street, the partnership, the two daughters, the private school, the invention of the new time-lock, the great factory, the Trust, the vice-presidency, the clear head in the panic, the board of directors, the mass of capital, the amazing power.

"And of course we brought the girls up very different from what we'd had."

"Of course."

The old epic of America; the wonderful, cruel destiny of its sons and daughters ... I seemed to see them, climbing, climbing, their dainty feet on the bent, grey heads of the human stairway love had built and thrift had mortared and habit had hardened there!

"It was all right while mother was with us," he went on. "I used to get home late after one of those big dinners, and she'd be sitting up and warm me a little soup or something on the alcohol lamp (she'd never touch electricity, mother wouldn't) and I'd get my coat off and sit awhile; she'd send the servants to bed. Minnie never liked that, but while mother lived, Minnie didn't have so much say. Not but that Minnie wasn't a good girl and a good daughter, for a minute, mind you! Wasn't she?"

He turned to his old housekeeper.

"Miss Vail had a very fine mind," she said quietly, "a great deal of faculty."

"That's it—faculty," he repeated contentedly. "But Irene was easier to get along with. A good deal easier. You said you'd never met Irene?"

"I never had that pleasure."

"She was married over in Italy. The Queen of Italy asked for it to be that way, and with mother gone, I didn't see it mattered much, though Minnie didn't like it. But the Queen was Hannibal's godmother. She was at the wedding. We didn't think, when Irene used to lie in her little crib in the front bedroom in Kansas City, sucking on that rubber doll, that a queen would be at her wedding, did we?"

I looked out of the window for a minute, frowning a little in the effort to adjust my ideas to the surprise of the Vails' having had a housekeeper in those early days. When I turned my face to the room again, Mrs. Leeth was gone.

"Minnie got me to give up the business, and after a while I did. So long as I was working for mother and the girls, I'd never have stopped, but with them gone, and the rest I had to take, after the pneumonia, I sort of let things slide. What's the use? There's Vint, now—he kept at it till he died. No one to do for, really—his girl had all her mother's money, too, and she gives it all to foreign missions, anyhow.

"She's here, you know. Thinks she's—well, I guess I couldn't tell a lady just what she thinks she is, poor thing!"

"I see why she's here, Mr. Vail; but tell me, why do you stay here?" I cried suddenly; the quiet, sensible little man forced it out of me, fairly.

He looked whimsically up at me—I sat higher in my chair than he.

"Didn't the doctor tell you?" he asked quietly.

"No, he said you would, perhaps."

"Well, I don't mind. It happened when she died."

"Mrs. Vail?"

"No, Mrs. Leeth."

I jumped—I couldn't help it.

"Wh—what?" I gasped. What a horrible thing—like a bomb thrown into the quiet room!

"Yes," he said placidly, "sounds queer to you, doesn't it? Well, it is queer, I guess."

It was with the greatest difficulty that I held myself to my chair. My throat went perfectly dry, suddenly, and if I did not scream, it was merely because I have a fairly strong will and a horror of making a scene. The little room had turned dreadful to me, all at once—dreadful and unnatural; Absolom Vail, in his pepper-and-salt, a nightmare.

He seemed to read my thoughts and put his hand out reassuringly.

"Oh, I don't think she's dead, *now*!" he explained, "I'm not so crazy as all that comes to! Goodness, no!"

"Oh...," I faltered, soothed in spite of myself by his kindly smile.

"No, no. It was this way."

He leaned forward slightly and tapped the arms of his chair rhythmically.

"After mother left me, there wasn't much to keep going for, you see. Then Irene, she went off, and though she was mighty kind about it, and there'd always be a room for me, and all that, and I liked Hannibal well enough, still, I'd never be happy in Italy. Hannibal saw it himself. In a good many ways Hannibal used to see what I meant, now and again—funny, wasn't it, with him so foreign? You'd have thought Barkington, now ... but that's neither here nor there.

"Well, we stayed in the house together, Mrs. Leeth and me, and we got on very well. She knew all mother's ways, and we used to talk about her, evenings, and she as good as gave me her promise she'd never leave me while I wanted her.

"Then I had pneumonia. We had three trained nurses, but I guess there's no doubt she pulled me through. She was up all the nights.

"Irene and Hannibal came right over—it seems they cabled. Irene was expecting to have her baby, too, and it was in March, the worst time to cross the water. But she came. And Hannibal listened to the doctors and the nurses and then he turned to Mrs. Leeth—'How do you find Mr. Vail to-day?' he said.

"'He'll live, sir,' she said, and he said, 'All right,' and that was all there was to it. There was always something about Hannibal ...

"Then *she* came down. Pleurisy. I'd been South and got back, and I was well enough, you understand, but when they told me that they couldn't save her, something turned right over inside me, and I knew I couldn't bear it. It was too much—everything just slipping away from me, one by one, and me all alone—no, I wasn't good for it, that's all. I suppose it sounds dreadfully weak to you, but there it is: I wasn't good for it.

"I was sitting by her bed, looking at her, thinking of all the old days she could remember with me, and the girls she'd seen grow up, and mother, and all, and all of a sudden she opened her eyes and she knew me. She was sinking fast, but she knew me for the first time in days.

"'Mrs. Leeth,' I said, 'it's no use. If you go, I'll go too. I can't stick it out alone! Must you?' I said. 'Must you? Isn't there any way?'

"'Wait!' she sort of whispered to me, 'wait! There'll be a way, Mr. Vail—a way'll be found!'

"And then her eyes closed.

"I just sat there, staring ahead. I was too miserable to notice anything different about her, though I knew she was very still.

"By and by one of the nurses came in very soft and lifted up one of her hands—I had mine over the other. She was a nice girl, that nurse—we both liked her real well. Dr. Stanchon—the old doctor, not the boy, here—brought her, and he said to me, 'Now, Mr. Vail, here's the best nurse in New York: trust her.' And we did. She looked sharp at me, Miss Jessop did, and listened over her heart, then she put her cheek down to the lips.

"'Why, she's gone!' she said. 'Mr. Vail, when did it happen?'

"And then she called the doctor and he said yes, she was gone. *That's* why I say Mrs. Leeth died."

He looked calmly at me and I found to my surprise that during this story I had grown as calm as he and had quite forgotten, in my sympathy for the little man, just why he had begun to tell it. It was most perplexing. The room had taken on its homely comfort again: the horror had disappeared.

"So I sat there. The doctor said to let me stay, if I felt so. And I just saw my whole life pass right by me like pictures in a book—if you see what I mean. I saw Min when she graduated and Irene playing tunes to her mamma and me on the piano, and the day the new gold furniture came in, and Mrs. Leeth leading me by the hand out of mother's room after I'd sat all day and all night by her....

"And I looked at the face lying so quiet there, and while I looked, it sort of shook—more like when you throw a little pebble into a pond—and the eyes opened. And I knew mother was looking at me. That's all."

Poor, lonely little man! How could I have felt afraid of him? It was not difficult to see how it had been.

"Then she—Mrs. Leeth—had not really died at all, had she?" I said hastily, only to bite my lips at my tactlessness.

But he smiled tolerantly.

"That's what they said," he answered quietly. "It was very interesting, they said. The doctor was pretty hard on Miss Jessop, I thought. But I guess they always lay it off on them.

"They were all so excited about it, they didn't seem to notice what had happened. And by and by I saw they never would notice it, anyway. I just spoke a little about it to Irene and it frightened her, so I kept quiet. She said she saw Mrs. Leeth was different, somehow, but it was the sickness, she thought. They had to go right back. He wanted the baby to be born in Italy. That was all right, of course."

"And Mrs. Leeth—what did *she* say?"

"Oh, she was never one to talk, Mrs. Leeth. She talks less than ever, now. I don't know as I put it very clear to you: it's a pretty hard thing *to* put clear."

He looked appealingly at me.

"Of course, of course," I said soothingly. "Those things are not to be set down in black and white."

"That's just it. When I say that mother looks out at me from her eyes, it seems to be more what I mean. I seem to have 'em both by me, if you can see.... And when I look in her eyes, I understand it all—and I can wait," he added simply. "You've noticed her eyes?"

I nodded.

"Does she ever speak...?"

"I couldn't make you see what I mean very well, about that," he said contentedly. "She just looks at me. It's all plain, then. Maybe that's how we'll all do, in the next life. Don't you think so?"

I found my way to Will's office through a mist of tears.

"Well, what about it?" he asked abruptly.

"I think it's one of the most touching things I ever heard."

"Believe it?"

"Why, Will!"

"Oh! Then you don't blame me any more for committing him?"

"Certainly not. What else could you do?"

"Um-m-m. That's what Minnie, Countess of Barkington, said. She put it stronger than that. When a man of that age spends half of his time in the housekeeper's room, sorting linen, she suggested, there's something wrong. We shall certainly question the will—if he alters it."

"Alters it?"

"In favor of Mrs. Leeth, of course. The fair Minnie hasn't lived among the English aristocracy for nothing."

"Why, Will, how ludicrous—you mean that she suspects——"

"Certainly she does. And very hard-headed of her, too. Stranger things have been."

"But one has only to look at them!"

"That's what Irene thought. But not Barkington. He suggested an asylum. The doctor called me in. (The doctor, by the way, swears the woman died, aunty. 'Only, of course, she couldn't have,' he always adds.) To everybody's surprise Absolom agrees quietly, immediately.

"'I wouldn't have Irene worried, as she is now, for anything,' he said. 'I never meant to leave Mrs. Leeth a penny more than the thousand a year mother and I always planned, but if Minnie can't believe me, all right.'

"Now, here's an odd thing, aunty. No one of that family ever heard of this place, including Absolom himself. Precious few people know about it, anyhow, you see. It pays every one not to. Well. Mrs. Leeth is dismissed, arrangements made, I take him in a motor out here. We walk through the hall, and the first person we meet here—Mrs. Leeth. New housekeeper. It seems the old one died of heart failure overnight. Dr. Jarvyse finds this one, by great good luck just out of a job. Highly recommended by Mr. Absolom Vail. Never occupied just this post, apparently, but Jarvyse feels perfectly certain she's just the woman for it. I don't know how he knew it, but she certainly is. Best woman we ever had."

"How perfectly extraordinary! Was Mr. Vail surprised?"

"Not at all. He just smiled politely, and neither of 'em has ever discussed it."

"What did the Countess have to say?"

"Oh, she was furious, till I pointed out that we couldn't have the woman in a safer place, because every employee signs a bond on entering, never to receive by bequest or otherwise a penny from any patient. We all sign."

"What does the Italian Count think of it all?"

"Hannibal? He's all right, Hannibal. He and I and Barkington had a little session in this very room about a fortnight ago. I was saying something about the question of Mr. Vail's insanity.

"'Question?' says Barkington. 'Question? Why there is no question! As a man of science, Count Hannibal, you know as well as I do——'

"'But I am not a man of science, my dear fellow—I'm a Roman,' says Hannibal, grinning away (those Italians speak wonderful English, you know). 'Very odd things happen in Rome, now and then, my good Barkington!'"

I looked at him steadily. He sat surrounded by his mysterious electric machines under shining glass domes, among costly leather-bound volumes whose very titles questioned the foundation of reason; telephones and telegrams ready to hand upon his orderly desk. And it seemed to me that he smiled mockingly at me behind his baffling eye-glasses.

"I don't understand you, Will," I said slowly, "you seem to be leading me to ... do you mean me to understand that you believe that Mrs. Vail's—spirit—entered—came back ... do you mean you think Mr. Vail is right, all the time?"

"Not at all," he returned promptly. "I acknowledge no such conditions. I know nothing of spirits nor what they do. I do not know that there are any. I study the human brain: when it ceases to respond to nervous stimuli, I cease to study it, that's all."

"Then why do you—why do you look at me..."

He struck his fist on the table.

"I look at you," he cried, "because you amaze me so, you people who assume that you know all about the human brain, where I leave off! Granted your premises, yours and Trix's and the Barkingtons', why*don't* you believe him? I should. Look at that woman's eyes! Try to talk to her! Do you suppose we haven't tried? Ask Jarvyse what he's got out of her! Get something out of her, yourself! Then ask yourself: *if what Absolom says is so, how would she act differently from the way she does act?*

"God! I wish I *could* believe him!"

He struck the desk again, and it seemed to me that behind his glasses he scorned me for the nondescript I was.

I went quickly out of the office into the corridor. I would find Mrs. Leeth and have it out with her. I would—she stood directly in front of me.

"Oh—how do you do!" I stammered. Her hands were full of cut flowers.

"How—how do you feel about Mr. Vail?" I demanded brusquely.

The ordinary, stocky, black-dressed figure raised its head slowly; the eyes met mine.

And suddenly I knew that the flowers in her hands were hyacinths, hyacinths and damp fern and mignonette. It grew and grew and surrounded me with a penetrating cloud of rich perfume, perfume and old, sweet memories that cut and soothed at once. I thought of the lily-of-the-valley bed under my mother's window, and her brown, brown eyes held mine and she—my mother, back again and smiling—filled my heart so full that I stood drowned in the old days and listened for the school-bell and the other children's voices!

It seemed that it had all been a mistake, a long mistake, and she had been there all the time.... I cannot tell you how sweet and certain it all was.

And then I knew the odour for what it was—hyacinth. Hyacinths in a round, spaded bed, with a robin singing near, and myself picking a stalk, and the man stepping up behind me that had blotted out all the other men, who were mistakes and slipped away ... and yet we would not begin again, my dearest! No, no, there is plenty of time!

And just as I was swimming back, staring at her eyes, it came over me that there had been hyacinths on the piano, almost overpowering in the dusk of the room that will always be nearest to me—I hope I may lie there, dead. I was playing Chopin, and life looked so rich: the boy was not born yet. I said, "If he should die"—but of course I couldn't believe that he would. And then —and then it was as if he had *not* died, after all, and I saw that this had been a mistake, too! It was so calm, so simple—no shock at all. Why had I never known? And all this while the girls and I had kept flowers on that tiny, tiny grave! I must tell his father....

She dropped her eyes to the hyacinths and I put my hand on a chair to steady myself. My cheeks were all wet.

"Mr. Vail seems very contented," she said. "Of course, I am accustomed to looking after him."

She stepped quietly through an open door, the keys jangling softly at her belt.

I went South with my husband for a fortnight, and on my return Will dined with us.

"By the way," he said, "were you surprised at Vail's death?"

It was three days' news and I had forgotten to mention it.

"He never was the same after the pneumonia, and he worried about his daughter Irene. She came through all right, though. Well, he was over sixty."

"How—what became of Mrs. Leeth?" I asked eagerly.

He smiled oddly.

"Nobody knows. She's never been seen since the funeral."

"Never been seen? But who is the housekeeper, then?"

"Oh, they've got another. Never'll be Mrs. Leeth's equal, though. She left on the first of the month."

"But when she was paid off, didn't anybody inquire?"

"She never was paid off," he said quietly. "She never came for her money."

THE UNBURIED

The talk shifted at length—as it inevitably must—to women, and the unalterable and uncharted mystery of their mental currents: the jagged and cruelly unsuspected reefs that rear suddenly under rippling shoal-water, the maelstrom that boils just beyond the soft curve of the fairest cape.

"There's no good asking 'why,'" said the great doctor slowly, "you might as well ask, 'why not.' They're incomprehensible. For thirty years I've studied them. Thirty years...."

He leaned forward over the table weightily. The others unconsciously bent toward him.

"Once I thought it was spasmodic—unrelated," he went on thoughtfully, counting his words, it seemed, "but not now. No. I believe there is a law—a big law—they follow, an orbit so extended that any examples one may collect count for too little to help. They seem to vary..." he stared at the siphons and rings of wet on the table.

Outside the club windows the rain fell, glistening and grey; it was making for dusk and the black stream of hansoms and umbrellas were homeward bound. They motioned away the servant who had come to turn on the lights in their corner.

"There are influences," Stanchon began again, abruptly, "currents ... I don't know—they feel them more than we do. And they exert them more, too. We admit one and doubt the other."

He squeezed a half lemon into his glass with a beautiful, firm-wristed wrench, extracted the pips with one deft circuit of the spoon, and poured rock candy into the acid. Over this he dropped in silence a measured amount from a squat foreign bottle at his elbow and filled the glass from a carafe of distilled water.

"It's a queer thing altogether—I don't know what makes me think of it," he began, "and I wouldn't have dared tell it when it happened. Now I can tell anything—I suppose—being sixty and an eminent alienist. Lord! Times goes and goes, and just as you get to where you could use it to advantage—well, the young ones need the room.

"Nervous! What are nerves, anyhow?

"Sometimes I think I know ... a little ... but the time is so short, so short!"

He drank half his glass.

"There comes a time," he said abruptly, "when you first discover what a gnat in a whirlpool you are. I mean that after you've done everything, played perfectly fair and followed all the rules, arranged your combinations and observed the reasonable results for so long that you begin to think you've got hold of the System—something happens, and it's all upset again—flat anarchy. We get it different ways, I suppose. As if a runner bumped into a brick wall on the home-stretch ... strange!

"I was in one of those little cities—Detroit, Cleveland—it doesn't matter. I've lived in both. It's a good size for a doctor—I got all kinds—and I learned fast, there. Nice people, too. I always had an eye for real estate, and what I made, I put into that. I had a good horse, and as I drove about I kept my eye on the property and the way the town was growing. One day I noticed that an oldish looking, comfortable sort of house, a little off from the centre of things, was for sale, and it struck me suddenly that there was a pretty good sort of house to own. It had trees around it and nice paths and a neat little new stable, and there was something in the long, low lines of it—no gingerbread or 'Jim Fisk' business or bands of coloured paint—that appealed to me. It attracted me—you see? Good God!

"I saw the agent and he put a price that surprised me. But the owner wanted to leave town immediately and had made it very low, to get the cash. He'd had hard luck; his wife in a mess with another man, ran up big bills against him—he wanted to get away and never see the town again. So I bought the place and asked the agent to rent it for me, for I was pretty busy just then. A little later he told me he had seen an especially good tenant—a well-to-do jeweller and his family, who seemed disposed to take a long lease and improve the property.

"'You certainly have the luck, doctor!' he said.

"I remember I leaned out of my buggy and lectured him.

"'Luck!' says I. 'Nonsense, man! I get good tenants because I keep good repairs in good houses. You put down two and two and you get back four. Mathematics is under this world!'

"Pompous, wasn't I? But I was only forty. Only forty..."

His eyes gleamed at them from under his shaggy, grey brows; he seemed saturated with life, full of experiences.

"Well, I got my rent every month, and I gave 'em permission to put an evergreen hedge around the place, and I paid half the costs of piping water into the stable; the jeweller kept a horse and runabout for his wife. Then, just before the year was up, the agent called.

"'I'm afraid we won't get any renewal on this, doctor,' he said.

"'Why not? Not good enough for him any longer?' said I.

"'I'm afraid it's too good,' says he. 'You'll see it in the papers to-morrow, but I had it straight from him. His wife has skipped with his head clerk and they've taken most of the stock and all the money. He's nearly crazy.'

"'For heaven's sake!' said I. 'I thought they were a decent lot enough.'

"'So they were, I'll swear to it,' said he, 'but lately—I've seen her off and on'—and he looked rather conscious, I thought—' she's struck me differently. She's a queer woman.'

"Well, the upshot of it was, I let him off as easily as I could—he had three children on his hands and big debts to pay—and I bought a lot of his stuff and paid for the evergreen hedge. The woman never came back and he moved East. So much for them.

"I advertised the house, and that week the rectory of the principal Episcopal Church burned to the ground, and while they were building it again—in stone, of course—they decided to rent that house of mine, and of course I was pleased, because a lot of good, solid people see the property, in a case like that. I've always thought I'd like to develop a whole new section somewhere ... I had ideas ... but I never got the time. O Lord, the time! Slipping, slipping, under your palms, between your fingers, crumbling and running away!"

He shook himself like a big, loose-skinned bear, and long breaths were drawn all around the table.

"One night my wife asked me if I thought the rector liked his new rectory.

"'Why, I suppose so,' I said. 'I've had no complaints—why?'

"'He doesn't stay in it very much,' she said, rather slowly, for her, and when a woman measures her words, I always listen very carefully.

"'What do you mean?' I asked.

"'He practically lives in the study at the church,' said she, 'working there on parish business all day, and a good many evenings, too. That leaves her all alone, and that's not good for any woman.'

"' What on earth do you mean?' I said. 'Are those long-nosed old tabbies gossiping already? Shame on 'em!'

"'Oh, John,' she broke down and cried. 'They're talking horribly! It doesn't seem possible! But why isn't she more careful?'

"Well, there's no good going into that much further. It was a very unpleasant business. He was a pig-headed parson who wouldn't look after his own, and she, I thought, till my wife finally persuaded her to call me in, was simply one of those women who have mistaken their natural vocation. They hadn't been in the town long and they didn't stay long, for as soon as I really understood her I put her into a sanitarium—the sanitarium boom had just begun, then—and he went into the Salvation Army. He'd got his eyes opened, I fancy, and he made a great success in Chicago; he told me he never wanted to see another fashionable congregation in his life—said they were sinks of iniquity. But I don't think there was ever anything actually iniquitous in that business—it hadn't got that far. Only for a clergyman's family, of course ...

"You see, I got her out in time. Ugh! It makes me sick to think of it! She was a nervous wreck.

"That was the first time that Miss Jessop ever went back on me. She was a trained nurse not long out of the training school, and nurses were scarcer, then. A handsome, plucky creature—we worked together for years, and I got to depend a good deal on her. But after a week of the parson's wife she flounced in on me with that regular bronze-mule look of hers and informed me she was leaving the next day—she had to go back East, home, she said.

"I reasoned a bit with her—she had a great influence on women, Jessop, but it was no use.

"'There are two good nurses for to-morrow, doctor,' she said, 'I happen to know. I'd rather not argue about it. I'm tired. I need a change. I've had no vacation this year. And that woman would be better off in a hospital, anyway.'

"I was cross, and I kept my patient in her own house. I thought she wasn't fit to move.

"'I believe I'm going mad!' she used to tell me, with that glitter in the eye—gives the effect of a rearing horse—perfectly symptomatic. 'I tell you I'm not responsible, doctor, for what I do! You must keep me away from—people. But don't leave me alone—oh, don't leave me alone! Why don't the women come to see me? Oh, I can't stay alone!'

"And so on, and so on. It poured out in the regular way—how the poor things spend themselves! —and I listened to it all. They're perfectly typical under those circumstances, but one phrase struck me:

"'I have fought— Oh, I *have* fought! It's killing me, but I have fought!'

"She had, poor little woman. But what was she? When I realised ... when I *knew*..."

They sat now in a circle of dark. The room was nearly empty; the rain had grown to a torrent and lashed the windows furiously.

"Well, I couldn't help taking stock of the thing, and it looked odd, anyway you looked at it. I remembered that the reason I got the house in the first place was very much the same reason that had emptied it twice. Of course the agent remembered it, too.

"'Where's those mathematics of yours, doctor?' he asked me with a good-natured grin.

"'Stuff and nonsense!' I said to him. 'I'll get a tenant for that house, myself.'

"You see, whether or not there was any sense in it, I couldn't let that house get a bad name. There were neighbours and they will talk—they don't always know so much about mathematics as scientific men, you know!

"What a great thing it is, if one could get hold of it and use it—the collective spirit of a community! It's utilizable—or ought to be—like water power....

"There was a woman in town then, a 'mental healer,' she called herself. I'd run across her more than once and she interested me very much. She was a clever woman—sensible, too, which doesn't always follow, you know. So far as I could tell, she never handled a case she wasn't able to attend to, which may seem an odd thing for me to say, but happens to be so. I know of a dozen nervous, hysterical women—emotional spend-thrifts—that she bullied into shape and got so they could stand up without her behind them, too. They were cured, and they stayed cured. More than that, I sent more than one to her, myself!

"'Mrs. Mears,' I said, 'there's nothing the matter with these women that I can see but pure, piggish, bone-idle selfishness. I haven't got the courage to tell 'em so; if you have, and the long words you use disguise the fact sufficiently, go ahead and cure 'em, and God bless you!'

"'Thank you, doctor,' she said, and she cured 'em. They had no use for me after that. No, indeed —they told my wife they'd found a higher law and that calomel was sinful. But the poor old calomel wasn't so bad for 'em, after all, maybe.

"Well, I met her on my rounds one day and I stopped and asked her if she was satisfied with her house—I knew the neighbourhood was rather running down, there—the darkies were creeping up. She admitted she wasn't particularly, and, to make a long story short, I offered her this house of mine for two-thirds the regular rental.

"'I want a good steady tenant, Mrs. Mears,' I said, 'and people may as well get used to bringing their headaches over there—I may move out there sometime.'

"So she moved in and I never gave the matter another thought—I knew she wouldn't run off with anybody! No, she'd had her lesson, I take it. No blue-eyed woman gets as sensible as that woman was without a good, solid reason. And the reason is pretty certain to wear trousers.

"Well, sir, in a month she came to see me. I can see her now: a firm, stocky woman, long body and short legs and big head—the efficient type. She had the smooth pink cheeks and smooth forehead and straight eyes those healer-women have when they're first class of their kind—oh, there's a lot in it—a lot! We fight 'em and get the law on 'em and absorb 'em, finally, as we've fought every advance in medicine. It seems to be the only way in this world...

"She always looked so clean and taut, that woman, never a loose end anywhere.

"'Doctor,' says she, 'you must get a new tenant. I'm leaving to-morrow. How much will it cost me, giving no notice?'

"'Why, what's the matter?' I began. 'Anything I can attend to?'

"'Not a thing,' she answered promptly, 'and we won't discuss it, if you please. The van is there, by this time.'

"'Why, see here, Mrs. Mears,' I said seriously. 'This—this is hardly professional, it seems to me. If there's anything wrong with my property, I want to know it. Of course I know your theories— God's in his heaven and all's right with the world, and if you discuss it, the devil may creep in— I've read Emerson's Essays, myself. I know what you think about medicine and surgery and hygiene—you think Emerson! And that's all right, as far as it goes. But just for ten minutes, between you and me, what's the matter? You can keep on being serene, after that, all you want. Come now—as man to man!'

"She flattened her lips a little and tried not to scowl.

"'Put it that I don't like old houses, doctor,' she said finally.

"'Ah! House haunted?' I suggested, to tease her a little.

"She turned on me.

"'You said it, not I,' she answered, 'but it is true. The house is haunted, doctor, and if I lived there a day longer, I couldn't do my work. I didn't wish to discuss it—you know we don't believe in that—but you meant to do me a service. It's a crime to rent that house. It's slimy. It crawls.'

"'Slimy!' I cried. 'Why the agent told me that the cellar was new cemented, all whitewashed, every room new papered, fresh matting, hard wood on the lower floor, and I attended to the plumbing myself! It was gone over thoroughly three years ago—there must have been a thousand dollars put into it. It hadn't been lived in for years before that. Slimy!'

"'You don't understand me,' she said quietly.

"'For heaven's sake, what haunts it, then? Who's the ghost?' I cried testily.

"'Evil,' she said slowly, 'evil thought, evil lives ... you breathe it in ... it tangles you ... another night there ... I should have no more power, absolutely—I could help nobody. I must ask you not to refer to it again, please. I should not have mentioned it. How much do I owe you?'

"'You owe me nothing, of course,' I said shortly. 'I'll return you the amount of your cheque this afternoon. I'll move into that house, myself.'

"'You will be making a mistake,' she said very placidly, and left the office.

"It took me about forty-eight hours to make my arrangements. It was hot summer weather, fortunately, and I sent my wife off to the mountains, started in to have my own house renovated and decorated, as an excuse, left the housekeeper in charge there and moved my office paraphernalia into that old house with the evergreen hedge. My wife was a Southern woman and we always had darky servants. I took the waitress with me, a quiet little mulatto we'd had for more than a year, and sent for her mother, a very capable woman that I'd often used as nurse in cases where they couldn't pay a professional. She could do anything, the way those Southern darkies can, and she would cook and look after things generally.

"Well, in three days it seemed as if I'd always been there. You know how quickly a man manages a change like that; it's hard to see where the women generate all the friction they make out of a move of that sort. Althea was frying chicken contentedly and Mynie was sweeping and dusting as quietly as she always did.

"She was a slender, oval-faced little yellow girl with almost straight hair, parted and drawn down like a madonna's, very low voiced and capable, with only one fault; she was almost too shy and always timid that she'd make some blunder—which she seldom if ever did. She was devoted to her mother, who had brought her up particularly well, and delighted to be living with her. The patients all liked her and she was especially tactful with children.

"One day, after I'd been there a week, I strolled out in the kitchen.

"'This strikes me as being a pretty good house, eh, Althea?' I said. 'New and clean. Everything all right?'

"'Yes, Dr. Stanchon, thank you, seh, it seems like a very good house, seh,' she answered respectfully.

"'It's right surprisin' Mrs. Mears didn't like it!' says Mynie with a little giggle.

"It struck me then that I had never known Mynie to speak, in her life, without being spoken to, and even so, when I had occasion to speak to her, she started and looked a little scared. I supposed living with her mother had given her more confidence and felt rather glad of it.

"It might have been a week later one morning, as I leaned out of one of the office windows to knock my pipe clean, I heard a low laughing and murmuring on the side porch, and glancing carelessly in that direction, what should I see but Mynie twisting the lapel of a young man's coat; his arm was around her waist. It occurred to me that he was pretty well dressed for any beau she'd be likely to have, and as he turned his face partly, I realised with a disgusted surprise that it was George, my colored office-man. It would be hard to make you feel the way I did then, and you'll probably smile when I tell you that I couldn't have been more shocked and startled if it had been any one of you—but it's the truth.

"You see, George was a most exceptional fellow. Everybody in—in the city I'm telling about— knew him and respected him. Everybody among my patients knew that except for his colour he'd have been my regular office assistant long ago. As it was, he knew more medicine than many a lad with his gilt shingle up, and his English was perfect—he'd been in school till he was eighteen and was a great reader. He'd come to me as a coachman, but I soon saw his value and promoted him to the office, where he took all the telephoning, received the patients, got out the bills and kept all my accounts, personal and professional. He'd helped me more than once in operations, and had a perfect genius for administering anaesthetics. Nobody but our two selves knew what his salary was, but I never grudged a penny of it. Why, the fellow read French and German almost as well as I did, and tact—Lord, I wished every day of my life I had George's tact and resource! My wife was tremendously fond of him, and lent him all her books, and they used to have great discussions on political economy and theosophy and prison reform—oh, everything!

"He had lots of white blood, of course, and his wife you'd never guess to be anything but pure American, she was so white. One of the children, though, was black as my hat. The other had almost golden hair and deep blue eyes—a beautiful little girl, brought up like a duchess, too. They lived in a nice little house on the extreme edge of the negro district, and we all understood that when the little girl was fifteen or sixteen, she and her mother were going to move to Paris and train her voice; then if everything went well, George and the boy would join them and never come back—he was specialising in dentistry, mind you, in his spare time. It's different, of course, abroad.

"I'm telling you all this, so you can see how I felt; I'd had George nine years, and we'd always had darky servants, and—oh, well, to find him with that yellow streak in him after all, nearly floored me. I could have sworn he wasn't that sort of pup, and when he came in for his orders I talked to him like a Dutch uncle.

"'You've got to stop this, George,' I said directly, 'I can't have any such performances here. To tell you the truth, I never thought it of you! The idea—a quiet little thing like Mynie! She's as timid as a kitten and as innocent. Now I want your word of honour before you leave this office and I want it quick!'

"He opened his mouth once or twice in a confused sort of way, looked at me curiously, and then gave his word quietly. So far as I knew, he had never broken it.

"But I wasn't satisfied with that and I spoke to her mother.

"'You'd better keep an eye on Mynie, Althea,' I said carelessly. 'She's a pretty girl, you know, and men aren't always too careful what they say to a girl as pretty as Mynie.'

"'Yes, seh, I'll look out,' she said, 'I'll look out, doctor—ef I kin. Seems like I may have trouble, though. Is Mis' Stanchon comin' back soon, seh?'

"'Probably not,' I said. 'It's too hot for her here. Why, what's the matter? Anything wrong?'

"'I guess not, seh,' she answered, hesitating. 'I try to do my best, doctor. But I will sholy be glad when she comes back. And would you mind to speak to Mynie yo'self, seh?' and she slipped away.

"Well, I did speak to her. I spoke when I ran across her, strolling with George in a deserted walk of an old park. I called her right into the office the next morning.

"'Mynie,' I said sharply, 'what were you doing yesterday afternoon? Out with it!'

"She opened her eyes and looked full at me for a second—something she had never done.

"'I reckon 'twas my afternoon out, doctor!' she said softly, and that was all. But it was enough. It wouldn't have made any difference what she said, anyhow—the look was enough. It wasn't the look of our shy little Mynie; her eyes had never gone any farther than my breakfast table and the office door. But these eyes were slanting, curious, audacious—conscious. That's what it was, they were conscious of something—something I didn't know. And for a quick moment I remembered, with no connection, apparently, that queer look in the eyes of the parson's wife— the one that had the house before. I didn't know why, and I dismissed it as irrelevant, for that poor creature had been frightened to death, and Mynie was more self-confident than I had ever seen her and not at all pleasant with it. I've never been of a temper to stand any nonsense from servants, and the class of Northern darky that was growing up in that city wasn't always easy to deal with. But I remembered what a sterling creature the mother was, and I tried to be gentle with the girl.

"'You understand, Mynie,' I said temperately, 'I only speak for your good. I know the world better than you can and I don't want to see you get into bad ways. Do you want to lose George his place? You've got a good home, and you're with your mother, and there's no excuse for you if you slip up, you see. Understand me?'

"'Yes, doctor, I understand you,' she said, and walked out of the room with her head high and her hips swinging. Something in her carriage—so different from the way she used to slip in and out —struck me all of a sudden, and there flashed into my mind an old story about Althea's being the direct descendant of one of the oldest African kings and a princess in her own right. Absurd, of course, but it makes a lot of difference whether you regard those people as creeping up to our democracy or sliding down from their royalty, you see. And with Mynie the scale had shifted suddenly, and it was the last of an old line that swung by me, not the first of a new one. Straight across the commonplace air of my office a wind out of the jungle had blown, a whiff of something old and unmanageable, and beyond rules, or beneath 'em, perhaps; something there wasn't any prescription for; something not to be weighed and measured by any of the new methods, because it antedated method.

"Yes, it was all that. I don't know if I make myself clear at all.... You may think I was working up a fanciful theory just because a pert servant maid was getting a little wayward, but it wasn't only that—Lord, no! It was a great deal more than that, and it was just beginning; just beginning."

There was no doubt that he had the strained attention of all of them: their hands held the glasses, but they did not drink, looking mostly at the wet rings on the polished table, or the little heaps of white ashes. A servant passing through scratched a match with a rasping splutter, and they twitched angrily at the interruption, fearing it would throw him off the track—he was so easily quieted, and when once one of his great gulfs of silence received him, it was hopeless.

But this time he went on.

"After that the house got very still, by degrees. Althea sang less and less and by and by not at all. There seemed to be no clatter, no bustle, no homely, chattering machinery of life. Sometimes I would step out through the dining-room and listen, purposely, to see where they were. And it was always the same thing: Althea sitting in her clean kitchen, by her clean table, with a bowl or a pan or what not in her lap, her yellowish hands lax, her knees as still as marble, her eyes set ahead of her, thinking, thinking, thinking. Her brows would be knit and her face all drawn. She had the look of a fighter, a struggler with something—but there was nothing there. And out on the side porch Mynie would be sitting, her head thrown back against the wooden column of the porch, her hands clasped about her knees, smiling, smiling, always smiling. Sometimes she would hum a sort of low tuneless chant—it sounded like a pagan ritual of some sort, all repetitions, rising and falling in a monotonous, haunting drone. And once, as I stood watching her curiously, the word for that noise flashed suddenly into my mind—incantation. That was it, incantation.

"Well! All this sounds very feeble, doesn't it? The truth is, I haven't got the right vocabulary—as a matter of fact, I don't think anybody has. When you can describe a thing, a sensation, perfectly, I doubt if it's very important anyhow. It's always so. The big things simply elude description. And yet we all know them. Falling in love, for instance: God knows it's as definite as measles, but who ever described it? The most these writing fellows can manage is to tell you what a lot of people did who happened to be in that way, and sometimes they catch a lot of the tricks, but that's all. Then there's dying. There's a specific atmosphere about that—everybody knows it. The people know it mostly, themselves. I mean, if any one ever had occasion to die twice, he'd recognise the symptoms immediately. But nobody can describe it, though plenty of us know what it is.

"So with that house and the atmosphere in it. Something was happening there. Something so strong and so actual that it defied all appearances, all the ordinary influences that might be supposed to act on the imagination of, say, a sensitive, hysterical, under-occupied woman. For as a matter of fact there was nothing morbid in the look of the house—nothing at all. It was sunny and fresh and painted. It was clean and dry. But it ought not to have been. No ... I've sat there, late afternoons, when it seemed to me if I touched the walls they'd be damp and the woodwork rotted and mouldy. The boards should have creaked there and the stair-rails ought to have given under the hand—but they didn't. I had them all repaired, you see! But there were a few things I hadn't had the chance to repair and they ... oh, well, they were there, that was all.

"There? You'd have said so, any of you, if you'd seen Althea as I saw her one morning. I stepped into the kitchen suddenly, to give an order for some beef-tea I wanted to take away with me, and there she sat, cross-legged on the clean floor, a red silk scarf twined around her shoulders and—of all things—a red and blue kerchief twisted into a turban on her head. She was rocking back and forth and singing, and I give you my word, I was as shocked as if I'd seen my own mother in that rig, swaying there!

"She turned her head as I came in and I saw that she had big blue glass earrings in her ears.

"And all of a sudden it came to me—what was happening there: I felt very queer for a moment, I tell you! Everything seemed to be rolling backward, like one of those cinematograph things, reversed. Not I—I swear nothing touched me. I was the same. *So was the jeweller. So was the parson. So was the man before that...*

"'Althea,' I said roughly, 'what are you doing there? Take those rags off you! Get up immediately! I am ashamed of you.'

"Her eyes met mine for a moment, glittering like a savage's—it was nip and tuck between us there: she might have thrown a plate at me. But she didn't; I won. You see, she was not a young woman, and unusually controlled for one of her race, and she owed me a good deal, besides.

"'I'm thoroughly ashamed of you,' I repeated.

"She staggered up and burst into hoarse, frightened sobbing.

"'Fore God, I am, too, doctor!' she cried and stumbled into her pantry, shaking and muttering. I waited till she came back, and she was quiet and trim again—herself. She stuffed a bundle into the stove before my eyes, and I don't think she ever met my look again. She was a good woman, Althea was.

"But the other—Mynie—well, the game was up with her. Heavens, the change in that girl's eyes! It wasn't that they were bold, it wasn't that they were beautiful, nor even that they were conscious of it. No, it was more than that—more and worse and deeper and older— Oh, as old as Hell! That look unsettled ... disorganized ... how shall I put it? The flimsiness of civilisation, the essential bedrock of animalism—the big, ceaseless undertow of things ... anyway, it was all in that girl's eyes and it touched that spring in poor George that Nature has coiled in every one of us. The Old Lady wound us up with that spring and she daren't let it run down, you see."

The room was absolutely empty but for the four of them; they stared at him steadily, his rumbling, husky voice held them like a vise; they could not miss a word.

"She got fat on it. She bloomed in that infernal house like some tropical bog-flower; she expanded, she shot up.

"Once, at twilight, I peeped out and saw her sitting on the side porch, her chin in her hand, staring and staring, and laughing, now and then, and shutting her eyes. It made me shiver.

"That warm, damp dusk was like a Florida swamp; the air seemed to thicken, thicken, as I looked. A quick instinct warned me to look for George in the shadow: it seemed to me that he stood there, in ... glue ... like a caught fly. To let go—to drift in a warm, relaxing current ... I had to shake my shoulders, actually, as if there had been a net ... I felt for him so.

"I went to her mother.

"'Call that girl in!' I said roughly. 'What's the matter with her?'

"She wouldn't look at me.

"'Come, what's all this? Out with it!' I said. But she stood there, obstinate as a mule, and perfectly silent. You can't do anything with them, then.

"Well, it was like fighting filthy cobwebs: walking through them, breathing them, pulling them off from your mouth, your wrists, your ankles! Not that I felt anything directly, mind you—I could have lived there for years—alone. But it was all up with Mynie and George, they were done for, like the others ... like the others.

"What worked there, rotting like some infernal yeast? What terrible energy, what malignant, vindictive lust infected that place? What distorted, unhappy soul first sickened there? How long ago? *How long ago?* Are there centres of negation? Oh, I tell you, the table-tippers are harmless beside the sickening truths, the simply incredible possibilities of this little crevice we walk along!

"Was it like a grain of that nasty musk that gets into a woman's drawer and taints endlessly?

"I tell you, I saw that girl disintegrate, decay, turn fungoid under my eyes—ugh!

"There had to be an end, of course. I asked where she was going one afternoon, and then she smiled and looked up at me sidewise.

"'You needn't come back,' I said abruptly. 'I'll settle with your mother. Do you understand?'

"She arched her shoulder and flashed a glance straight above me, out of the open window.

"'I'm sorry you don't want me, doctor,' she said softly. I could see poor George tremble—the porch vines shook.

"Then I took her by the shoulders and shook her.

"'Get out of my house, you black slut!' I said—but I didn't say 'slut.' And she went. It was the only time I was ever brutal to a woman."

He gulped the rest of his tumbler.

"The next day I moved my office stuff back, and that damned house was empty.

"'I'm sorry about Mynie, Althea,' I said to the mother, the day afterward. 'If you ever need any money——'

"'Thank you, Dr. Stanchon, thank you, seh. You couldn't help it. But I guess she'll never need money, seh,' she said quietly. And she was right enough, of course.

"She knew. They're not far from the apes, and they know a lot we've forgotten, I believe. Perhaps forgetting it is what civilised us.

"I never saw Mynie again. She went off East, and George with her. They're both dead, now. His wife stayed on in the cottage.

"I gave her all the help I could ... it was my fault, I suppose. And yet, God knows, I meant nothing. I thought *I* was undertaking that damned house, you see—how could I tell how the thing worked?"

They watched him eagerly: his face showed that he had more to tell. Not a man moved, unless it were to knock the ash from his cigar or to light a fresh one.

"There was a Catholic priest there, then," he said slowly. "He's been moved higher up, since, and you'd all know his name, if I gave it. We'll call him Father Kelly—though that wasn't it, of course. He and I were great friends—he was a little older than I was—and we used to have many a good talk together, meeting on our rounds, you see. Often I'd take him miles on his way, and drop my driver out on the road, just for the pleasure of his company. Of course we disagreed entirely on what he considered the most important points, but leaving them out, we were thoroughly congenial, and we were often glad of each other's opinion, I can tell you, for we often had the same patients.

"Well, a day or two after I'd moved my stuff out of that cursed house, he came to the office with a drug case he was trying to reform: he'd persuaded the fellow as far as the pledge went, and I was to talk to him about diet and exercise and all the rest. After the man left, Father Kelly looked at me once or twice, talked a bit about the weather, and finally pulled out his old blackened pipe and looked around the office.

"'Have ye a bit of tobacco about ye, doctor?' says he. 'If so, and you're not too busy, I could do with a little rest—I was up all night.'

"I was glad enough, for I felt blue and out of sorts, and we pulled our chairs in front of the fireplace, from habit, and after a few minutes I found myself telling him the whole business.

"'Now what do you make of it, Father?' I asked.

"'I make the devil out of it, doctor,' said he, very placidly.

"'Oh, well,' I began impatiently, 'of course I can't be expected——'

"'Now, wait a bit, doctor,' he put in. 'If you don't go with my diagnosis, what's your own? What do you make out of it?'

"Well, there he had me.

"'Of course,' I said, 'it's a mere coincidence.'

"'Ah,' says he, 'then would you be willing to go and live there with your wife?'

"'Good God, no!' I burst out, before I thought. And then I wouldn't back out of it. You see, there had been five women. Five good, ordinary, honest women—six, if you count Miss Jessop.

"'I thought not,' said he quietly.

"He sat and puffed awhile.

"Finally, 'I'll have to be taking a look at your house, doctor,' he said.

"'All right,' said I. 'When?'

"'This evening,' he said, 'after my confessions. Say about nine. And I'll go home and have a nap. I'm thinking I'll need one.'

"And he knocked out his pipe and left.

"I was busy all the afternoon, so busy that I almost forgot the whole thing, and as a matter of fact, I had had no time for dinner, when he called for me. He was so fresh and bright and jolly that you'd never have suspected he'd just got a murderer to agree to give himself up, gone with him to see him safely jailed, and sent his confession up to the governor—oh, he was a remarkable man, that man! And it's a remarkable institution, the Confessional. We're learning to do more with it now than we did twenty years ago. But they've always known ... they've always known..."

He ruminated long, and crushed the ashes in the brass tray before him. The men nodded, but kept silence, dreading lest he lose the thread.

"I had the horse ready and drove myself. When I unlocked the door of the house I lighted the lamp in the hall, and so on in every room we went through, kitchen and all. In every room there was a fresh shining lamp, filled and ready, for Althea had left everything like a new pin, and in every room that lamp was lighted, when we left it. You know what a nice, warm glow an old-fashioned kerosene lamp gives a place—electricity's nothing to it, in my opinion.

"'This seems a good sort of house, doctor,' said Father Kelly to me, as we came back and sat down in the pretty little sitting-room, with a palm in it, and cushions my wife had made, and books on the table. 'I can't see any harm here.'

"'All right,' said I, 'then let's go home. I missed my dinner. Since you see there's no devil here ____'

"'I don't see that,' said he, calmly, 'I only see that I haven't found him yet. If a woman has a cancer, doctor, you don't know it the moment you shake hands with her, do ye? So with me and my patients. Now let's think a bit, and if you don't object, I'll call a little consultation.'

"So he takes a little black book out of his pocket, and actually sits there reading! I humoured him, and smoked. After a while he looks up, crosses himself, puts away the book and nods at me contentedly.

"'Now, which room would all of these women use the most, doctor?' says he.

"'The kitchen,' I said directly, thinking of Mynie and Althea. Then, 'No, no, for Mrs. Mears used this for her consulting-room. But the parson's wife spent most of her time in her bedroom. Still, the jeweller's wife didn't—they used the dining-room to sit in. There's no one room, you see.'

"'Unless they all had the same bedroom,' he suggested quietly.

"'By George, they did, then!' I cried, 'for I gave it to Mynie and Althea because it was the coolest. I always sleep on the ground floor.'

"'Then we'll try the bedroom, doctor,' says he, and we went up-stairs. He was a stocky, short little fellow, strong as a bull, with iron-grey hair, very solid on his feet, yet quick and active, like a thin man. He sat down in the rocking-chair in the neat, empty bedroom and I brought in another lamp from across the hall.

"'You don't think you'll need the dark for your materializations, Father?' I said, half laughing, as I set my lamp on the bureau.

"'No, no, doctor,' he answered, smiling. 'The Church doesn't work in the dark, you know. We're all for candles, and plenty of 'em.'

"I had to grin at that. He was as quick a man with his tongue as I ever met.

"Well, we sat there, and sat there, and he shut his eyes and tipped back and forth in that chair like a woman, and I might as well have not been there. I mean I was out of his consciousness entirely. Finally I got nervous and bored.

"'There's nothing here, Father,' I said, rather testily. 'Haven't I been here hours on end with the parson's wife? Wouldn't I have known it?'

"He never opened his eyes.

"'Probably not, doctor,' he said pleasantly. 'It's not your job, you see. You were thinking about her liver.'

"'And you?' said I.

"'Her life everlasting,' said he.

"And his eyes shut, all the time!

"So I shut my mouth and watched him. And suddenly his lips began to work, and he was mumbling to himself, and I saw that his hands were grasping the arms of the wooden chair tight, so tight that as he prayed, he actually worked himself over the floor, as a child will, you know. After he'd moved several feet that way, between me and the fireplace—I was counting the inches, to keep myself quiet—he stopped suddenly, opened his eyes and loosened his hands.

"'I've got it now, thanks be!' he said, looking straight at me. 'It's this room, sure enough, doctor!'

"'What do you mean, for heaven's sake?' I said, getting up and coming to him, interested enough, now, you can believe.

"'*For hell's sake*, would be nearer the mark,' he answered me, gently enough, but his jaw was set and there was a light in his eye I'd seen there once or twice. 'This is a bad business. This'll take more than sitting down, this will.'

"And flat on his knees he plumped, ahead of his chair, and crossed himself and started praying in Latin. He made no special noise nor movement, but after a while I saw the sweat stand out on his forehead and his face was drawn and pale—and grew paler. Every now and then he'd give a sort of deep sigh and hitch along, almost imperceptibly, on his knees, from fatigue and nervous tension, and after about ten minutes he was almost in the fireplace. With anybody else I could never have stood it, but it was impossible not to respect Father Kelly, and I can tell you that whatever prayers he prayed, they were no perfunctory mumblings: they took it out of him! He was like a man fighting, blindfolded—he breathed like a prize fighter, I tell you! And just at the edge of the hearth, when I thought I must stop him (that sort of auto-hypnosis will take a person straight out of an open six-story window, you know) he stopped himself, opened his eyes with a jerk, and pointed ahead of him.

"'Mother of God,' he said in a husky whisper, 'but it's there!'

"'There!' said I. 'What's there, Father? There can't be anything in that fireplace—I've seen a dozen fires in it.'

"He got up from his knees as unconcerned as he'd gotten down on them and cleared his throat.

"'Not in it, perhaps, doctor,' he said, 'but then, under it. Or over it, perhaps. But there, somewhere, it is.'

"'You mean the bricks?' I cried, and he nodded his head like a man too weak to talk.

"'Maybe,' he whispered. 'Look and see."

"There was a full set of fire-irons there, and I took the poker and tapped all about the hearth, as excited as a boy on a treasure hunt, though of course I didn't believe in it, any more than the boy does, really.

"'No, Father,' I said, 'there's nothing to show—' and then, just between the andirons, I hit a blow that rang as hollow as a drum!

"'But there's no brick loose!' I cried, and he whispered, 'Then break it!'

"It took more than a few blows and I broke the poker, but finally I loosened the mortar and there under the two centre bricks was an iron box, about seven inches square, made like a little trunk. I fished it out and opened it—it opened from the side—and pulled out two thick handfuls of yellow letters, without envelopes. I opened the top one eagerly, but it had no date nor address. For signature there was only the name 'Olive.'"

He stopped abruptly and stared at the thick-bellied decanter before him. His voice sank lower.

"I have never heard or read that name since," he said slowly, "without a thrill at my nerves like a picked violin string. They were the wickedest letters ever written, I think. Even for a woman, they were incredible."

The men stared at him, mystified, confused, eager.

"One, the third, I think, said something like this: '*They may bury me, now that you want me no longer. They shall never bury these letters—I swear it. Here in the room where I wrote them, they shall live after I am gone.*'

"And they lived—God, they lived! As I pored over them, cross-legged by that little hearth, I believe that I was as lost to the world about me as Father Kelly had been a few moments before. They were not written for me, they offered me nothing, the writer was beyond doubt dead and gone; but for the moment those yellow papers held me, soul and body, in such a grip as I have never known before or since. I can't tell you ... I didn't know such things could be written...." He shook his head slowly.

"I'd always been fairly decent, you see—there were circumstances ... I couldn't take advantage...

"Did you ever turn over a good old sunny rock, flat, a little mossy, but clean and wholesome? And underneath it crawls—it crawls! Black, slimy slug things ... muck of the Pit!

"That was me. And every time my eyes fell on one of those amazing phrases on that yellow page, I had to hold the rock down!

"Suddenly I felt a hand on my shoulder. I jumped like a woman. Father Kelly stood over me, and he looked, from where I sat below him, unhumanly tall. He held out his hand.

"'Give them to me,' he said.

"'But, Father, you don't want to see them!' I burst out. 'I'm going to destroy them. You—you mustn't see them! Let me burn them——'

"'Give them to me, my son," he repeated, and I gave them up like a child. It was remarkable.

"'At any rate, I warn you,' I began. But he only smiled.

"'When you are warned of fever in a house, do you pass it by, my son?' he asked me softly. 'But this is a different matter.'

"I admit that I couldn't meet his eyes.

"Well, he read them all through placidly, and then he sighed and shook his head.

"'Poor things, poor things!' he said, 'and now we'll burn them. There is nothing I can do.'

"So we burned them there and put back the bricks and he muttered some short prayer or other and made the sign of the cross over the fireplace and then turned to me.

"'Didn't I see some bread and ham and a cheese in that wire safe in the cellar, doctor?' says he. 'I had no supper to-night.'

"We went down and got them and a bottle of Scotch, too, and I remember perfectly that we polished off half a small ham, a whole Edam cheese, a loaf of bread and nearly a bottle of the Scotch—the bottle wasn't quite full, to begin with, you see.

"After we'd finished we had a smoke, and then I stared at him straight.

"'What's the meaning of it all, Father?' I asked.

"'I can't tell you, my son,' said he (he never called me so before or since that night) 'but you may be sure of one thing—God reigns. And now, what are you thinking to do?'

"'Burn down this house,' said I, 'and send for my wife to come back.'

"'By all means send for your wife,' says he quickly, 'but if you're bound to destroy this house—which strikes me as a very good sort of house—why not give it me?'

"'To you?' I cried. 'You don't mean that you'd use it?'

"'I could put a parochial school for girls there next week,' he said cheerfully. 'We need one at this end badly, but I hadn't the money."

"'And you'd put innocent girls in this place?'

"'Give me a chance, and then come hear Sister Mary Eustacia sing with 'em, next Sunday,' he said.

"So I deeded it to him, land and all, and they had a great kick-up there with little boys in lace night-gowns, and incense and what not. And, by George, the girls did sing for me, too, with Sister Somebody-or-other bowing and blushing behind 'em—all in white they were, with blue sashes, and voices like larks ... I never had a daughter...."

He half rose, heavily, leaning on his elbows. "Mind you, there's something there!" he said slowly.

"There's a Pit below—you have to count on it. Perhaps we're shovelling it in, all the time, shovelling it in...

"And the more you whistle, the better you'll work, of course. Very well, then, whistle! But don't mistake—it's there ... it's there."

They drew long breaths and pushed away from the table; the rain had stopped.

And still in silence they walked out together into the fresh, damp evening.

THE ORACLES

You'll wonder, no doubt, at me having the daring to make what you might call a sort of romance out of her life—now all's over. And, of course, it's not in my way at all. Not but what I've read enough of romance-books—many's the many! My mother was always at me to lay them by and take up some bit of work that 'ud bring me in more in the end—and yet, there's no doubt it was my readings and dreamings and such-like that brought me about Miss Lisbet's friendship, at the first, and that friendship was the making of me, one way and another, as mother never denied.

It was Dr. Stanchon that set me about it. He came into my cottage, a matter of a month or so back, looking fair grizzled and white—the heat, he said. And if I knew better, I never said so. He never minded the heat till this summer. And on his vacation at home, too! But he showed his age, fair.

"You haven't some kind of drink for me, have you, Rhoda?" he says, sort of faint-like. "It's been a hard day at the hospital."

Now that might do for some, but not for me, that's known the doctor fifty-four years come Easter. I looked at the wheels of the gig, and they were all clay, red clay from the one road hereabouts that's made of it—the graveyard road. And I knew where he'd been. But of course I says nothing, but brings him a palm-leaf fan, and seats him out of the glare, in the entry that looks over the little garden, and I waters the red bricks of the porch with a spray or two from the garden-pot (nothing so cooling as watered brick, I say!) and hurries in to beat up his drink. He settled down in the old chair I always keep for him—a Windsor, cushioned in some English chintz his wife brought me out from home, twenty years ago—and I heard him sigh and stretch as I got the lemons and the eggs. I beat up the whites, stiff as silver, added the lemon juice by littles, dusted a bit of castor sugar, and stuck in a sprig of mint from my sunken half-barrel where the cress grows.

"Ah, that makes a man new!" says he, handing back the glass. "It's a pity you can't patent that, Rhoda!"

And then he pulled out his old pipe, and smoked for a quarter-hour, without a word. But he rested.

"And how's Miss Jessop, these days, doctor?" says I, when I saw he was ready for talking.

"Finely, finely!" says he. "Her little girl wrote me a letter yesterday. Ten years old! Image of her father, that child. You're as bad as Lisbet, though, that never would learn to change."

"I'm sure I beg her pardon—Mrs. Weldon, of course, and her with a boy fourteen, too!" says I. "How Miss Lisbet did take to her, surely! I always thought having her to help with Master Louis's children when they were so bad, just helped poor Miss Lisbet to bear with her sorrow at not starting the hospital, and all that."

"Yes, yes," he said and nodded.

"She was a fine woman, Jessop was. Best nurse I ever had. Yes, yes—Weldon's a lucky fellow."

The cress smelled strong in the heat, then, and I couldn't but say:

"Do you remember when Miss Lisbet and I started the cress-bed, doctor, down in the Winthrop pond?"

At first he didn't answer, and I saw the old times in his face.

"How she did enjoy your cress-and-mustard salad!" he says, finally. "Mrs. Stanchon spoke of it this morning—have you a little mess I could take up to the house?"

And so we passed to talking about her, and it eased us both.

"It's like a sort of tale, sir, isn't it?" says I, thoughtful-like. "Often and often when my niece has left everything tidy, and made my tea and cakes, and put away the wash, and watered the brick, and gone home, and I sit here while the pot draws and there's only the cat for company (not that I complain! I've my thoughts, and plenty of books, and all the old days to live over!) often and often, as I say, it'll come to me in a sort of tale, like, and I wish there was some one to take it down; it would read off like a book!"

"And why not take it down yourself, Rhoda, my girl?" says he. "There's one, as I needn't tell you, would have no little pleasure reading it."

And so I began. You'd be surprised at the many that's offered to help me, and piece out bits of her life that maybe I wouldn't know. But I knew enough for what I had in mind to show, namely, what Miss Lisbet was always planning to do—and what she really did do.

So now I'll begin at the beginning.

It was the morning of the day I was ten years old that I first saw her. A Saturday it was, and a holiday, and mother gave me a piece of currant bread, buttered, for a treat, and the day free till sunset, after my morning tasks were through. I was all that was left her—five others buried, in fifteen years—and she was very easy with me, for which you could scarcely blame her, poor soul! Three lost in England, of the smallpox, and one that hardly opened his little eyes, and my sister of something that they had no name for rightly in those days, doctor says, but they call it appendicitis now. I was born over here, and never saw England, though I've always loved to read about it and always called it "home," not thinking, as one often will. Mother had black memories of the old country and was anxious for us to grow up little Americans, though I can see now that she went to work very wrong to bring that about, for we always curtseyed to the rector and old Madam Winthrop when she rode by in the coach, and never, in short, thought of looking higher than we were born.

So when I saw a lovely young lady drive up in a pony cart, hand the reins to the groom, get out, and walk through the gate toward me, I held the currant bread behind me and dropped a little curtsey.

"Is this Mrs. Pennyfield's house?" she says, stopping and staring at me.

"Yes, miss, she's my mother," says I.

"What is your name?" says she.

"Rhoda Pennyfield, please, miss," says I, and then, the goodness knows why, for I was a shy enough little thing commonly, "It's my birthday!"

"Why, how funny!" she says, smiling the loveliest smile in the world. "It's mine, too! How old are you, Rhoda Pennyfield?"

"Ten, miss."

"Isn't that wonderful!" she cries out, blushing like a rose peony. "I am ten to-day, too! What were your presents? Mine were the pony phaeton and this gold watch (she held it out to me on a chain about her neck) and a macaw from South America from my Uncle Mather, on an ebony perch. And a French doll from my aunty in New York, but I don't care for dolls any more. What had you?"

Now, as you can see, if I had really been a little American, I should have been jealous and ashamed that things were so different between us, but such a notion never entered my head.

"Mother baked currant bread, miss," I said, "and Madam Winthrop's gardener gave me a spotted kitten, and I have a string of blue beads and the day to myself. I'm thinking I'll go up to The Cedars and Mrs. Williams will let me read some of the books from the library for the afternoon."

"Why, that's where I live—The Cedars!" she says, surprised. "Madam Winthrop is my aunt, and Mrs. Williams dresses me! Come into the phaeton and I'll drive you there!"

She had forgot the errand she came on, bless her, with the excitement, and if mother hadn't come out to inquire, there'd have been a great to-do. There was a maid all over blotches at The Cedars, and a doctor and nurse was wanted, and mother was ready very quick, as she always was. So I got into the phaeton and Miss Lisbet drove me to The Cedars, and I had a birthday dinner with her: roast fowl and mashed potatoes and new peas and a frozen pudding with figs and almonds in it. I can see her now, at the head of the table, with me and Mrs. Williams on either side, and the macaw, all indigo and orange color and scarlet, on his perch opposite! She had on a worked muslin frock with lace-trimmed pantalets, blue silk stockings, and black French kid ankle-ties. Her hair, a light golden brown, was all in curls, and a blue velvet snood kept it back: the young girls today wear ribbons about their heads something like it. Her eyes were a dark, bright blue, and her cheeks, like most American children's, a sort of clear pale, that flushed quick with her feelings. She was tall and slim and looked quite three years older than me, that has always been stocky-like and apple-cheeked, even at sixty-four!

She had been away at a school for two years, having lost her father and mother, and old Madam Winthrop had adopted her, in a sort of way, being her great-aunt, and was to leave her all her money.

While we were eating, old Dr. Stanchon pops in, leading a little red-haired boy, very plain and clever-looking, by the hand.

"Can this youngster have a bite with you, Mrs. Williams?" says he, looking worried like. "That precious girl of yours has the fever, and I'll be busy some time. I promised him the fish pond for a treat, for it's his birthday, to-day, and now perhaps Miss Elizabeth will take him there—hello, little Rhoda! How fine we are!"

The little lad pulls out a great pocket-knife and lays it on the table.

"I am Dick Stanchon, and I'm ten years old to-day!" says he very quick. "I have this Barlow knife and the 'Arabian Nights,' and I'm to be a doctor, like my father. Do you have frozen pudding often, here?"

Well, you can see how startling it would be to three children to be at the same birthday together! We couldn't be tired talking of it.

"We will all be firm friends for the rest of our life," said Miss Lisbet, very excited, "and never have secrets from each other. And when I get Aunt Winthrop's money, I will divide it into three parts, one for each. And we will do a great deal of good in the world."

"Come, come," says Mrs. Williams, sour-like, "not so fast, missy. You've not the money yet, nor shouldn't speak of it, and as for being friends, it's all right so far as Dick Stanchon is concerned, but I doubt if Madam will feel the same as to Rhoda Pennyfield! So make no more plans till we know."

But of course we did make plans, for all her stiffness. We sat in the red cedar grove, playing at tea-parties with a beautiful china tea-set, and Master Dick was to marry her, and I was to live with them and be nurse to the children, with one named for me!

Dear, dear! I've forgot much that's come in between and many that's been kind to me (more shame to me!) but I can see the sun on her curls now and him sharpening his new knife on the granite rocks that were so thick in the grove.

"Rhoda and Dick," says she, very solemn, after a little, "I'm going to tell you a great secret. Come close to me."

You can believe we listened with all our ears; we worshipped the ground she trod on, both of us, do you see, even then.

"I mean to do a great deal of good in the world before I die," says she, "as I mentioned before, at dinner. I don't mean just ordinary *being*good, you know, but *doing* it. At school I always meant to go as a missionary, and I was saving all my money for a fund for it, but I couldn't seem to keep it, somehow. Two or three of the girls were poor girls, and if they hadn't their birthdays remembered, it would have been dreadful. And the cook's little boy was lame in his spine and he was so fond of flowers! And I hadn't so much money, anyway. Then, all my time was full, because we had to do things every hour, just so. But now I'm to have a governess and I shall have a great deal of time, so I can study hard for a missionary and perhaps go to South America —if there are any heathens there, as I suppose there are."

"Yes, miss," says I.

"So now my new life is beginning," she says very low and solemn, "and I feel that everything will be different. I wish I could be *sure*, though, that it would be!"

"Why don't you try the larkspurs, miss," says I. "They'll tell you."

My mother, you must know, was a great believer in signs. Not being much educated, she went by them, I suppose, the way plain people will, be it ever so. There's no use saying it's against religion—mother was as religious as any one, take who you will—they will do it. If a bird flew into the house, there was death for sure, and she never would let three candles be lighted, no matter whose the house. And so my sister and I had many of these ways and signs, and always told how things would be by larkspurs. So I told Miss Lisbet how to strip them off for "yes, no, yes, no," and she asked her question very solemn:

"Larkspur, larkspur, tell me true,
Or never again I'll trust to you!

Is there to be a great change in my life?" And she stripped them off, mumbling-like to herself, "Yes, no, yes, no"—and the last off was "no."

And then she cried, poor thing, and I with her, for we both believed in 'em, but Dick only laughed and said it was all foolishness.

"If you want to do different from what you have been, Lisbet, of course you can," says he, and then the old doctor came and fetched us both home.

"I'm going to begin my studying, just the same!" she calls after us, and I watched the sun on her hair till the coachman's cottage cut us off.

Well, the governess came and they'd lessons all morning long and music practising afternoons, but there was no missionary study, because she took it into her head that I must be educated and know all she knew—as if that was likely! Still, I picked up a good bit, here and there, and the gardener's little boy, that was backward and dumb-like, isn't forgetting to-day what he owes to Miss Lisbet, I'll warrant. Three days a week she'd read to him and spell the letters and sums plain —and him that was the mock of the scholars, so that he'd never go near the school, what is he now, I ask you? Professor in Yale College, and helped Dr. Stanchon in the planning of a big school for those children that are backward-like, as he was, and many of them as bright as bright, really. They manage such as them better than they did in those days, doctor says, and most of it owed to Henry Wilson's boy.

Often and often we'd walk up to her tea from the lodge, her setting her little teeth to keep from crying at the time she was wasting, with all her heathen waiting for her in South America!

"But I can't leave poor little Ezra Wilson, Rhoda, I just can't!" she'd cry out. "Wait till these old music-lessons are over and I haven't to use those horrible dumb-bells every morning, and I'll do something for the world, yet!"

"Surely, miss," I'd soothe her.

Well, the time went by like sands in a glass, and we were grown maids before you'd think twice. She looked full two years more than her seventeen, and Master Dick was away at Harvard College two years already, for he was wonderful forward and clever always, and first in all his classes. What time she'd had from her lessons and her paintings and sketching (which she hated dreadfully, poor thing, though seeming a master of it, to my eyes!) she was teaching him French and German from her governess, for they didn't teach it in the village school and his mother couldn't spare him away, and those languages helped him a good bit in his studies at the college. The old doctor was terrible proud of him.

And then came the day that he came home so sudden. It was a grand April morning and Miss Lisbet and I were directing Henry Wilson about changing the vines and laying them by for the house painting: Madam was scolding and fussing about, annoying everybody with her sharp ways, and I remember thinking that she was failing for sure. I was sad, too, for mother had decided to put me out to service, after all, and that meant a parting for Miss Lisbet and me. Mother felt that I was getting above myself, like, and spoiled for anything that would happen me in the usual course if Miss Lisbet ever changed, you see. And who could deny that? But the dear thing knew nothing of it, yet—I hadn't the heart.

Well, Madam was scolding away famously.

"Mind that wistaria, Wilson!" says she. "There's not its equal in Westchester County!"

"Yes, yes, Madam," says he, crusty-like. "Why good-morning, Master Dick!"

And there he stood. At the first glance, I saw he looked different. Older and graver.

"What's this, what's this, Richard?" Madam cries. "Neglecting your studies?"

"Studies? Studies?" says he, as quick and sharp as she. "What, is the matter with the people about here? Are you dreaming? Fort Sumter down, the flag insulted, the President calling for seventy-five thousand volunteers, and you talk of studies! I'm going to try to get into the Seventh, and I'm only here to see Elizabeth before I go."

"Nonsense, boy!" says Madam, trembling, though. "We'll see what your father has to say, first."

"My father only wishes he had a dozen sons, ma'am!" he told her, proud as Lucifer. "Lisbet, can I speak with you?"

She went directly to him, and they walked, holding hands, behind the cedar grove. She told me afterward that he just said:

"Will you wait till I come back, Lisbet?"

And she answered, "Why, of course, Dick!" They parted a promised couple. Madam was all shaky, but she kissed him good-bye, and let him put a little blue-stoned ring on Miss Lisbet's hand—there was a splash of red paint on it from the house, and mother fair turned white when I told her. "They'll never wed," she said, "that's certain sure! Poor young people!"

But the paint wasn't for blood, after all, for he never got a scratch. He was handsome enough in his new uniform, and more than one envied my Miss Lisbet when she waved him good-bye on the train—they were off for Baltimore.

"Rhoda," says she to me, after a few weeks of waiting, "I can't bear this! Us eating and drinking so easy, and those poor boys dying—it's not right. I must and shall go as nurse!"

And we could do nothing with her—she'd hardly sleep. It was Dr. Stanchon found the way to handle her.

"Dear child," he says at last, "why not do as I do—send a substitute? I sent my boy, because I'm the only doctor left here, now, and people must be born and die, you know, war or no war," says he. "I'd far rather have gone. Now, it's out of the question for you, for many reasons, but if your aunt would give you your dress-money and you gave up a summer at the mountains, you could pay a good, settled woman, of experience, and there's many would love to go."

Well, she seized on that, the generous creature, and got it out of Madam, and we fitted out a respectable widow-woman mother often had to help her, and sent her to one of those Southern cities—I forget now. She wrote up only that there was mostly blacks for waiting on one, and food poor and scarce. But Master Dick sent word that she kept the fever away for a mile around her, and the officers thereabouts gave her a long piece of writing and a medal after all was over, and the Rebels a silver cup—she cared for all alike, whatever the uniform. The little house she had was built up into a hospital, later, and she lived and died there, and only came up to the north to beg money for it. It was the only one in thirty miles around. Eighteen years she lived there, and left the cup to Miss Lisbet; the medal to her daughter.

Well, I must hurry on. I could talk about those days forever, but in the books, I have taken notice often, they pick and choose.

So I will pass to when it came to her of a sudden how she could collect clothes and food for the army, and keep one place open for the lint-scraping and bandage-rolling, as all the ladies were doing in the big cities. She had a tongue of honey and every one knew about her having hired Mrs. Jarvis to go nurse, so she was sure to get what she begged for. She took over a vacant office in the village, part of Madam's property, and I never saw her happier than the day we were fitting it up. It was all cleaned and new furnished and there were desks and tables and nursing-books and shelves for the jellies and medicines, and everything to be sent orderly and where needed at the time, not rushed forward all helter-skelter as so much is at such times. Dr. Stanchon saw all, and heard the plans, and patted her shoulder.

"Well done, Blossom, well done!" says he. "I might have let you go, after all!"

And he offered to advise and find out the quickest and best trains and such like.

It was July and a hot, clear day. The notice was in the village paper for all the women that could help, to come to a first meeting and take hours for duty there, and routes to collect, and offer wagons if they had them, and give fruit for jelly, and Miss Lisbet led off with the old pony and cart for steady work.

We were resting in the garden and she had just told me that she meant to give all her time to the "office," as we called it in a joking way (for nice young ladies didn't go to offices then, I promise you! Madam thought little enough of it) and she put her hand on mine.

"Rhoda," says she, "my dream is coming true—do you see? I'm to do something for my country, after all! Just as a man would—just as Dick does, Rhoda! Isn't it a grand thing?"

"Yes, miss," says I.

"The change is coming now, Rhoda," she says, and then, laughing at herself, "I'm going to ask the larkspurs!"

And she pulled a great stalk and held it over her head, as I had taught her seven years before.

"*Larkspur, larkspur, tell me true,*
Or never again I'll trust to you!

Is there to be a great change in my life?"

And she stripped them off, *yes, no, yes, no*—and they said *no*! The sweet face fell, and I hurried to comfort her.

"Maybe they always say no hereabouts," says I. "Let me have a try!" And I asked the same question, but it came *yes*, and that I knew must be true, though she did not.

The next day, after she had made a speech like the Queen's (I thought) and every one wondering, with her so young, and a hundred dollars pledged, and all so eager to work under her—for she was one of them that's born to lead—who should run in but Henry Wilson, all out of breath, crying to her to hurry home, for Madam was down with a stroke, and one side of her all powerless!

Well, to make a long story short, she never left her poor aunt for above an hour at a time till the fighting was over! Madam, who had never seemed overfond before, was mad for her now, and she was pushing her chair or reading to her or stroking her hand or playing old tunes or sitting in sight, the livelong day. They tried the sea and they tried the mountains and there was a nurse and a maid, but it was always Miss Lisbet behind it all. She was rich, she had real French convent lace on her body-linen, and asparagus and peaches in winter, and a conservatory as big as a house, oh, yes. But she was more tied down than many a poor girl 'prenticed for her living, and I often wonder if it's not that way with many of the rich ladies you see! I know I was working hard with a dressmaker the first year—before they kept me as seamstress and mender at The Cedars —and *I* wouldn't have changed with her, except for love of her, poor dear!

I was back in The Cedars when Madam went off in her sleep one night as easy as a baby. There was no need for grieving—'twas a blessed release, and just the soberness and the thoughts that must come to one when even an old body of eighty-odd passes away. Poor old Madam hadn't many friends, for everybody was so afraid of her, and we all felt the best that ever she'd done was to leave the lonely old place to Miss Lisbet. Master Dick was coming home, for the war was over, and the black men freed at last, and he was full captain, and never a scratch or a headache even, to show for the four years!

We were in the garden waiting for him, she as lovely as ever I'd seen her in a white dress, all frilled from the waist down, with violet ribbons (Madam made her vow never to wear black for her) and a violet band in her hair. She'd a great brooch of amethyst stones at her neck and Master Dick's blue ring on her finger.

"Rhoda," says she, of a sudden, "what if we tried the larkspurs again?" and she smiled at me, a mischievous little smile, like a child's.

"Nay, now, miss dear," says I, "what's the good of such games, and you a grown woman? No doubt now but your way is clear to do as you like—a fine husband and plenty of money. Let it be."

"But I will," she says, reaching for a spray of the blue stuff, "I will, Rhoda, once more, for luck."

"Well, then, miss," says I, "put the question different like, why not? Make it plainer—you're forever talking about 'a change in your life,' and there's always changes, you know."

So she laughs and holds it up and sings:

"*Larkspur, larkspur, tell me true,*
Or never again I'll trust to you!

Am I going to be able now to use all this money to help some great cause?"

And the flowers said, *no*!

Well, I couldn't say I was sorry for that, just because she was all for schooling and helping the blacks, now they were thrown on themselves like; for old Dr. Stanchon would have it that they were bound to make more trouble now in the South than they had before, and that those who had freed them owed them a living—or something like that. Most hated him for it around our parts, but doctor says the country has found his father was right, to-day. Nevertheless, there's other uses for good family money than that, as we all know.

"You've bewitched the larkspurs, Miss Lisbet," I said, laughing. "Why not fool them a bit? Pick a tiny short spray like this, and ask a question you *know* the answer to, and then you'll see how things are."

"Well," says she, "I'll ask 'If I'm to marry Dick'!"

I didn't half like that, but I happened to peep out of the tail of my eye and who should I see but Master Dick himself, leaning over the low cedar hedge, looking for us. He was out of her sight, and so I made haste and picked a tiny stalk with but three blossoms and handed it to her.

"Quick, quick, Miss Lisbet, dear!" I said, knowing well what the answer would be. She asked quick enough, but when she stripped them, *yes, no*—and stopped there, I saw that the third had somehow fallen off and lay on her white lap. It gave me a turn, but she only brushed it away and laughed softly.

"It *is* foolish," she said, "isn't it, Rhoda? For there he is! Here, Dick, this way!"

I started to leave them, but she wouldn't have it, and gave him her cheek to kiss as easy as a child —or started to, but there was a man in uniform behind him, just rounding the turn, and she drew back.

"Major La Salle," says Master Dick, proud as Punch, you could see, "Miss Elizabeth Winthrop."

She curtseyed and the Major bowed to the ground, and I couldn't but notice a tiny bald spot amongst his curly dark hair.

"An old fellow for Master Dick's friend," thought I, and so he was, being all of thirty-six, and more like Dr. Stanchon's crony than his son's! Thirty-six was something in those days, you see, and Master Dick was all ready to settle when the young men of his age to-day are playing their football games and heedless as school girls.

The Major had lines about his mouth and eyes, and had buried a wife, we learned, three years before the war—a sad marriage, by Master Dick's accounts, as she wasn't worthy of him and had made him grave before his time. Our young Captain couldn't talk enough of him and had written many's the letters about him before ever we saw him. But we were both surprised to find him so much older than we had thought, and Miss Lisbet was afraid to talk much before him at first, for fear he'd find her missish and ignorant. She didn't realize, the sweet thing, how any one would think, to see her at the head of that great house, managing all and doing so much good in the village, that she was the equal of any woman.

They'd been but three days in the village, and all the time they had from the doctor's wife's proud tea-drinkings, to show off her boy, they'd spent with us. She always had me by her, for Mrs. Williams was getting on, and best off by herself, and Miss Lisbet didn't feel 'twas quite as it should be for her to be off with them alone. So when they spoke of Madam's will, I was sewing near by.

Miss Lisbet was telling of her schemes for the poor blacks and the Major was agreeing with her, and said that Master Dick's father had the right of it.

"Now, for heaven's sake, Louis, don't encourage Miss Winthrop in any of her plans for the human race," says Master Dick, laughing. "It's bad enough to have my father executor. All that money depends on me, you know, and I don't approve of women's rights as much as you do."

"Depends on you? What do you mean?" says the Major.

"Why, unless she marries me she doesn't get Madam's money at all," says Master Dick. "The old lady was afraid of unprincipled fortune hunters, and of me, at least, she knew the worst!"

"But the larkspurs said I wouldn't marry you, Captain Dick Stanchon!" she cried, half laughing, half displeased, for she couldn't bear him to question what she said.

The Major got up at that and walked away, and I left them, too, as was quite correct for a promised pair.

It might have been an hour later that I walked to the cedar grove to find my thimble and saw Miss Lisbet hurrying there ahead of me. I slackened a bit, and when I caught her up I saw she was talking with the Major—he must have been waiting there for her. I thought it odd, but stooped over and looked through the grass, and all of a sudden they were level with me, the other side the hedge.

"You sent for me?" said she, breathless like.

"Yes. Can you guess why?" said he, and my knees began to shake.

"N-no, Major La Salle," said she, still breathing strangely.

"I sent for you to tell you that the larkspur told you true, Elizabeth," he said, very deep. "You will never marry Dick Stanchon, you will marry me."

"Why—why..." she began, and I couldn't move then, try as I might.

"As sure as that little star belongs in the moon's arms, Elizabeth, you belong in mine!" said he. "Don't you know it?"

"But, Dick," she said, still breathing as I had never heard her.

"Dick is a boy," he said. "You are fit for a man. I loved you when I first took off my cap before you. But I would never court an heiress. Could you come to a western army post and live on a Major's pay?"

"It's not me—I could live on nothing, almost—it's how to tell Dick!" she began, crying and breathing that strange way, both together—and then I knew it was all over, of course.

"My star!" I heard him say, and I crept away, somehow.

Well, that was all. One week, she was a great heiress and engaged to a bright young fellow with life opening out before him; the next she was married to a poor widower, fifteen years her elder, and off to some place in the western prairies, with only a chest of linen and silver and some old mahogany and her clothes! It was like a dream. But only to see her look at him, you'd know she'd met her master. Before, she hadn't sensed things rightly, she told me.

I was wild to go with her, but no such thing as a maid for his wife, the Major said, and anyway, mother was near doubled with the rheumatism and I couldn't be spared. So I kissed her on the station platform and cried myself blind that night. And Master Dick went off to Germany, to study, and never a word was mentioned: he held his head high, the Captain did!

We got news regular from little Essie White, that Miss Lisbet's outworn dresses used to go to. She used to read an hour a day, did Miss Lisbet, to Essie's mother, who went blind, and she stocked Essie with flannels and such, as she grew. I trained her in as kitchen maid when I was at The Cedars, and when help turned out so poor and scarce in the West—all ignorant Paddies, as we called them then—she sent to me and I sped Essie out to her, and a good job, too, for she was in no state to be worrying out her precious health over dust and dirt and victuals!

Essie wrote us long letters, how Miss Lisbet was the belle of the post and had a night school for the private soldiers started, with officers' ladies to teach, and took all the charge of the little hospital. Mrs. Jarvis sent her rules and saving ways and many clever contrivances from all her experience in the South, and long after the La Salles left that post the night school was kept up— and may be now, for aught I know, for it seemed that all she planted, grew. Balls they gave and private theatricals and riding parties, and Essie said she was happy as the day was long, but for that she felt she might have done so much for the world with Madam's money. She wanted schools in all the army posts and the negroes taught farming and goodness knows what not, you see.

But when little Louis came there was no time for all that, I promise you! It broke my heart not to be with her, but mother was failing, slow but sure, and 'twould have been sin to leave her.

But I heard all his sweet ways and when he was creeping, and how he called my poor old picture "Dody" (bless him!) and hardly was he ready for his kilts but his brother was stepping into his shoes! Named for her father he was, and the image of the first, that was the image of the Major. She took the care of them mostly, herself, for she didn't like the rough girls out there, and had only Essie and a woman for washing, and I didn't need Essie's letters to tell me she was tired and worn-like. It seemed a poor kind of life for one that had had a half dozen of servants and gardens and grape houses and her saddle-horse—but she wouldn't have changed for Windsor Castle, I well knew.

And next I heard, they were to move, very sudden, and the garden just planted and all, and worst of all, Essie had lost her heart to a corporal and was to stay behind. At the time I blamed her sorely and wrote her a bitter letter, but, dearie me, life is life for all of us, and Miss Lisbet wasn't her treasure as she was mine. We made it up later, Essie and me.

My dear wrote me herself, the saddest letter that ever I had from her, I believe. The old mahogany pieces had been stored, very careful, and burned in the storage, and the linen was out and the china broken, and the new baby would find but a poor house, she feared, when they should be settled. Could I find her one for Essie's place? And oh, if only she could see my face, for she dreaded her coming trial, with every one strange!

I was sitting in my new black, when I read the letter, with poor mother free of her rheumatics at last, and all soft as I was from it, I cried and cried!

I wrote her that I'd find some one, and then I went to the old doctor and we talked and twisted it this way and that, and he went up to The Cedars and called on Madam's heir-at-law, a crabbed old cousin that lived much to himself and saw only the doctor, and the end of it was that I was to pick out what I thought Miss Lisbet would like in the matter of furniture, for he used but a third of the rooms, and what linen and stuff his housekeeper thought could be spared.

And wasn't I glad to hear that, for well I knew the housekeeper, a good woman who'd nursed turn about with mother for years, and had seen my young lady grow up!

Well, if I do say it of myself, I stripped The Cedars thorough! And yet a stranger would hardly know. It was full, do you see, from many generations, and overflowing, and I furnished three bedrooms, complete, from the garrets! Blankets I got, and a trunk of towels, and seven woven bedspreads, and a dining-table that Miss Lisbet's mother's mother had eaten a wedding dinner at, and the stuffed macaw on his ebony perch! Eight dozen dinner napkins that had never seen the laundry, and carpets that the moths were sure to take if I didn't! And brass fire-irons and a great chest of books and some heads of statues she'd always liked, and big engravings of foreign places, broken old ruins and such. And her nursery fittings, that had never been touched, I took entire—fire guard and small chairs, Moses in the Bulrushes, little kneeling Samuel and all! And nearly everything from her lovely bedroom—chintz valances, and the little South American dressing-cabinet, and the china-set in a strawed barrel. *I* knew what she loved—who better? And the old doctor got the whole car-load across the country free as air for me, through a gentleman that had heard how much Miss Lisbet had done in the War, and that as good as owned the railroad. He had us met with mules, too, at the end of the horrid, dusty trip; and when me and little Maria Riggs (niece of a tidy widow-woman Miss Lisbet had had chair-caning taught to, so that she had no need to come on the town) got to the new home, we found only a neighbor to give us the keys. The Major was off on army matters for a week, and she had taken the two boys and gone on a visit to a new friend she'd made, and left things all hugger-mugger, from despair and tiredness, poor girl!

I was quite as well pleased, and Maria and I swept and cleaned and nailed carpets and hung pictures and clear-starched muslin curtains and filled shelves and drawers, as happy as queens. And round the house I planted out the five old vines I'd brought all moist and good in an open basket, from The Cedars, and in the garden that a fine, fresh-faced soldierman, English as could be, dug and spaded for me, what did I put in but *larkspur seeds*, amongst the sweet williams and pansies and mignonette!

Well, she came back, expecting nothing, do you see, and there at the door was I, in black, with white cuffs and apron, and little Maria curtseying behind me. And the old claw-leg card-table in the hall and the glass with the gilt eagle above it.

"Rhoda! *Rhoda!*" she screams, and gives one look at the statues and pictures and new carpet in the drawing-room and faints on the floor! And I nearly crazy for being such a fool at such a time!

None the less, the third boy was born in his mother's old four-posted bed, as beautiful as a king, and her living picture. Stanchon La Salle he was, for the old doctor, who never bore her a moment's grudge, mind you, on Master Dick's account.

"He's a fine man, Rhoda, and I doubt if Dick could have managed her right," was all he ever said to me. "She has a great spirit."

And then the time went by like the water under a bridge. She'd no more worries about drudging, for Maria and I did all, with the English soldierman for rough jobs; but she had her hands full with the boys, for the Major didn't want them sent back to the East to school, and she had all the teaching and training of them, to say nothing of the care of them, growing. Nine years we lived there, and then Master Louis was off to West Point, and in two years more his brother, and one day—it seemed the next day but two or three!—we were packing Master Stanchon's trunk to go to Yale College, where his father went! We rubbed our eyes and sat alone, and there was the macaw she got for her tenth birthday looking at us! And I do assure you, I felt much the same as ever. Which I had heard people say, as a girl, and felt to be unbecoming.

The Colonel was pretty nigh to white hair, but firm and strong, and she was grey, but not a wrinkle, and very beautiful. He was to leave the service and had been offered a post in government, somehow, at Washington, when just as we were beginning to worry if his eyes could stand the book-work, the lawyer's letter came.

It seemed too good to be true. Old, crabbed Mr. Hawkes was long ago dead, and The Cedars closed, and his heir, a very curious woman, had felt that Miss Lisbet was defrauded, and left everything to her in her will! So we were to go back, and it cleared so many worries that we cried together.

"And now, Rhoda, now for a chance to do something!" she says, suddenly.

I only stared at her.

"Why, Miss Lisbet, you've been doing since you were born!" I cried.

"Oh, Rhoda, you know!" she says, coaxing, "only for those near me, and in such a small way! Now the boys are started, and no more worry for the Colonel, and you and I can do something that will last!"

And laughing like a girl, if she didn't fly out to the garden and find our frost-bitten, yellow larkspur, the last!

"See!" says she, and began to wave it.

"Oh, don't, don't!" says I, anxious-like, "and you to be a grandmother next year, maybe!" (for Louis was to be married to a New York young lady in the winter).

But she would, and when she asked, half laughing, half frightened:

"*Am I to do what I have longed for all my life, at last?*" and stripped off the rotting blossoms, *yes, no, yes, no*—the last one fell.

And before ever we reached The Cedars the Colonel had gone blind!

Well, for five years she was never from his side one half hour at a time. He said he blessed the blindness that gave him her hand at every moment, and it was a beautiful sight to see them together. Riches makes such an affliction as light as it can ever be, that's certain, and he lived in luxury. He held Louis's twin daughters in his arms and hoped to "see," as he called it, smiling, the next brother's, but it was not to be.

Dr. Stanchon, as I learned at last to call Master Dick, said that he couldn't have had a moment's pain, and his own boy, named for the Colonel, carried him to the grave with our three.

Mrs. Stanchon was a sweet soul, tied to a wheel-chair for life after five years married, and Miss Lisbet was forever doing things for her entertainment and to make her forget, like. She never did too much, but just enough, and didn't stop with grapes and books, as many rich folk will, you know, but sat with her every other day, at least, with the Colonel by her side, listening to her bright talk. I doubt the two of them realized, at those times, how afflicted they were!

She never talked as if he was gone—always as if they'd only parted for a little. Her hair was soon whiter than his, and she walked and moved very slow, for her, but the boys seemed to see no difference.

Louis's wife was delicate and came to us, finally, till he should have an easier post, and the twins were not strong, like our babies. Once we nearly lost them, and after that Granny Lisbet (as they called her) never took her eye off them, and pulled them through. It seemed the village was full of sick children that year, and the mothers were crazy for her to look at every one.

She was anxious to set up a regular nurse for the district, and gave a room for that purpose, with a lending closet, and arranged money for the nurse to be paid for ten years. (They are quite common, now, but hers was the first in our parts.)

"She's working too hard, Rhoda, my girl," says Dr. Stanchon. "Her heart's not what she thinks. Keep her quiet, can't you?" But what could I do?

I nearly cried, last June, when I'd got her out in the garden, that day, for a bit of quiet, and she began on her plans for the villages to be taxed for nurses and doctors, to keep off sickness!

"The babies are all well, now," says she, "and Louis comes for his family to-morrow, and the twins are no trouble. The nurse is all started in the village and I am going to see the Governor at Albany next week—I have an appointment. Isn't it strange, Rhoda, that I am all but fifty, and only ready now to do something with my opportunities? I've ten good years before me, and the Colonel shall be proud of me yet!"

I felt so weak and sad all of a sudden—God knows why. She rarely spoke of him. I held her hand.

"Why, look, Rhoda, there's a stalk of larkspur out!" she said. "Go pick it for me, will you?"

I started to say no, but then I saw but one bud on it and I thought to myself, "I'll see her pleased for once, I will!" knowing she'd never notice, and so brought it. She waved it, blue above her white head (and me only iron grey to-day!)

"Larkspur,   larkspur,   tell   me   true,
Or never again I'll trust to you,"

she mumbled like, and I thought her voice sounded strange and far away, somehow.

"Is a change coming at last in my narrow little life?"

"Oh, hush, Miss Lisbet! you that have been so much to so many!" says I, sobbing at her dear stupidness, and then she begins, yes—and that was all.

"Why, Rhoda!" she cries, "at last, at last I've won!" and half rises in the garden-chair. Then suddenly her hands went to her heart.

"Why, Louis—Louis! My dear!" she said, staring at the cedar hedge. *"Can you see?"* And fell back.

The change had come, indeed, and I and all that loved her hope that now she knows what a life like hers meant to those she lived among and blessed!

THE END

Made in the USA
Coppell, TX
20 April 2024